WARRIOR-PIONEERS II

Extracts from the Boone Papers

Volumes 14C-15C of the Draper Manuscripts

Anne Crabb

HERITAGE BOOKS
2025

HERITAGE BOOKS
AN IMPRINT OF HERITAGE BOOKS, INC.

Books, CDs, and more—Worldwide

For our listing of thousands of titles see our website
at
www.HeritageBooks.com

Published 2025 by
HERITAGE BOOKS, INC.
Publishing Division
5810 Ruatan Street
Berwyn Heights, MD 20740

Heritage Books by the author:

And the Battle Began like Claps of Thunder;
The Siege of Boonesborough - 1778
As Told by the Pioneers

Warrior-Pioneers: Extracts from the Boone Papers,
Volumes 4C–13C of the Draper Manuscripts

Warrior-Pioneers II: Extracts from the Boone Papers,
Volumes 14C–15C of the Draper Manuscripts

International Standard Book Number
Paperbound: 978-0-7884-5217-8

Daniel Boone Portrait, 1820
Chester Harding
National Portrait Gallery

Portrait of Lyman C. Draper
from his book entitled "King's Mountain and Its Heroes." 1881

CONTENTS

ILLUSTRATIONS

INTRODUCTION

> **Sir you are amedtly to Call on Duty One third of our militia as well mounted as posable...**
>
> Daniel Boone. February 15, 1783

> **Draper rescued from oblivion the history of America's first Far West.**
>
> Ted Franklin Belue

Lyman Copeland Draper (1815-1891) was a chronicler of the late 18th to mid-19th century. By his own estimation, he traveled more than 60,000 miles, on foot, horse, mule, wagon, stage coach, and train from the 1840's to 1890 in the course of his research. He interviewed eyewitnesses and descendants of those who stood fast on the western frontiers, and Native Americans holding onto their homelands. The Mohawk Tribe named him "The Inquirer."

The "warrior-pioneers," as he called those pushing west, provided accounts of frontier life, sieges and battles, Indian captivities, and trees marked with Boone's initials.

This work contains transcriptions and excerpts from volumes 14C and 15C of Draper's Boone Papers and follows transcriptions from Volumes 4C – 13C (*Warrior-Pioneers,* 2019).

In rough chronological order, Draper compiled these two volumes to trace Daniel Boone's life from his last years in Kentucky to his old age in Missouri, where even then he was still hunting.

Boone's letters and depositions are scattered throughout these two volumes. His communications are clear and can be read phonetically.

Lyman Draper's Collection

During his years of research and extensive travel, Draper held the position of Corresponding Secretary of the Wisconsin Historical Society.

On his death the partly-organized collection, stored in a stone building near his home, was left to the Wisconsin Historical Society. A succession of distinguished librarians and historians organized the collection of several hundred volumes into Series designated A to Z and AA to ZZ. Josephine Harper's *Guide to the Draper Manuscripts* (1983) offers a description of each volume. Calendars have been published for some of the Series, but there is no such guide for the thirty-three volumes of the Boone Papers (C Series).

Draper's Source Materials

A meticulous historian, Draper kept a set of notebooks for each trip and cited sources throughout his work. Often cited is the collection of interviews compiled by Presbyterian minister John Dabney Shane (1812-1864).

Another key source is the two-volume *History of Kentucky* (1874) by Richard H. Collins. It was Collins who sent Draper the depositions from Kentucky Land Suits found in Volume 15C.

Draper's interview with Nathan Boone, Daniel's youngest son, is frequently cited, as is Niles' *Register*, a national magazine published in Baltimore from 1811 to 1848 by Hezekiah Niles.

Draper and Boone

Draper had long anticipated completing biographies of Daniel Boone, George Rogers Clark, Simon Kenton, and others, but only his *King's Mountain and Its Heroes* (Draper, 1881), an account of the American victory at King's Mountain in 1780, was ever published. His Boone biography (B Series) was eventually published by Ted Franklin Belue in *Life of Boone* (1998).

Among the stories Draper collected are colorful anecdotes about Boone's hunting expeditions, one being that Boone came upon a herd of buffalo so large that he had to climb a tree and stay perched there for hours. Another story told to Draper was that Boone, sensing an unknown human presence in the woods, took refuge behind a tree, and poked his hat out on the end of his ramrod to see if anyone shot at it.

Draper was welcomed into the homes of Boone relatives in Missouri for extended visits and interviews. He wrote of Daniel Boone's character:

> **His faith and charity were large and tolerant, his thoughts outran the creeds, and his sympathies embraced all who were good.**
>
> Lyman Draper.
> DM 16C 34

Pioneer Narratives in the Boone Papers

Included in Volume 14 of the Boone papers are captivity stories sent to Draper from members of the Sharp, Flinn, and Tackett families. They wrote of their last glance at burning cabins as they were carried off to Indian towns to be adopted, sold, enslaved, or killed. Sensing her captors' plans, one young girl warned her elderly relative:

> **Grandmother, it is time for you to pray. They are going to kill you!**
>
> Betsy Tackett
> DM 14C 100

This transcription of Volume 15C contains Collins' Depositions from the Kentucky Land Suits and journal entries not original to this volume. The last part of the volume contains correspondence and interviews from Missouri, where Draper heard from transplanted Kentuckians. They told of building cabins and forts all over again for defense in Missouri alongside sons of Daniel Boone. Eyewitness accounts of battles in Missouri and Black Hawk War close the volume.

Boone's visitors in Missouri described him as modest and well-spoken, and as an avid hunter. One wrote:

> **Boone... exhibits a liberality of feeling and enlarged views of policy, which it would be well for the more refined statesmen of the present day to imitate.**
>
> S. G. Tucker
> DM 14C 107

Note to the Reader

This is a collection of primary sources: letters, interviews, military correspondence, maps, and other documents which are nearly all handwritten or hand-drawn. Given that schooling was at best sporadic on the frontier, correspondents' handwriting varies in spelling, punctuation, capitalization and accuracy. "Best guess" transcribing is all that is possible in many instances. One of Draper's correspondents made his own disclaimer:

> Please excuse Bad writing for I am no scolar.
>
> James Mollett
>
> DM 15C 39

To add my own disclaimer, I am no historian, and this is not a complete transcription. I undertake this work to make available the most valuable accounts from these two volumes of the Boone Papers. The reader is encouraged to consult Draper's original notebooks, available on microfilm.

All letters here were addressed to Lyman Draper unless noted. Draper's memos and notes appear within brackets followed by LCD as in the original notebooks.

I have added explanatory words and corrected spellings in brackets without initials. My brief comments are italicized. To distinguish longer comments from those of Draper and his correspondents, my comments appear in Calibri font throughout the work.

I have added punctuation sparingly; original spelling and capitalization is usually retained. Draper's underlining is omitted except where he cited published sources. Original page numbers have been retained; numbering within documents is omitted.

Illustrations and quotes from other volumes of Draper's collection are cited as DM.

Terminology which would be considered improper or insensitive today was used throughout this work by Draper and his correspondents.

14C

This volume begins with Daniel Boone's correspondence regarding his militia duties in 1783. The Boones were then living at Boone's Station a few miles from Fort Boonesborough, Kentucky,

During these years Daniel Boone was a landholder, surveyor, representative to the Virginia legislature, trader in ginseng, and a Lieutenant Colonel in the county militia. There are letters and military reports from Boone himself, along with Indian captivity stories, one of which pertains to Boone. He may have rescued young captive Chloe Flinn, whose mother, brother and sisters remained in captivity.

In addition to many letters from children and grandchildren of the Flinn captives, there are other captivity accounts from the Sharp and Tacket families describing frontier attacks, massacres, and long or short captivities. In some cases, family members were welcomed home after being exchanged at treaties, but some captives chose not to return. One captive, unwillingly brought home to her family, disappeared though her family tried to keep her home by tying her to the bedstead at night

This volume also includes a copy of an original slave document dated 1785 and signed by James Harrod, Thomas Kennedy, and Joseph White.

During the three years leading up to Draper's timeline for this volume, Daniel's brother Ned Booe was killed by Indians (1780), Daniel was captured by the British in Charlottesville

(1781), and his son Israel and nephew Thomas were killed at the Battle of Blue Licks (1782). After losing his land title at Boone's Station, Boone moved his family a few miles away to Marble Creek, and then to Limestone (now Maysville, KY). The Boones then lived several years in the Kanawha area of western Viginia near Point Pleasant, returning to Nicholas County, Kentucky briefly before moving to Missouri in 1799.

14C 1 LCD: **Daniel Boone 1783**
May Courts Established, some opposition.
Trip 1860, 41, 52-53 (*Draper numbered his notebooks).*

Wood's Affair at Crab Orchard – April 13, 1783
Boone's Narrative; Nokes notes; Col. Fleming's Journal for date &c; Robertson's Scrap Book, 273; Autobiography of Rev. J. B. Finley, 145-146.

Joseph Hall*, in his pension statement, says in the Spring of 1783, the Indians invaded Kentucky, & encamped on the head of Sandy. Col. Benjamin Logan, with Col. John Logan, raised a force & marched against them. Isaac Shelby was along, but Indians had decamped before their arrival. Henry Wilson gives particulars.

* Pension Statement in DM 36J 203-5

14C 2 LCD: **Boone's Military Orders – Jan. & Feb. 1783.**
An Escort for Col. Marshall & A Scouting Expedition.
Sunday, Jan 12, 1783. Lt. Col. Robert Patterson.
Thursday, Feb. 20th [William] Calk's Cabin – near Mt. Sterling, Montgomery County. Collins Ky II: 516, 633-634.

Following are two military orders in Boone's handwriting. "Amedetly" is immediately, "Shone Expedition" refers to Shawnee Expedition. "Strode" refers to Strode's Station. "Sine" indicates sign of Indian presence, "Patison" is Col. Robert Patterson. "Hour" is intended as "our."

You are amedetly to call over on ____ 3 of hour Company guard ____ to _____ Col. Marshall _____ to the Falls of Ohio You will call on those who was Excused from the Shone Expedition and those who come into the Country ____ the army marched; they are to meet at Lexington on Sunday next* with out fail given under my hand this 6 Day of January 1783.

Dal Boone

*Sunday, Jan. 12, 1783. LCD

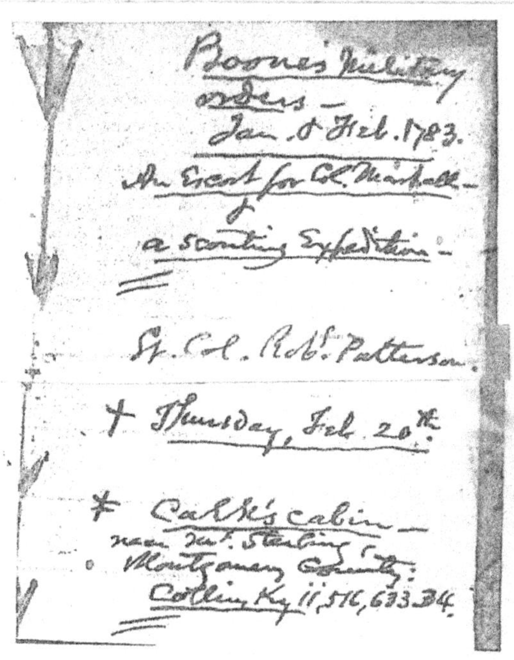

Boone's Military orders — Jan. & Feb. 1783.

An Escort for Col. Marshall — & a scouting Expedition —

Lt. Col. Robt. Patterson.

+ Thursday, Feb. 20th.

* Calk's cabin — near Mt. Sterling, Montgomery County; Collins Ky II, 516, 633-34.

LCD: Boone's Military Orders – Jan. & Feb. 1783. DM 14C 2

Daniel Boone letter, 1783. DM 14C 2

Orders the 15th february 1783

Sir you are amedtly to Call on Duty one third of our militia as well mounted as posable and Eight Days provision to take a town as follows Commanded by Lieut. Col. Patison and Rondevous at Strode on the Tuesday next the 20th + from there to March to Calkes Cabin++ thence on an East Corse til they get 10 miles above the upper Blue Licks then Down to the Licks thence to Limestone and if no Sine found a Straight Corse to Eagel Creek 10 miles from the head from thence home . If time be found the Corse Commander to act as he thinks most _____.

+ Thursday, Feb. 20

++Calk's Cabin near Mount Sterling, Montgomery County. Collins ii: 516. *Other page numbers are illegible.*

14C 2(1) Daniel Boone Military Orders, *cont.*

The first several lines of the William Watson survey are obliterated and the last lines are missing. Shull/Scholl family were Boone relatives. "Shuger trees" would be sugar maples.

You will be ___ ___ will first Call on all who were Excused from the Expedition Except those that went to the falls with Col. Marshall; and then call them off as they Stand on the List: ___ ____ ___ Given ___ my hand

Daniel Boone CLT

Certificate given to the [*Land*] Commissioners Joseph Shull, William Shull, John Coney[?], Thomas Brooks, Jacob Hunter, Dal. Boone Sadels and guns Ordered that Lieut. Capt. Robert Johnson have ten pounds of powder
March the tenth 1783

Dal Boone

Survaid for Wilm Watson 400 acres begin in said Watsons Line of an Entry of 950 acres at a Shuger tree W 253 poles to 2 Shuger trees... 253 poles and Linn ____ 253 poles to ____.

14C 3-3(6) J. P. Hale, Charleston, W. Va., Aug. 26, 1882
LCD heading: Boone in West Virginia – 1788.
[George] Washington in West Virginia in 1773.

J. P. Hale (1824-1902) was the great-grandson of Mary Draper Ingels who escaped after being captured by the Shawnees. He was a physician, businessman, and historian who published his own works. J. P. Hale was the founder of the predecessor of the West Virginia State Archives. His work is cited by several of Draper's correspondents.

Boone will touch the heart of the great Public... [they] will read the life of Boone as they will "Robinson Crusoe," the "Arabian Nights," &c.

Hon. L. D. Draper

My Dear Sir

Your favour of 10th & 15th July were duly received as the Boone paper, returned...

You say you would have taken some notes of the Boone paper with my consent. I regret you did not. I intended you to make any use of it you pleased, in fact I hunted up the facts chiefly for you...

I am very sorry to learn that your "Kings Mountain" was not a financial success...but as a financial measure I think your life of Boone will have far greater chances of success.

Kings Mountain may have greater literary merit & may have cost you greater labour & research... Boone will touch the heart of the great Public... [they] will read the life of Boone as they will "Robinson Crusoe," the "Arabian Nights," &c.

You ask me where Boone's 500 acres of land was & say that the ownership of land is no evidence of residence. In this case I don't suppose he ever lived on the 500 acres. The land was on 18 Mile Creek over 30 miles from & below here. Tradition fixes his residence 4 miles above here.

He probably settled at the Mouth of Kanawha first, when coming to Western Virginia, but afterwards came up here. He & his wife & presumably all his family were at Point Pleasant (the mouth of Kanawha) in 1786. A deed dated in April 1786 to land in Kentucky is signed & acknowledged by himself & wife at Point Pleasant...

You ask me if I can identify a visit of General Washington to Wheeling & this Valley in 1772 or 1773. I am now in pursuit of a document in the Clerk's office of Augusta County which I think will establish that visit & put it in 1773. A friend promises to send me the facts next week. When I get them, will report them to you. I want to find evidence of another visit, probably in 1782 to 1786.

His trip of 1773, above, attended to and which I am hunting up, is distinct from his earlier trip to the lower end of the ____ in 1770.

I have finished writing up the history I detail of the Captivity & remarkable escape of Mrs. Mary Ingles, also the rescue of her son & his remarkable career. I shall publish it soon in pamphlet or small book form & will send you a copy.

With many kind wishes,
Yours Very Truly
J. P. Hale

P. S. In another envelope I send facts about Kenton, ____ ____. JPH

14C 4 LCD: **Daniel Boone, 1784**

1784, March 10, Boone Surveying – Dr. J. A. Snowden, of Right Angle, Clark County, Ky., loaned me a copy of a survey made by Boone at above date – said copy made by Robert Parker, Surveyor of Fayette County Ky. (No date of making said copy but it has an ancient & authentic appearance.) It is a survey for 1000 acres in compact form – no angles – made 10th March 1784, commencing at the mouth of Lulbergrud __ is a branch of Red river – on the upper side of the Creek – a little of the upper portion extending by the meanderings of the stream, to its north side. Surveyed for Thos. Austin.

Signed: Daniel Boone, Deputy Surveyor Fayette

County

Examined[?] T. Marshall, Surveyor Fayette County

Chain Carrier Joseph Scholl*
C. C. Edmund Callaway**
Daniel Morgan Boone, Marker***
A Copy – Test: Rob. Parker,
Surveyor Fayette County

Col. Marshall resigned his surveyorship in 1787, so as to [go] to the Legislature of Virginia. Green's Spanish Conspiracy, 194. LCD

*Joseph Scholl was Daniel Boone's son-in-law.
**Edmund Callaway was a nephew of Col. Richard Callaway of Fort Boonesborough and brother of Flanders, James and Micajah Callaway
***Daniel Morgan Boone was Daniel Boone's son

14C 5 Daniel Boone to Lawrence Thompson, Aug. 6, 1784.

Copy of original is water damaged. It is addressed to Thompson at The Whitoke [White Oak?] Spring when Thompson was Surveyor of Lincoln County KY/VA. Daniel Boone seemed to be asking him to settle ["Satel"] a surveying debt. A postscript initialed by Daniel Boone is illegible

I am to pay a Large sum of money at Court on tues day next the ____ you promised to pay up for Moore and tatum. hope you will Com Down and Satel on Monday next at my house as I am ____ _____ myself ____ and to set aside all Doutes on the bisness _____. I have sent you Col. Marshall _____ together with P_____ and the Chan men _____ _____

14C 6 LCD: **Daniel Boone, 1784-1785**
1785 &c – Col. Thomas Hart &c – trading in Kentucky. Nathan Boone's notes show that his father, Col. Daniel Boone, was gathering ginseng & selling goods at perhaps a later period – 1787.
Aug. 23, 1785 – Boone's Letter. Boone lost his land at Boone's Station.
April 1784 – Col. Boone pilots a surveying party to Fleming County, meets 600 buffaloes at Upper Blue Licks. Shane I, Woodford County p. 15
1784-85 – First Bees in Kentucky. Shane's Collections [*remainder blotted out*]
Aug. 16 – Col. Boone, then County Lieutenant of Lincoln, his letter on the state of the frontiers: Trip 1860, iv, 51 &c. September 1785 – Boone served as Sheriff near 3 years. Trip 1860, iii, 206.

14C 7 Newspaper clipping dated July 27, 1889 from Lockport, NY sent by John H. Rochester from the papers of his late uncle, Henry E. Rochester.

The clipping contained two letters from Daniel Boone written to Col. Nathaniel Rochester at Danville, Kentucky, printed from originals and described as being "written in a plain hand." Boone was beset by debts and lawsuits during this time.

The first letter was sent from Fayette County; the second has no return address; the two letters may have been delivered together by one of Daniel Boone's sons.

The land described in the first letter, Boone said, is "in quality equal to any you have seen on the South Side the Kentucky River," that it is known to be the first claim there. The land lay on Silver Creek and adjoined William Hoy's settlement and preemption. By Capt. aestel Boone may have meant Samuel Estill. In the following letter, Boone would speak "plain"...

> **Sir, I must be plan with you. I am intirely Out of Cash and the Chane men and Markers Must be payd.**

Fayette County, July 17th 1785

Sir – The Lands Mr. McFadden is offering you in Qulety Eacqul to any you have Seen on the South Side the Cantuck and never has been disputed by any man as it was known to be the first Clames thare by Satelment and preemtoin and I believe his Wright to be good From John Hart and Hix It Lyes on Silver crick Joining a Satelment and premtion of William Hoy assignee of Wiliam Deel on his South and Capt. Ervings also on his south and Capt astells on his West and Luis Craig on his North; thare are a Smart Crick Runs through the Midel of it an Som Likely Springs on the Land Jesse Benton in No wise Consarns With it It ____ Near 8 or 4 miles from it and Your own Land Lyes at the fork of Millers Crick on the North Side Cantuck Near 2 Miles from the Rever a bout 12 Miles from astels Station up the Rever; this from your omble servent

Daniel Boone

July the 17th 1785.

Dear Sir Times are a Litel Difegult at present about Indians; 2 or 3 Companys have Lately been Droveen from that Qurter Col. Hart's Land Which is about 18

Miles from Limestone and 9 miles from the uper Salt spring; however the Land Shall be survvayed at all avents. If I live before the time you mentioned So as they[?] May be Returned to the ofis at your Lasure. When you come over, Sir, I must be plan with you. I am intirely out of Cash and the Chane men and Markers Must be payd on the Spot and I want 2 or 3 ginnes for my own use Sir if you will send me Six ginnes by my Litel Sun it shall be Sateled on our first meeting by Sir your omble Servent.

Daniel Boone

14C 8-8(1) N. C. Tuttle, Clark County, Ky., April 18, 1885

LCD: Pilot Knob, Powell County, Ky. – Boone's Survey, 1785. Nelson Conkwright Tuttle was surveyor of Clark County, KY.

Dear Sir

In complying to your Request, I went among the Evans Family yesterday in Search of the Old Boone Survey made for Thomas Y. Austin in 1785. I failed to obtain it. I found the Old Lady Evans who I found from her Statement to be 90 years old. Her husband has been dead many years – he served in the war of 1812, was in Dudley's defeat. His name was John Evans and the Son who had this Old Survey was named John D. Evans. She says that the Paper in mention was left at Mr. Everman's – the Father-in-law of John D. Evans. He and his wife both being dead she says the Paper in mention was left at Mr. Everman's in the Clock. I have imployed Miss Lurena Passley, a Grand daughter of Mrs. Evans, to go to Mr. Everman's and Make a Search or it. She thinks she will obtain it. I gave her your address and told if she succeeded in finding it to mail to you immediately. Her address is Lurena Passley, Vaughn's Mills, Estill County, Ky. I have not been on Pilot Knob since I wrote to you, but have been told by several relyable men the initials of Boone are there on the south side of the cliff, as follows, from the description: D. B. 1785. They say they have seen it.

My recollection of the date of this Survey is that it was in June, 1785, and I have always heard it said, that Boone named this knob when he made that Survey.

Since you have been communicating with me, I have taken some study & thought concerning this mountain. I passed within a mile of it last week, running the old Clark, Montgomery and Estill County lines, about which there is some litigation. This Knob in the first arrangement of counties was in Bourbon, afterward Montgomery, and now in Powell.

Yours truly,
N. C. Tuttle

14C 9 Newspaper clipping enclosed with 'A Bit of History" gives a description of Pilot Knob and Daniel Boone's initials cut on a tree there. The clipping was probably sent by N. C. Tuttle. Kentucky Union Railroad is mentioned; it ran 95 miles from Lexington to Jackson, KY.

A Bit of History
Coral Hill, Ky., Feb. 9 [18__]

I noticed in your paper a month or two ago that information was wanted by Mr. L. C. Draper, of Madison, Wisconsin, in regard to Mr. George Rogers Clark. I was in Clark County, Ky., in January 1885, and there *[met a]* surveyor by the name of Mr. N. C. Tuttle, who said he had received a letter from one L C. Draper, Corresponding Secretary of the Historic Society of the U. S., wanting information in regard to George Rogers Clark, and, also, desiring a description of a section of country known as the Indian Old-fields. He did not answer Draper's letter, but gave me the facts as he knew them.

When this section was settled by the whites these "old fields" were cleared, and there is not a stump visible... Daniel Boone made a survey in 1785 of one thousand acres of land in this vicinity for Thomas J. Austin. In sight of the "old fields" is a noted mountain known as Pilot Knob, which it is said was named by Boone at the time of this survey. Pilot Knob is a mountain standing in the forks of Brush Creek, and is connected with other mountains in the vicinity. It is 1,000 feet high and about three miles East of the "old fields" and about one mile East of the K. U. R. R. A cliff on the South side of the mountain, upon which it is said Boone cut his initials, is about 100 feet high, and is composed of three kinds of stone: sandstone first, mill-grit next, and limestone on top, which is visible for ten or fifteen miles around.

14C 10 Nelson C. Tuttle, Clark County, Ky., July 31, 1884[?]. *Omitted: a discussion of "an Old Boon Survey."*

14C 11-11(1) Nelson C. Tuttle, Clark County, Ky., December 18, 1884[?]. *The letter has been copied over by LCD.*

Dear Sir

Yours of the 12th Just is at hand and contents noted. The Pilot Knob is Situated in the County of Powell...about 3 miles east of the Indian Old Fields... This knob is situated in the fork of Brush Creek. Not being connected with the other chains of Mountains in that vicinity on the south side of the Pinacle is a Cliff about 100 feet in height composed of Sand Stone ____ and Limestone. The Mountain is mostly well Timbered though about the cliff the Timber is scrubby but down on the Base the Timber is gone. It is about 1000 feet above the Level of Brush Creek and is accessible on horseback or Buggy almost to the cliff – and near the cliff is a Pass which it is said that L. M. Berry in Pursueing a Fox with his hound rode clear over the mountain on horseback. It is said that Daniel Boone carved his Initials in the Stone in the cliff when he made the Survey for Thomas Y. Osten [Austin] in 1785. This Survey, in Daniel Boone's hand-writing, was in the hands of John Evans of Powell County, who deceased some time since, & who promised to give me the said survey, & if I can procure it, I will send it to you.

It is said that when Boone made this Survey, he gave this knob this name – Pilot Knob. I have surveyed across the Knob and around it & know its situation...

The K. N. Rail-Road, almost finished, runs within a mile of the foot of the Knob...

Yours truly
Nelson C. Tuttle

14C 12 Nelson C. Tuttle, Clark County, Ky., Jan. 25, 1885

...I have delayed writing to you hoping...to visit the Pilot Knob...though it has been very cold and disagreeable and I am Getting Old and cannot Expose my self... I have a survey to make in that vicinity... I will see if Boons Initials is there carved in the rock and Give you a bird-eye view of the Situation...

I made inquiry and learned that ...Mr. William Everman was Administrator [for John Evans who had the Boone survey].

Now my dear sir I take this page of my Letter in thanking you for the Book you sent...as I naturally love books... *[Draper had sent him his King's Mountain book.*]

14C 13-13(2) N. C. Tuttle map: "A bird Eye View [sic] of the Pilot Knob and its vicinity," Powell, County, Ky., Feb. 10, 1885.

My Dear Sir

The above [referring to his map] is a bird-eye view of the Pilot Knob and its Vicinity. This Mountain is Situated in Powell County, Ky. About 1 ½ mile n. e. of the K U. R. R. and about 3 miles East of the Indians Old Fields...this mountain can be ascended or descended on Horseback... The cliff is on the South end of the Mountain, and the path is just north of the cliff... after arriving on the top, you may walk out to the top...which gives the greatest view of any mountain in Kentucky mountains in this vicinity. It is by estimation about 900 feet up to the foot of the cliff in perpendicular height from the bed of Brush Creek...

After arriving the top is oblong. You may walk back north for 100 or 150 yards though very narrow, and finally terminating with a small cliff, the top being covered with small timber and shrubbery, such as cedars, small hickory and red brush. This mountain is oblong, and covers several hundred acres, being disconnected from the other ranges of mountains... They are the last mountains reaching the Bluegrass regions of Kentucky...

I live about 10 miles from this Knob... The Indian Old Fields is about 3 miles nearly west of the Knob. Mr. John H. Goff is the owner of the greater part of the Old Fields...

Yours truly to be heard from again,
N. C Tuttle

14C 14-14(1) LCD: **Col. Boone & Land Matters, May 1785.** From "Memorials of the Crawford Family." Privately Printed, New York, 1883.

Copy of a letter from Col. Daniel Boone to Capt. Charles Yancey, transcribed by LCD from the original at the Virginia State Library. Thompson mentioned in this letter was Lawrence Thompson, Surveyor of Lincoln County, Ky./Va. Transcribing is uncertain. "Brother grant" probably refers to William Grant, husband of Boone's sister Elizabeth. "Patan" would refer to a land patent.

Dear Sir,

I rec'd yours Date the 20th febury 1785 and am very sorry to here you Never Rec'd a Later from me as I have wrote you three times Since I Saw you at Brother grants and sorry to here of the Dath of your brother as I make No Doubt it puts you to many Disadvantages. However We must submit to providence and provide for the Living and talk of our Lands

Your plots ware all Returned that we Survayd ameditly but Bridges and Boone's preemption and that of Boone's for a Most Simple Reason, in Making out his plot and Cald for my beginning the Enterry Said Runin North then East South and West to the beginning So I had another plot to make out and having no other bisness at the Regesters ofis I Lat Bridges Ly till a bout 7 months ago however I Expect them at Richmond by this time there are no Dispute reason on any of your lands at all The Land you got from Col. Todd is Not yet laid of for good Reasons Mr Parker his pardner was gon to philadelphia and Returned but a few Days ago and there patan is Come.

I went the other Day to Todds on that account and he is free to Do what he promised you but parker could Not be got at that time I also wanted Capt.

Hayes with me at the Layeing of the Land as he is Bater at the Bisness than myself . the u____t fees you desired me to Recall from the general Survayers I Exspet is useless until Col. Marshall Returns from Virginia at which time I Shall Demand it as for Mr. Thomson of Lincoln County he utterly Denide taking the Dubel fees and told me at that time he had no Right to them

My Best Respets to you and all your family and Remean your Most obedient omble Sarvent.

Daniel Boone
[in facsimilie – LCD]

14C 15 Original document dated Nov. 8, 1785 pertaining to slaves owned by McCartan Campbell and David[?] Zubly in possession of John Kincaid of Lincoln County, Ky.

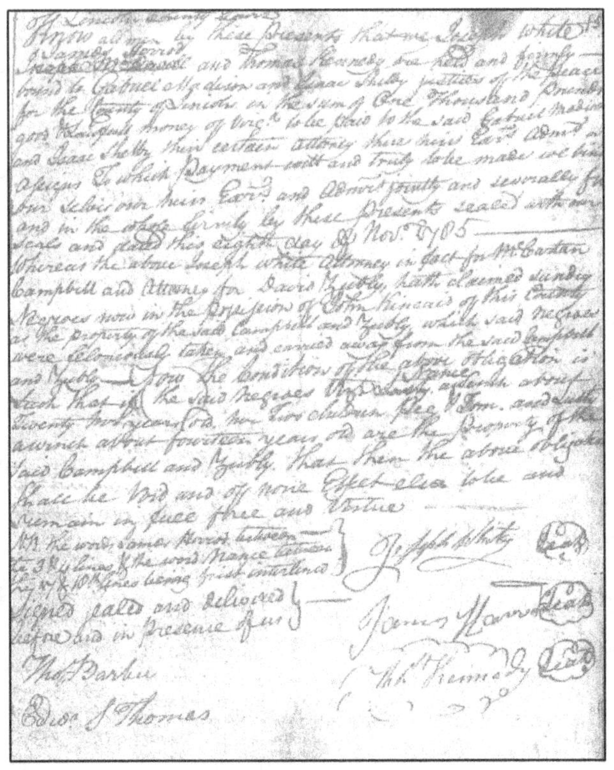

Slave document, 1785. DM 14C 15

[*words missing*] ... Lincoln County Court

Know all men by these presents that we Joseph White, James Harrod and Thomas Kennedy are held and firmly bound to Gabriel Madison and Isaac Shelby, justices of the peace for the County of Lincoln in the sum of One Thousand pounds good Lawfull money of Virginia to be paid to the said Gabriel Madison and Isaac Shelby their certain attorney their heirs, Executors, Administrators or Assigns To which Payment will and truly to be made we bind our selves...jointly and severally for and in the whole firmly by these presents sealed with our seals and dated this eighth day of November 1785.

Whereas the above Joseph White, Attorney in fact for McCartan Campbell and Attorney for David[?] Zubly, hath claimed sundry Negroes now in the possession of John Kincaid of this County as the property of the said Campbell and Zubly, which said Negroes were feloniously taken and carried away from the said Campbell and Zubly. Now the Condition of the above obligation is such, that of the said Negroes that Nance a wench about Twenty two years old, has Two children, Pec & Tom, and __usty, a wench about fourteen years old, are the property of the said Campbell and Zubly, that then the above obligation Shall be Void and of none Effect, also to be and remain in full force and Virtue.

N. B. The words James Harrod between the 3 & 4 lines of the word n___[?] between the 7 & 10th lines being first interlined.

Signed sealed and delivered before and in presence of :

Thos. Barbee

Edwd. S. Thomas

Signed:

Joseph White

James Harrod

Thos. Kennedy

The Sharp Family Captivity

The first captivity account in this volume are letters from the Sharp family and others telling of the capture and return of Rebecca Armstrong Sharp and her three children: Catherine, age 6, Mary, age 4, and William, age 3.

Rebecca, daughter of William Armstrong, was married to Abram Sharp and moved with the family to Kentucky about 1783 to settle in a cabin near McAfee's Station. Abram was away at the time of an Indian attack in 1786. Rebecca and the children had just returned from visiting her mother, Mrs. Armstrong. Rebecca's sister accompanied them home where Indians were concealed but did not attack until early the next morning. The sister, identified as Miss Armstrong, was killed as she ran out of the cabin after wrestling with an Indian at the cabin door.

The captives were taken to different Indian towns. Rebecca, the mother, was exchanged at the Limestone Treaty in 1787 and was in such poor health that she remained with a family there until such time as she was able to ride home. Her husband was there to receive her. By one account, he brought clothing for the captives and enough horses to ransom two captives.

It is thought that Catherine was exchanged at the same time with her mother. Mary and William, still very young children, remained with the Indians until sometime later. William was skilled with bow and arrow when he returned to Kentucky. Mary was eventually ransomed by her father and brought back to Kentucky. Though tied to the bedstead at night, she disappeared and was not heard from again. Family lore and even Draper suggested that she was married to Wyandot Chief Tar-Hee (The Crane).

See Katherine L. House, "Kentucky Biographical Notebook, Abraham and Rebecca Sharp, Ordeal at the Salt River, Autumn 1786"; *Filson Club History Quarterly*, vol. 61, no. 4, October 1967.

14C 16-16(1) James C. McAfee, Danville, Ky., 1868[?] LCD: **The Capture of Mrs. Sharp & Family, 1786.**

Lyman C. Draper Esq.

Dear Sir: After a long silence at last I am possessed in part of the information you desire. I have just read the Enclosed papers in reference to Col. Sharp.

You did not state in your letter what information you desire of Col. Bailey's relations, consequently I did not write to them.

I refer you to Judge Winifred Bailey of Stanford, Ky., I think a grand son of Col. Bailey, also James Green of Houstonville, Lincoln County, Ky. who married into the Family of Col. Baley. You speak of having written to me more than a year ago. Perhaps I was then absent from home east or south whither I spent some time. Would be pleased to answer any letter of enquiry you may make regarding old settlers of Ky.

Respectfully
Your friend
James C. McAfee

14C 17-17(1) Abram Sharp to Mr. McAfee. No date.

Abram Sharp was the son of the captive William, and grandson of Rebecca Sharp. The family were visiting at the Armstrong cabin before the attack.

> **Thinking there was no danger, they returned home in the evening...**

Mr. McAfee

The family of Col. Abram Sharp were captured under the following circumstances.

They had been to Mr. William Armstrong's, [*who was*] father to Grandmother [*Rebecca*] Sharp. (He lived where the Rev. D. P. Young now lives.) Thinking there was no danger, they returned home in the evening unaccompanied with any person except Miss Armstrong, sister to Mrs. Sharp.

The Indians were encamped on the creek near the house which was a log cabin. Hearing the calf balling [*bawling*] as they afterwards stated, [*the Indians*] went to the house that night before the family went to bed and peeping through the cracks of the house, saw them churning... No man person about, they did not interrupt them until next morning.

[*The Indians*] came at daylight. There was but one Indian that brought his gun with him and he did not go into the house but stood out in the chimney corner. As the others entered the house one of them seized Miss Armstrong and she being too stout for him, got away from him, and as she got over the fence, the man out of doors in the chimney corner shot her dead on the spot.

You can well cull out from these Scraps such information as you may think proper to send Mr.

Draper. I would like to have a Copy of his History when it is published.

If there is anything else I can furnish I would do so.

Yours &c
Abram Sharp

14C 18-18(1) Abram Sharp. *No salutation, no date.*

> **I do not know that grandmother saw any of her children until after they were exchanged.**

Col. Abram Sharp was born in Bedford County, Virginia, near the Peaks of Otter, in the year 1741. He was a Soldier in the Revolutionary War and participated in the Battle of Guilford about the year 1778 or 1778 [1781 – LCD]. He was married to Rebecca Armstrong, daughter of William Armstrong of Botetourt County, Virginia. He emigrated with his family to Kentucky in 1783, and was engaged frequently in Indian fighting, and helped to destroy an Indian town not far from Chillicothe, Ohio.

...his family, consisting of his wife, his daughter Catherine (born March 28, 1780), Mary (born Jan. 7, 1782) and his son William (born June 7, 1783) were captured by a band of Indians who had come to Kentucky for the purpose of plunder and hunting.

The family were separated soon after they arrived at the Indian Town. I do not know that grandmother saw any of her children until after they were exchanged.

Grandfather did not get all his family back at the same time; how long they were with the Indians I do not know. I have often heard my father (William Sharp) say, that he could shoot a bow & arrow very well when he got back. Grandfather did not find Aunt Mary for some time after he got the others. When and where he did find her, he had to pay a ransom for her.

She did not want to return with him. He, however, started for home with her and at night whilst he was asleep, although he had her inside of the fort, and tied to the bed stead on which he was sleeping, she was stolen from them. And he could never find any trace of her from that day to this.

Grand Mother Sharp died about 1807, and grand father Sharp died about 1823, in the eighty second year of his age.* They both died and were buried near the place where the family were captured by the Indians. The place is now owned by A. P. Sharp.

Yours Respectfully,
Abram Sharp

*1823
81
Born 1742 LCD

14C 19-20 LCD Memo on letter from Rev. A. A. Hogue, Salvisa, Ky., May 17, 1873.

In notes I took of Col. John Johnston, long Shawanoe Indian Agent in Ohio, p. 20 – it is stated that Sally Sharp was taken prisoner by the Wyandotts when young, & grew up pretty, when Tar-hee, The Crane, married her. Tar-hee's white wife, Sally Sharp, was captured on Greenbrier, perhaps in 1782 – as she was too young to remember anything about her family. She was about 66 in 1847; & in 1843 emigrated to Kansas with the Wyandotts. (Wyandotts migrated in July, 1843 – Howe's Ohio, p. 549). Hence born about 1780. Cist's Advertiser, Nov. 23, 1847.

I am convinced that Sally is a misnomer – either Col. Johnston did not retain the name accurately or the Indians had ignorantly changed it. That she was Mary Sharp, mentioned in Abram Sharp's letter – born Jan. 7, 1782, & captured with her mother, brother & sister on Salt River, Ky., near Harrodsburg.

LCD

The above speculation by Draper is that Mary Sharp was the wife of Wyandott Chief Tar-hee. It is known that Tar-hee was married to a French-Canadian woman who died in 1803; he may have married again the next year. Shawnee Indian agent Col. John Johnston gave Sallie as the name of Tar-hee's second wife.

Rev. A. A. Hogue, Salvisa, Ky., writes, May 17, 1873: Mr. Abram Sharp is still living, & occupying one of the old McAfee mansions near Salvisa, on Salt River. Mr. A. P. Sharp is dead, but his widow still lives on his farm.

Col. William Sharp, father of Abram, and who was taken by the Indians (this was the last raid of Indians in Ky.) was returned, and occupied a part of the old Sharp homestead. The point from where he was taken by the Indians is three or four hundred yards from where I write this – 4 miles west of Salvisa [*Mercer County, KY.]* He died in April, 1840, in this room where I write. He was elder in the New Providence Church, to which old Dr. Cleland preached for many years. One of Col. Sharp's sons, David Sharp, occupies the family mansion and farm at present. Uncle William Sharp was fifty-seven years old when he died.

LCD: See Trip 1858, vol. 1 p. 34 &c. Mrs. Anna Nicholson's recollections. **
See Trip 1860, vol. 8, p. 209. *
Cist's Advertiser, 1847-48, p. 142

*This says, in a list of prisoners with the Indians, "Mary Sharp taken in 1786, by the Shawanoes near McAfee's." Shane's Collections, v. p. 131 [LCD]

**The following two paragraphs are from Draper's interview with Mrs. Anna Nicholson, daughter of Jacob Boone who participated in the prisoner exchange at Limestone in 1787. She was 5 years old at the time, but remembered Mrs. Sharp being brought in to her family.

Col. Boone, Col. Sharp, Jacob Boone, Capt. Kenton, Col. B. Logan and some others, passed over the river, and went back about half a mile where the trail crosses Fishing Gut, where they met Mrs. Sharp mounted a-straddle, with nothing on her head, and dressed in leggings and petticoat... She seemed broken in spirits and paid little attention to the whites; though recognized her husband who was deeply moved.

She was taken to Jacob Boone's, got soap, and went to the river, above the creek, among the willows, out of sight, and washed herself, and put on clean clothes brought by her husband, who also brought clothing for his little girl; but for some reason...the little girl was not brought in. [DM 7S 34]

14C 21 William S. McMurtry. LCD interview with Dr. William S. McMurtry, Los Gatos, California, Jan. 31st, 1890. Born in Mercer County, Ky., Aug 24, 1818, son of William [McMurtry] & Priscilla Sharp.

This is from the son of Priscilla; she was not captured with others in the Sharp family.

**The Indians broke into the house
Leaving tomahawk hacks on the door.**

LCD: **Mrs. Sharp's Captivity**

Abraham L. Sharp was from Virginia, settled early in Kentucky. In 1786 while Mr. Sharp was absent on a campaign (perhaps Clark's Wabash Campaign of Sept. 1786) a party of seven Indians – nationality not remembered – came mainly to steal horses. Finding the Sharp residence with no men for its protection, concluded to attack it – left their guns at their camp, except one who took his along. The Indians broke into the house leaving tomahawk hacks on the door. A sister of Mrs. Sharp seized a chain & made fight, but at length fled out of the house. When jumping the fence, was shot by the Indian who had a gun. Hence he was stigmatized by his fellows [*as*] a squaw who could only fight & kill a squaw.

Mrs. Sharp, & a daughter...& two sons, William and John... were captured, while Priscilla, the youngest daughter, about two years old, was absent at a neighbor's visiting & escaped.

The two boys when returned from captivity had become quite like young Indians – dodging behind the stumps & trees...

****

14C 22 LCD: **Daniel Boone, 1786**

Early Spring* removes to Limestone. Col. Nathan Boone's notes p. 159, Trip, 1860, iv, p. 67

May – Store at Limestone. Shane's Collections, ii, Montgomery County, p. 20

Limestone – Cooper's Information, p. 20 (Cooper, Finlay, & Filson)

July 20 – Surveying – Roosevelt i. 339

See Zach. Holliday's note for this period - 2nd vol. Clark's Campaign
Boone loses his "Station" tract – an earlier survey to one Gordon of Spotsylvania. Shane ii, Montgomery County, 79

*April 28th 1786 – was near mouth of the Kanawha River. Collins Ky ii, 562. He must have gone east – perhaps to get goods as in May he had a store of goods at Limestone, as cited above. Perhaps got goods of Thomas Hunt at Hagerstown [?], Md. LCD.

14C 23-24 LCD: **Daniel Boone, 1786.**
From the Tri[?] Weekly Kentucky Yeoman, Feb. 15, 1881. Proceedings of Annual Meeting of the Kentucky Historical Society, Feb. 11, 1881.

The newspaper clipping, too dark to transcribe completely, is a letter from Daniel Boone to John Overton of Lincoln County concerning survey expenses that Boone had incurred for Overton. It is dated July 20, 1786. Following that is a discussion of the characteristics of Daniel Boone's writing, and a paragraph on Elijah Smith, who kept one of the first stores in Lexington. Explanation is given that John Overton and his brother Waller Overton emigrated from Virginia to Kentucky in 1784, "in company with Daniel Boone." John Overton later went to Tennessee while Waller Overton settled in the Blue-Grass region of Kentucky.

LCD sources: Logan's Expedition - Magazine of American History, I, 435.

Pension Statements, i, 66; Sudduth's Ms. Narrative p. 9, Abstract 1st reference below.

Shane's Collections ii: Bath County, p. 33, 70-72, 51, 58; Montgomery County p. 78; Nicholas County p. 5; Shane ii Fleming County p. 5; Henry
Wilson's Notes p. 79 &c; Abraham Thomas Scrap Book. p.34.
Deserted Camp – History Clinton County [Ohio?] p. 233, 237 - see Kenton Notes 1786.
Boone & Kenton commanded the advance: Letter in Flint's Geography & History ii, 472.
Boone at Maysville – boat house. Shane's ii, Fleming County, 13, 22; Bath County 51; Montgomery County 20.
May [1786] – Indians at mouth of Eagle Creek – Shane's Collections ii, Montgomery County, 22, 23

14C 25 LCD: **Daniel Boone – 1786,**
*October Trustee of town of Washington:
Henings, xi, 361.
Attack on Sharp Family, Salt River – Shane Collection, v,
131
A woman out soap-boiling kills an Indian near Grant's Station. Shane I, Fayette County, p. 5.
October – Logan's Campaign:
See Nathan Boone's Notes &c
Hunt's Geography & ____, ii, 469 &c
Ms. Patterson Papers,
Mrs. _____ poem
Shane's Collections, xiii p. 99; ____ _____

*The town of Washington, in the state of Virginia at that time, was founded on Simon Kenton's land. Boone was among the Town Trustees.

14C 26 Col. Levi Todd to Gov. [Patrick] Henry, Fayette County, Ky., June 22, 1786

Something should be done to save the lives and property of the frontier inhabitants...

Col. Todd says “Since Col. Boone’s removal, he had made every effort to regulate[?] the militia. He cannot make an accurate return, but the number Exclusive of officers, is about 1100. Something should be done to save the lives and property of the frontier inhabitants who have happened these six months past, and were exposed to many inroads of the Savages, as we did in that length of time through the whole course of the war, particular actions excepted.

I think it probable that a separation will...shortly take place, though I am at a loss to judge. The Kentucky people appear less unanimous than formerly, and a great variety of sentiment prevails.”

***

The Flinn Family Captivity

Draper received this second series of captivity correspondence from children and grandchildren of the Flinn family who were captured in western Virginia in 1786.

John and Elizabeth Halstead Flinn had settled on Cabin Creek near Kanawha River in western Virginia with their four children about 1784 when the frontier was vulnerable to Indian attack. One day John, Elizabeth and daughter Mary (called Polly) were outside putting up a pole to hang clothes. Indians attacked, led by renegade Simon Girty. John Flinn was shot and killed. Polly fell to the ground uninjured near her father and was presumed dead by the attackers.

Taking Elizabeth with them, the Indians went into the cabin and found the other three children: Nancy, Chloe, and John (approximate ages 8, 5, and 4). The Indians plundered the cabin, set fire to it, and started off to the Indian towns with the children and their mother.

When the Indians left with her family, Polly, about age 14, watched from a hiding place as their cabin burned. She ran to a neighbor's cabin but found it unoccupied. She made her way to Donnally's fort on foot; she did not see her family for several years.

When the captives arrived in the Indian village, only young John was allowed to stay in the same village with his mother Elizabeth. She spoke English to him often so he would remember his name. Elizabeth died in captivity.

John lived in various Indian villages and was given the name "The Man Who Limped" due to an injury suffered in early childhood. Years later, John visited his family in western Virginia for a few months, but could not be persuaded to stay. In 1811 he married Agnes Priest, whose family had moved to Ohio about 1805.

Nancy stayed with her Indian family until she was about age 17 when she was married to a Shawnee warrior. There is much speculation on the identity of Nancy's Shawnee husband, some indicating a connection to Tecumseh's family. Nancy was brought home by James Halstead, probably her mother's brother; her child, born a few months later, was named Elizabeth. Nancy married George Miller in 1800 and raised a family. Elizabeth grew up among her Virginia family; she married Simian Jarrell

Chloe's time in captivity was brief. She was rescued by Daniel Boone and/or exchanged at the Treaty at Limestone in 1787. Afterward she was taken in by some of Daniel Boone's relatives, but eventually was brought back to live with her older sister Polly.

14C 27 LCD: **Chloe Flinn**

Chloe Flinn would seem to have been born in 1779: Captured when [age] seven (says her son J. F. Ballard, & her grandson Ensminger) hence in 1786, when an Indian war broke out. Kept seven months on some authority, which would make it Spring of 1787 she was brought in to Boone's treaty at Limestone. Here is a complete corroboration.

Died in 1863 (as her son Boone Ballard says) - & aged 84 as her son J. F. Ballard says – which should be if [she was] born in 1779.

July 25, 1885 The grave stone says she died 9th. Nov. 1863, aged 83. Perhaps well along in her 84th year.

14C 28, 29 Letters from **L V. Flinn**, Alcouy[?], Ohio, 1883 and 1884.

Information in this letter duplicates that of others from the Flinn family and is not included here.

14C 30-30(3) Elizabeth Flinn Hain, May 3, 1884, Port Jefferson, Ohio. Elizabeth Hain was the daughter of the captive John Flinn.

> **He built four fires – one on each side,**
> **one at the head, and one at the feet –**
> **this is the way he had to do to**
> **keep the wolves from devouring him.**

He raised his gun, took aim & fired & down came a coon. He was so hungry he could almost have devoured it raw. Now-days, people think they can't eat without preserves or jelly.

Dr Sir:

I lived longer at home with my father (John Flinn) than any of my brothers, & heard him relate about his father & family.

My grandfather lived in Greenbrier County Virginia in a fort. Went out in the evening to his farm to fix his fence. The oldest daughter had dreamed the preceding night that some red men came there, and tapped them all on the shoulder but her father, that they tapped him on the head. The next day her dream was made manifest.

They heard a halloo – four Indians approached, Simon Girty their leader. They were ordered to march out – Mr. Flinn & his daughter Nancy [Polly] marched out, the others staying in the hut or cabin. The Indians shot Mr. Flinn with two bullets. Nancy fell at the same time, though not hurt. They did not scalp their victims. After plundering the house of what they wanted, they set it on fire, & they started with their prisoners.

After they had been some little time gone, Nancy, who had been lying beside her dead father, arose, & gazing in the distance at her receding friends, her first impulse was to follow them & share their fate, but she did not. As night approached, she started for the fort. I had the pleasure of seeing her in after years.

Father said that he & his mother & two sisters marched 3 days. Father was only 5 years old, & having had his foot cut severely, the Indians let him ride, while the others had to take it on foot. Then they went three days, & came to a Shawnee village. They had three warriors stand guard over the prisoners. An old squaw took my father from the guard out behind a tree. When he learned their language, he found they were going to burn him. His mother lived about six months. So great were her hardships, that when one day she threw down a load of wood she had been required to carry, she fell dead.

At first they gave my father a bow and arrow to learn to hunt, & afterwards gave him a rifle.

The Indians said they believed he could put a hundred bullets on top of another at a mark. When he became a young man, he then became free to do as they did.

He was 82 when he died – made his will. When a young man, he was keeping store at Fort Wayne – having been hired as an interpreter. This was after he became grown up & free. That was all the opportunity of learning he had. He had learned figures on the scales while in the public store at Fort Wayne.

He gave land to all his children – had 100 acres when he died, & did not owe a cent. Never was known to be in a saloon – that is what I call a man among men.

Grandfather's name was John Flinn, as was my father's. He was a smart man. His girls were Nancy, 17, Couy [Chloe], 15; Lizzie [Mary/Polly], 12.

[Ages when taken? LCD]

One evening before he started to go [home to Virginia – LCD] he built four fires – one on each side, one at the head, and one at the feet – this is the way he had to do to keep the wolves from devouring him, just before he laid down. Not having eaten anything for ten days he looked up into the tree, & saw what seemed like two balls of fire – he raised his gun took aim, & fired & down came a coon. He was so hungry he could almost have devoured it raw. Now-days, people think they can't eat without preserves or jelly.

The names of my father's children are James, John, Jeremiah, Anna, George, Emilia, Lizzie, Benjamin, Adam, Peter, Dieh [Jedediah? LCD], Isaiah, Chapman, & Elizabeth.
He was twice a prisoner – taken in 1812, before he had any children.

He was hired by Johnston, the Indian agent, to go out to Fort Wayne & see if the Indians were going to make war against the Americans.

Simon Girty wanted the whites to hire him to be a leader on their side, & they would not – so he joined the Indians & did all the mischief he could. Write if you wish me to tell you any thing more. Could I talk to you instead of writing, I could tell you many things.

Elizabeth Hain

14C 31-32 Elizabeth Flinn Hain, May 15, 1884

> **A guard was appointed to prevent intoxicated Indians from burning him.**
>
> **The woods were his home – whenever night overtook him, he laid down to sleep.**

Mr. Draper Dear Sir:

Answers to you inquires.
1st The Flinn children were all born in Greenbrier County,
Virginia
2nd As to Aunt Nancy Miller, I do not know when she died.
3rd That was [what] the Indians did when they received a prisoner – a guard was appointed to prevent intoxicated Indians from burning him.

4th My father said it was only six months after captivity till his mother's death.
5th. My father's mother's first name was Elizabeth.
6th. Yes, it was Simon Girty that led the band that killed my grandfather & captured the family.
7th. My father's first captivity was as related when he was five years old.

His second captivity was after he was married – when Indian agent [John] Johnston living in Piqua, Ohio, hired my father in the War of 1812, knowing he was acquainted with the Indians, to go to Fort Wayne to ascertain if they were going to engage in war against the Americans. They had a battle that day, & they all knew him. They were angered because he left them. They called him a spy and took him prisoner.
8th. When the Flinn family were captured, they were taken to the Shawanoe village. I don't know how long they were there.
9th. He happened to look up into the tree, as mentioned in my former letter, & seeing the coon, shot him, & had his supper. 10th. The woods were his home – whenever night overtook him, he laid down to sleep.

If you are living in Madison, I will be out there this Fall to see my brothers. When I will tell you the rest. If nothing happens, I will be there this Fall.

Elizabeth Hain

14C 33-33(3) Amos Flinn, Frankfort, Kansas, May 11, 1884, son of the captive John Flinn.

> **He was about twelve years old when threatened to be burned. He was bought from the stake by an old French woman with a quart of whisky.**

Dear Sir:

In reply to your letter of March 30, 1884, I had forgotten a good deal concerning the captivity of my father's family. I have been studying on it is the reason I have not sooner written you.

My father's family was captured in Greenbrier County, Virginia. His father was gathering corn in a field. My father was five years old when captured - & was 82 when he died.

Your 2nd question: There were eight or ten Indians of the party – I don't know their leader's name. I think they were Miamies or Shawanoes. I can't tell which. Nor can I tell you the names of the Indian towns to which the captives were taken, but they lived near to a fort...

Your 3rd question: Father (John Flinn) lived most of the time of his captivity in Ohio and Indiana, but I do not know in what Indian towns.

He was about twelve years old when threatened to be burned. He was bought from the stake by an old French woman with a quart of whisky, and taken to the woods... & hid two or three days till the Indians got sober. He lived with this old French lady two or three years, & then she sold him to the Indians. I don't know to what tribe. He was sold three or four times for a quart of whisky each time.

4th question. The names of his sisters – the oldest was Polly, the other Chloe, both of whom were captured. Polly married an Indian, & had one child. Both of them were stolen from the Indians by Daniel Boone.

There was another girl that fell when her father was shot down in the corn-field, but was not hurt nor scalped. When the Indians left with their prisoners, she went to the fort, & here we lost track or her. Her name was Nancy. Their mother was captured at the same time. After killing old Mr. Flinn, & taking Mrs. Flinn & the eldest girl, they went to the house & took little John & Chloe, set the house on fire, & left.

They kept Mrs. Flinn to do their hard work – she fell dead packing a load of wood.

When Mr. Flinn was killed, there were three shots fired at him & they all struck him. As the girl fell at the same time, I suppose the Indians thought she was shot also.

Father left the Indians at the age of twenty-one years. They set him free. They gave him a gun and some ammunition. He then went to Fort Wayne, Indiana, & hired to a merchant as clerk to trade with the Indians. He remained seven years in this employment, and then concluded he would settle down. He got married in Virginia to a girl of the name of Agnes Priest. They had two children. The Government hired him to go out among the Indians as a spy – there he was taken prisoner again. He was gone about three months, and his family supposed he was killed. He stole away from the Indians when they were asleep.

After that he lived on his farm in Miami County, Ohio until his death. He left a wife & fourteen children, twelve boys and two girls, all living but three of the boys, & a daughter-in-law.

This is all I can recollect. I would like to see your book when printed - & maybe could sell some of them. I think all of the Flinns would by the work.

Yours &c,
Amos Flinn

14C 34-34(1) John B. Miller, Bald Knob, Boone County, W. Va., Sept 2, 1885, son of the captive Nancy Flinn. Note at end from A. J.[?] Miller.

Mr. L. C. Drapery [sic]

Dear sir: I received your Book and letter in regard to Chloe Flinn being captured by the Indians. You are mistaken. It was my mother Nancy Flinn and John Flinn. Nancy Flinn lived with the Indians 12 years, then returned to Virginia and married a Miller. If you want all the statement about Nancy Flinn you must write to me, and I will give you a full statement of her life.

John B. Miller

Mr. Drapery [sic], I could give you a full statement of Nancy Flinn if my mother was at home but I think father can giv a Correct Statement. He is giting veary old. You drop me a postal card and I Will rite it out.

A.F. Miller[?]

14C 35-35(1) A. F.[?] Miller, Oceana, Virginia, October, 1883, son of the captive Nancy Flinn.

She heard the Bones crush in him.

Nancy Flinn
1st She was Born in 1778 Monroe County, Virginia.
2nd They [her parents – LCD] was Born in 1700 I suppose in Virginia. I think so.
3rd Grand father hadn't been in Kanawha very long – they moved from Monroe County, Va.
4th There was about fifteen or twenty Indians [of the capturing party – LCD].
5th I don't know who was their leader.
6th She was taken to the state of Ohio near Detroit.
7th She died before the war about 1850 – She was about 80 years old.
8th They were living on Cabin creek, in Kanawha County, West Virginia; it was in the spring. Grandfather, grandmother, and mother, Chloe & John Flinn was out Fixing up the fence one morning. Then they was going to the fort for shelter. While grand

father was tying up the fence, the Indians shot him dead, and when they came up, they turned him over. She [Nancy – LCD] heard the Bones crush in him.

Grand Mother went to see mother, and mother said the Indians killed her – She was so old. Before they left, they burnt the house. Mother was young and staid with them till she was grown. You cant make her case as bad as it was. She was badly treated. She had one Child after She come back. The child died in 1878. It was half Indian.

The tribe took her to Detroit. You will know the tribe. I could tell you more, but you know more about their Customs than I can tell you.

This Republican wants J. G. Blaine For President in 1884.

Yours truly.
A. F.[?] Miller

14C 36 J. B. Miller, Bald Knob, Boone County, W.Va., April 15, 1884

Dear Sir
In reply to your letter I will question the old man for you again:
1st Mother [Nancy Flinn – LCD] was about [age] 8 I gu[e]ss [when captured – LCD]
2n John Flinn was about two years younger [than Chloe – LCD].
3rd I think Adam Hann raised her [Chloe Flinn – LCD] in Monroe County, Va.
4th I think it was Shawnees that took her to Detroit.
5th I don't know. She died in Missouri [when she died & age – LCD]. Reference Charley Miller, Mary Miller, Adam Miller's wife in Harrison County, Mo. They may have a record of her death.
6th I have no recollection of it [a narrative of her captivity – Nancy Flinn. LCD]

7th Roda Gillespie, Polly Miller in Coffee, Burg*, ___ Harrison Co., Mo.
Rite to William Gillaspie and he will give you the Post Office of the two sisters.

Yours Truly
J. B. Miller

*Coffeeburgh, Daviess Co., Mo. LCD

14C 37 John Jarrell, Winifrede, W. Va., Oct. 20, 1883, grandson of captive Nancy Flinn.

The writer referred Draper to his sister, Mary Williams, at Pattonsburg, Davis County, Missouri.

14C 38 Kemper Jarrell, Jan. 22, 1884, *son of Elizabeth, the child of Nancy born after she returned from captivity.*

> **She had a child while she was a prisoner, & this child was my mother.**

Mr. L. C. Draper: - Sir:

I wish to have a correspondence with you, as my grandmother [Nancy Flinn – LCD] was stolen by the Indians. She had a child while she was a prisoner, & this child was my mother. I am one third Indian blood.

Send me your Historical Society Collection, I will send you the record of my generation.

Browntown, Kanawha Co., West Va.

Kemper Jarrell

14C 39-39(1) Kemper Jarrell, February 10, 1884

Mr. Lyman C. Draper

Dear Sir I was very glad too think you want information of my Grand Mother and her generation as

I can not give you any Information in this letter. My Grand Mother wrote out her life in full before she died and as soon as I can get the life of her I will give you ever thing in full that you ask of me and A good meny more that is composed of the Indian party and soon as I collect ever thing I will give you full Information my Grand Mother and her _____ generation.

You wanted the names of the Grand Children and there Post Office address. they request me to ask you if those books are free reports for our party. if they are they say that they would be very glad if you will send them all one A piece and they will assist all they can in giving you information. I will give you the names of those requested me too ask you for the collections.

I will give you names of them and Post Office address Brownstown, Ka[nawha] County, West. Va. These are their names: Albert Jarrell, William Jarrell, Jasper Jarrell, Joseph K. Jarrell, John Jarrell.

there is A good ----_in Boone County composed of the meny Indian party whitch I am not able too give you eny information About them in this letter but I will give you ever thing you ask me in the next _____.

14C 40-40(1) John Flinn's Captivity – 1786.
LCD: Copy from letter in pencil.

> **Once he was in a hollow log,**
> **and they ran directly over it.**

Mary Ann Flinn, Shidler, Delaware County, Ind., April 15, 1884, daughter of captive John Flinn.

When Father Flinn's adopted [Indian – LCD] father was killed in a skirmish, then he thought he would go back to Virginia to see his people, but when he got there, he did not like to stay with them, for he did not like their way of cooking. He did not feel at home with them. So he told them that he was going back to the Indians again. They begged & plead with him not to go, but they could not persuade him to stay with them any longer.

After he returned to the Indians, he discovered that he did not like them any more. They took him prisoner, some of them declaring he was a spy, while some plead for him. They took his horses and guns from him, and left him with the squaws. The Indians went for plunder where they had a skirmish the day before. They allowed to attend to him the next day. He suspected that they would shoot or burn him when they returned. He went and got his gun, and the squaws asked him what he was going to do. He replied that he was going home. They said he had better not go, for if the Indians should catch him, they would kill him. He said he knew that as well as they did. He started. The Indians followed him three or four days, and once he was in a hollow log, and they ran directly over it. He traveled by night, hiding by day. He swam a large stream, & at length reached the settlements again, but underwent many hardships in accomplishing it. He was as much of an Indian as any of them, and knew all their tricks very well. He could talk nine different Indian languages.

Father Flinn got married in Virginia, Greenbrier County, to Miss Agnes Priest in 1810, & raised twelve sons and two daughters, all growing to be men and women, & all were at his burial.

My husband has been sick for some time. J. W. Flinn is here helping me take care of him. James Flinn's memory is not very good now.

Mary Ann Flinn

James Flinn writes a few lines saying he can add nothing to what his brother, J. W. Flinn has sent – time has blotted out incidents from his memory.

14C 41-41(1) Adam Flinn, Oregon, Holt County, Mo., April 17, 1884, *son of captive John Flinn*

> **The people had to stay in the fort. They would slip out & plant little patches of corn.**

.

LCD: John Flinn's Captivity – 1786. A copy from letter in pencil.

Lyman C. Draper – Sir:

I received your letter &c a few days ago. Forty years ago I could have answered your questions, as I heard my father relate the particulars of his captivity. He used frequently to talk to us on that subject. I am sixty years old, & have forgotten some, but will do the best I can.

1s The date of father's birth I can't give you. He was born in Greenbrier County, Va. He was four or five years old when captured. He died June 11, 1857, in his 82nd year.

2nd As to the number of Indians, their leader, to what towns taken, I cannot say.

At the time when taken, the people had to stay in the fort – part of the time they would slip out, & plant little patches of corn. His folks went to farm to look after their corn. Some Indians came on them. My grandfather & two of his girls were in the field; while grandmother & my father were at the house. The Indians fired on grandfather. He fell, having received seven shots. One of the girls fell, the Indians, supposing one shot struck & killed her. They took the other girl prisoner, & went to the house, took out what they wanted, and then set it on fire. Grandmother, my father & sister were taken. When they were gone, the surviving girl who fell in the cornfield, got up & went to the fort.

3rd Before father was able to hunt, & make his own living, he fared hard, & went hungry many times. As soon as he could carry a shot gun, the Indians furnished him one, & then he did better. As soon as he was large enough to use a rifle, they gave him one. Then, he said, he was all right.

4th He was with seven different tribes & could talk their language. He never took any part of their fighting. He was sent off with the squaws & young Indians to hunt for them. Can't say what towns he lived in. Don't know his age when threatened to be burned – must have been seven or eight. A French woman bought him from the Indians for a pint of rum.

5th His mother lived about three years, & fell dead as she dropped a load of wood from her shoulder. Father's sister – Chloe, I think, was her name. Don't know her age – was separated from him & he never after saw her till he was rising of sixty years of age. He then sent one of my brothers, & money to pay their expenses, and she came and paid him a visit – a meeting of great joy.

I cannot think of any thing else that would be of importance to you – or I would be glad to write it.

Yours respectfully
Adam Flinn

14C 42-43 J. F. Ballard, Reeses Mills, Boone County, Indiana. July 22, 1882.

LCD: **Chloe Flinn's Captivity**

Mr. Draper Dear Sir

I received your letter but not in due time for I was away from home. You wished to know about my mother's captivity. All that I know is as my mother has told me but I will give it to you as near as I can.

1[s] My mother was Seven years old when captured. 2nd The tribe was the flat head nation. The number in their company was about fifteen but I could not say who their leader was.

3rd She said she was with them about eight months.

4th Colonel Boone made a treaty with them and got her from them but I could not say what kind.

5th My father I think was born in 1779 or near that time and was 84 years old when he died. And my mother as well as I recollect was just seven years younger than my father and She died in her 84th year. I was born in 1810, 18th October – had three brothers older than me and one Sister. Three Brothers and two Sisters younger. my mother was sixteen or near that when married.

I have tried to answer your questions as near as I can. I am the only one of the children that is living in Indiana. Two of my brothers are living in Missouri. The rest are all dead. If you Should make a book I would like to have a copy of your work.

I remain your Friend.

When your first letter came I was about Seventy-five miles further west – had not been to Waldron for three years.

Yours
J. F. Ballard

LCD Questions, July 25, 1883.
1st Who [were] your mother's parents & where raised?
2nd How long in Cabin Creek when attacked?
3rd Shawnees or Cherokees who captured your mother?

4th With which did your mother live after her return, & where?
5th Record of your mother's death? Gravestones of her & your father – near Waldron? Who could I write to for inscription?
6th Names & address of your two surviving brothers.
7th What time in the year your mother was taken? One account says they were in the cornfield; if hoeing, then it was in the summer; if gathering corn, in the Fall.
8th Your aunt Polly Mann's[?] descendants.
9th Your Aunt Nancy Miller's descendants.

Answers to the above questions were not found.

During the time of Chloe's return, Daniel Boone was hunting and selling ginseng in western Virginia. Rebecca and two of their sons, Nathan and Daniel Morgan Boone, accompanied him on these keel boat journeys. Nathan reported to Draper that Chloe Flinn was with them on one of these journeys and that she was taken to live with the family of John Van Bibber, close friends of the Boones, until she could be returned to her family.

14C 44 LCD: Captivity of Chloe Flinn – Rescued by Col. Boone. From Dr. J. P. Hale's article in the Kanawha Gazette, Sept. 27, 1882.

The clipping is not entirely legible. Part of the article is paraphrased here in italics; direct quotes are without italics. The statement that Boone was in the area when the Flinns were attacked is not given in any other account. In this statement, Chloe Flinn's grandson, St. Clair Ballard, credits Boone with rescuing his mother.

John Flinn's cabin was "situated between two branches of the creek...known as "Flinn's wet branch" and "Flinn's dry branch," *and these are important landmarks in surveys and land suits.*

Daniel Boone happened to be near at hand... at once organized a party for pursuit, over took and killed the Indians and rescued the prisoner, who being an orphan, was brought up and educated by Boone...

St. Clair Ballard
Findagrave.com/memorial.49604739/st_clair_ballard#view-photo-139828030. Photograph, Richard C. LeRoy

The article continues that Boone County, West Virginia, was named for Daniel Boone when it was formed at the session of the Legislature in 1846-1847. St. Clair Ballard described the military services of Daniel Boone and claimed that his mother, Chloe Flinn Ballard, had proposed the naming of the county for Boone. The county seat was named Ballardsville.

On the same page is the following letter.

LCD to Sheriff of Logan County, W. Va., Oct 4, 1882

Dear Sir:

I write to you for information about St. Clair Ballard who some 35 years ago represented your county in the Virginia Legislature... I would like to know his address – [or] of any brother or sister... to whom you can refer me.

Be good enough to inform me – for which I shall feel thankful.

Very Truly Yours
Lyman C. Draper

14C 45 John E. Peck, White's[?] Mills, Logan County, W. Va., Oct.[?], 11[?], 1882

Dr Sir:

Mr. St. Clair Ballard died some 4 or 5 years ago of ____, rather suddenly...I think he has a son living in Boone County, W. Virginia named Ma---- Ballard, Madison Post Office, Boone County, W. Virginia. You might get information useful to you concerning Mr. Ballard from William Allen, Esq., or John Powell, Esq., same address...

Yours Respectfully,
Jno E. Peck

14C 46-46(2) M. S. Ballard, Madison, Boone County, W. Va., Nov 1, 1882. *The writer was son of St. Clair Ballard. Letter written in pencil has been traced over in ink.*

Mr. Draper Sir:

I received a letter from you in reference to the capture of my grand mother by the Indians and her rescue by Daniel Boon, in which you referred to a newspaper account by Mr. Hale, of Kanawha County, West Virginia. I saw the same account and it is correct, as I have always understood the case. My grand parents moved away from here when I was a small boy and I have no recollection of dates. I will give the names and P. O. address of persons that probably can give the desired information:

Boone Ballard – Bethany, Harrison County, Missouri

John F. Ballard – Waldron, Shelby County, Indiana

St. Clair Ensminger – Shelbyville, Shelby County, Indiana

Andrew Ensminger – Shelbyville, Shelby County, Indiana

The Ballards named are sons of my grandmother and the others [are] grandchildren.

There are some old people in this county that I think would know some of the particulars of the case. I will see them and, if so, will write to you. If you write to those referred to, tell them who gave you their address – as they know me and will answer your Letter more readily.

My name is M. S. Ballard, the oldest son of St. Clair Ballard.

14C 47-48 LCD questions *to Chloe Flinn's sons,* Nov. 5, 1882

1st What were the names of the parents of Chloe Flinn – were they both killed, & were others killed?

2nd What were the particulars of Chloe Flinn being taken – what [was] her age at the time?

3rd When & where was she born?

4th Where did her parents reside when she was captured?
5th How many Indians composed the party – of what tribe - & name of the leader?
6th How far was Chloe Flinn taken before she was rescued - & at what place was she rescued?
7th Under what circumstances did Col. Boone hear of her captivity – and how did he accomplish the rescue - & how many were with him?
8th To whom was your mother married, & when & where, & at what ages did she and her husband die?
9th How did the Indians treat her when with them - & how long with them?

LCD

Also sent the same in substance, to St. Clair & Andrew Ensminger, grandsons of Chloe Flinn – both of Shelbyville, Indiana, Nov. 5, 1882.

14C 49-49(3) M. S. Ballard, Madison, Boone County, W. Va., Nov. 19, 1882.

> **One sister hid in a sink hole in the ground and staid till the Indians left them.**

Mr. Draper

Sir: I have delayed answering yours of the 5th expecting to see some old people in this county that I think know something about the capture and rescue of my grand mother, but have not seen them, as my business keeps me close at home.

I will give you their names:

Andrew Kessinger and Nancy Ballard of this place.

I will try to answer your questions to the best of my recollection.

1st I think she was captured in Kanawha County, this state, on the Kanawha river, 25 miles above Charleston. 2nd I don't know what age she was when captured but think she was very young, some three or four years old. 3rd She had no brother or sister killed; one brother was captured with her, and staid with the Indians till grown, and then settled somewhere in Ohio – his name was John F. Flinn.

One sister hid in a sink hole in the ground and staid till the Indians left them, then went to Greenbrier County this state to a fort, about sixty miles and give the news of what had happened.

4th I know nothing about the number or the tribe of Indians. 5th She was taken to Ohio, but I don't know to what place. I don't think She was with the Indians very long.

6th I can give no particulars of the rescue.

7th I know nothing about how she was treated by the Indians. 8th She was married to John Ballard. She and her husband died in Shelby County, Indiana.

9th They moved to Indiana about 47 years back. [1795 – LCD]

I am fifty years old. My father [was] thirty-three years old when I was born, and he was her [Chloe's] second or third child, which would make her very old when she died, which was during the late war.

M. S. Ballard

14C 50-50(1) Boone Ballard, Bethany, Harrison County, Ill., Dec. 6, 1882. Son of Chloe Flinn Ballard.

Mr. Draper – Dear Sir: After some thought on the subject, I will endeavor to give you as near a correct history of my mother's captivity by the Indians as I can. In answer to your questions:

Chloe Flinn's parents' names were John & Elizabeth. They lived near the mouth of Cabin Creek on the Kanawha river. It seems that the old lady had a dream at night that caused uneasiness, and they all went out next morning to lay up some poles on the fence, preparatory to going to the fort that day. A band of Indians, I am not prepared to give the number nor the name of the leader, but my understanding is they were of the Cherokee tribe. They came upon them when in the act of laying a pole on the fence. Shot the old man while they were all lifting at the pole; they captured the old lady and three children – 2 girls and a boy. The 4th child, which was the eldest girl of that family, ran and fell into a sink-hole and escaped.

Chloe was 3 years old at the time of her capture. They kept her about one year. She never could ----- much at the treatment. They took them all from West Virginia into Ohio. Think Col Boone captured Chloe at or near the Sciota River. I think he was passing in search of some other children and came near their compound, found her with some other small children playing on the out skirts - told her to jump on his back and he would take her home and she done so. He traveled with her some distance. Came to a steep prespice and to avoid pursuit managed to swing himself over into the water, and by wading considerably, escaped.

Nancy was the other captive. She was older than mother. They kept her until she was about 20 years old and was married to a chief. She was discovered by some traders on the Ohio river somewhere near Maysville, decoyed[?] on their boat and captured.

John was the son's name; he stayed with them until grown, then became a trader with them, followed that until he became too old, then settled on the Sciota River and died there.

As regards the old lady's death, there is nothing definite. They kept her with the children for some time after they went into Ohio and there was a party went out on a hunting expedition. Took her with them, but she never returned. They reported that she died.

The girls when recaptured were taken back to Virginia to their friends. Nancy, the oldest, married George Miller, lived there to ripe old age and moved to Missouri and died in Harrison County.

Chloe married John Ballard, moved to Indiannia in 1833, lived and died there. Father died in 1862, mother in 1863. Mother being about 75, and Father 80 years of age.

Now, Mr. Draper, I have given you as correct a history of this narrative as my memory and health would permit. You can take and paint it over and make the best of it you can. I would just say to you that I received a very nice[?] title present in the way of a book and feel grateful to you for past favors but would feel moreso if when you get your history complete you would mail me a copy.

Boone Ballard.

14C 51-52 LCD to Boone Ballard, Feb. 14, 1882

Guess work in matters of history is not safe, & leads to many errors.

I am much puzzled about your mother's age when captured & when she died – the accounts I have conflict much with each other.

1st. Have you any record of your mother's birth & death?

Your nephew, M. S. Ballard was born in 1800, & [said] that there were one or two older children than St. Clair. Andrew Kessinger writes that Chapman Ballard was born in 1799, St Clair in 1802, you in 1804. I suppose he sort of guesses at these dates.

But if Chapman Ballard, your older brother, was born about 1798, St. Clair in 1800 – then your father & mother must have been married about 1797; & supposing your was about sixteen when married, that would fix her birth-year about 1781. Mr. Kessinger says she mother was born in 1781 or 1782. You say she was 75 when she died in 1863 – that would fix her birth year in 1788 – and would make her only ten years old when Chapman was born in 1798, if he was born then. That could not be.

At all events, you can see that I need some more accurate dates to guide me – guess work in matters of history is not safe, & leads to many errors.

You can, at least, tell me the date of your own birth - & how many brothers & sisters you had older than yourself:

Please name them in their order & their birth years.

2nd Where was your mother born?

3rd How long was she detained in captivity?

4th Were you named after Daniel Boone because he rescued your mother from captivity? And was she accustomed to speak of Boone as the person who had rescued or redeemed her?

5th What was your mother's age when married?

6th Are there any surviving children – your cousins – of your other sisters & of your uncle John Flinn? If so, give me their names and address.

7th How far above the mouth of Cabin Creek did your grandfather live, & on which side of it?

Which is your nearest rail-road station?

8th After your mother's return from captivity, with whom did she live & where?

One account says she lived with Boone.

LCD

14C 53-53(3) Andrew Kesinger, Madison, W. Va., Dec. 29, 1882, nephew of John and Chloe Flinn Ballard. *Andrew Kesinger had heard first-hand accounts from Polly and Nancy Flinn.*

LCD notes [partly obscured in margin]: The Flinns were all carried to Ohio that were captured except the mother. We have no history as to what became of her. The children never knew, supposed she was murdered.

Dear Sir:
Yours of the 14th instant is at hand. Below you will find information that I have in regard to the subject of your letter. I was born on the 12th day of January 1804, in the county of Monroe, Va. My father's name was Mathias Kesinger. He was born in Monroe, Va. My Mother was a sister of John Ballard, who married Chloe Flinn. My Grandfather and Mother came from Germany. My Grand father was ____ Matthias Kesinger and my Grand mother's maiden name was Juda Sipes[?].

I first knew Chloe Flinn after she had married John Ballard. When a small boy, living in Monroe County, Va., John and Chloe had three [LCD: four] male children: Chapman, St. Clair, and Medley. Chapman was born in the year 1799, St. Clair [in] 1802, Medley [in] 1804, & Boone Ballard, named for Daniel Boone.

I think from the best information that I have that Chloe Flinn was born about the year 1781 or 1782, and was married to John Ballard about the year 1798.

Chloe's father & mother were living on Cabin Creek, then Greenbrier County, now Kanawha County, at the time of their capture & killing of her father. Do not know the name of Chloe's father & mother. They had four children named respectively, Polly, Nancy, John, and Chloe.

At the time of the capture, their father was killed – was at the time engaged in putting up a pole on forks to hang clothes on after being washed. The Mother, Nancy, John, and Chloe were captured. Polly secreted herself in a hollow log and remained all night. Have heard her say that during the night she imagined she heard the Indians walking about near her concealment, but was relieved by hearing a deer jump off and whistle.

The next morning, she, being satisfied that the Indians were gone, made her way down to Fort Donnally, about 10 miles below, about 2 or three miles above where the City of Charleston is now situated. Polly afterwards married Adam Mann in Monroe County, Va., where she lived until her death. My recollection now is that she has been dead about 30 years.

Nancy Flinn was with the Indians several years. Likely she was 16 or 17 years old when she was taken from the Indians. She was stolen from the Indians by a man by the name of Halstead in Ohio. He was a relation of the Flinns. At that time, she had married an Indian and was enceinte by her Indian husband. After her return to Monroe County the child was born, a girl, who afterwards married Simeon Jarrell and settled about 3 miles above this place over Little Coal River where she lived & died. Her name was Elizabeth. Nancy after her return to Monroe County, Va. married a man by the name of George Miller and moved to Coal River a short distance from here. About the year 1830 they moved to Jackson County, Ohio. I went with them to assist them in moving. Miller and his wife afterwards moved to Missouri; they are both dead.

John Flinn remained with the Indians in Ohio until peace was made with them. He then settled there, the Indians giving him a large tract of land. He afterwards accumulated considerable property.

Chloe Flinn was married to John Ballard in Monroe or Kanawha County and moved afterwards to Coal River near here[?], thence to Indiana, Shelby County.

Chloe was very small when she was captured. My understanding has been that Daniel Boone exchanged a small Indian for her in Ohio. At the time she was exchanged, she was sitting on a bear skin. Boone brought her back to Kanawha and gave her to a man by the name of Slaughter – who raised her.

I have visited the spot where Flinn was killed on Cabin Creek. When I was young I have listened with great interest to Nancy Flinn, who married George Miller, relating her life among the Indians. She could make a nice moccasin, made a pair and presented to me.

I think it was the Shawnees that captured the Flinns, but I am not certain. Having given you a brief account of my recollections of history of the Flinn family as I learned it many years ago,

I remain yours truly,
Andrew Kesinger

John and Chloe Ballard have been dead ----_years, have a large connexion in this state & Indiana.

14C 54-55 LCD to Andrew Kesinger, Jan. 12, 1883
LCD: **Chloe Flinn's Captivity.**

1st At the time of this attack on the Flinns, were there other families residing on Cabin Creek[?]. And how far above the mouth of the Creek, on which side, did the Flinns live?
2nd Can you describe the locality where Flinn lived – whether in a valley or on upland?
3rd Can you refer me to any surviving children of Polly Flinn, afterwards Mrs. Mann; & Elizabeth (Nancy's

daughter) afterwards Mrs. Simeon Jarrell (if I read your letter aright) - & of Mrs. Nancy Miller - & of John Flinn, in Ohio?

4th If you can recall anything further about Col. Daniel Boone's going after Chloe Flinn – where he went to get her; or how long she was a prisoner, or how old when released – whether any one went with Boone on the trip – or anything else connected with Boone's journey? Or was the exchange for her effected at Maysville, Ky., where Indians would sometimes bring their prisoners, & where Boone lived before moving to the Kanawha country?

5th Can you refer met to any of the Slaughter family who raised Chloe – or at least, tell me where they lived?

14C 56-56-56(2) Andrew Kesinger, April 23, 1883, Madison, W. Va. LCD: **Chloe Flinn's Captivity**

Dear Sir,

Yours of 5th January and also of the 5th instant have been received...

...No other families resided on Cabin Creek at the time of the captivity of the Flinn family. I lived on Cabin Creek a number of years ago and the spot was pointed out to me where the Flinns' Cabin stood. This was about the year 1833 when I was there. A man by the name of Charlie Spurlock was living near the spot, took me to the ground where the Cabin stood, the remainds [sic] of the chimney was plain there to be seen. Nothing but a pile of rock of which the Chimney was built remained to mark that spot. This was about one half mile distant from the Kanawha River up on Cabin Creek, on the right hand side of the Creek as you ascended the Creek. The Cabin had been built in a bottom or valley between the hill and the creek.

I was well acquainted with Polly Flinn who married Adam Mann. [Chloe] Flinn who married John Ballard, and Nancy Flinn who married George Miller. Polly Flinn was not captured by the Indians. She secreted herself in a hollow log until the Indians were gone. She then went to Donally's Fort.

The Indians killed John Flinn, the father of the Children, and took the Mother whose name I do not now recollect, and her daughters Chloe and Nancy & her son John prisoners.

Chloe was very young, could not have been over two or three years old. Nancy was young but old enough to remember. I remember of her saying that her mother disappeared and she could not tell what the Indians did with her but supposed they killed her.

John Flinn, son of John Flinn, was captured by the Indians, was taken to Ohio. There he staid with the Indians until a treaty was made. I think he lived near Chillicothe. He was out in Monroe County, W. Va., to see his people. My Mother spoke of seeing him. Said he could not speak English well. Spoke C___ of Indians mostly.

Nancy was stolen from the Indians by a man by the name of Halstead, was brought back to her friends. She had married an Indian, and after her return she had a daughter whom she named Elizabeth. I do not know of any other Children of Polly Mann living except Jo Mann who was alive a few years ago. He has been traveling for years, do not know where he is now. Do not know of any [of] the children of Chloe, Nancy, or John living. Think they are all gone.

I have no definite information or recollection about how Boone got possession of Chloe but that which I wrote you heretofore. Cannot now recollect where she was when the exchange was made. Several reports as to her Capt_____.

I have heard that she was stolen by Boone & his comrades.

The Slaughter Family was all gone...

I saw an article written by Dr. J. P. Hale published in the West Virginia School Journal, February 1883 giving a very interesting account of D. Boone and the Flinn family, but I think it is in some respect incorrect...

I have...done the best that I could. Accept my thanks for the book...

Yours truly,
Andrew Kesinger

14C 57-57(1) Andrew Kesinger, Madison, W. Va., Aug. 20, 1883

Yours of the 1st have been received. Have delayed trying to...get information...

1st – From the best information I can get Chloe Flinn was born about 1783, was married about the year 1798, and died 1863. Chapman Ballard, the elder son of Chloe Flinn was born 1799.

2nd – Do not know anything further in relation to Jo Mann.

3rd – Names of Children of Chapman Ballard. Ryland Ballard, Henley Ballard, Elizabeth Smoot, Lucy Hager, all of whom reside near Madison, Boone County, W. Va. Chloe Henly, another child of Chapman Ballard, she lives now on Fields Creek in Kanawha County, W. Va.

4th – Elizabeth Jarrell has three children surviving her: Mrs. Thomas Nelson, Sallie Jarrell and John Jarrell, P. O. address Madison, Boone County, W. Va.

5th – Don't know the given name of _----, think it was Reuben.

6th – Have no tradition of Daniel Boone further than heretofore given.

7th – Nancy Ballard cannot give any traditions of Boone.
8th – There is man by the name of John B. Milller whose P. O. address if Bald Knob, Boone County, W. Va. Write to him, likely he can give some information as to the Flinn family.

Yours truly
Andrew Kesinger

14C58- 59 LCD to Andrew Kesinger, additional questions on Chloe Flinn captivity, Aug. 26, 1883

1 Did the Flinns live in Monroe County, Virginia before settling on Cabin Creek?
2 Were there children, or some of them, born in Monroe County?
3 How long had they been living on Cabin Creek when attacked by the Indians?
4 Have you any recollection of hearing what time in the year it was when attacked? I judge it was in the Fall.
5 I infer Nancy Flinn was four, & John Flinn two years older than Chloe. If you think differently, state it.
6 Did Slaughter live at Point Pleasant or Monroe County, or where?
7 About what year did Mrs. Nancy Miller die & what was her age?

I will write to Ryland Ballard as the oldest of Chapman Ballard's children & to John Jarrell – urge the latter to reply.

14C 60 Andrew Kesinger's answers, Madison, W. Va., April 14, 1884

Andrew Kesinger wrote that he didn't know whether the Flinns lived in Monroe County before settling on Cabin

Creek, and that he did not know where Ruben Slaughter lived.

14C 61-61(1) LCD: Chloe Flinn's Captivity

> Left a little girl at Van Bibber's whom Col. Boone had brought up from Maysville, where she was delivered up from captivity by the Indians.

The autumn of 1786 was the time of her capture, but her return is less certain. LCD

She was doubtless given up at the Limestone Treaty – May, 1787 – or brought in not very long after. She lived with Col. Daniel Boone at Limestone till the Fall of 1788, when he went up to Point Pleasant with ginseng. [See vol. of Boone Notes, p. 333, as fixing this date. LCD]

Speaking of this trip to Point Pleasant, in the Fall of 1788, & sinking of boat, & getting his ginseng wet, Col. Nathan Boone, who was along, & then in his 8th year, says:

"Reaching Point Pleasant, by John Van Bibber's invitation, Col. Boone & family went & stopped while at his house, while Col. Boone was getting the boat & cargo in readiness to resume his journey. Left a little girl at Van Bibber's whom Col. Boone had brought up from Maysville, where she was delivered up from captivity by the Indians, probably at the treaty of 1787, & had since lived in his family. Her name was Chloe Flinn, some ten [8 - LCD] years old, who had been taken prisoner from Greenbrier, where she was subsequently sent to her friends."
Boone Notes, &c, 185.

P.S. Since noting the above, I am confirmed in 1786 as the time when Chloe Flinn was captured. In the Fall of that year, by a letter received from her son, J. A. Ballard, who says she was seven months with the Indians, & given at a treaty with Col. Boone, which was in May, 1787. St.Clair Ensminger, her grandson, also says she was seven months a prisoner, thence captured in October in the cornfield – doubtless gathering corn.

Boone and Van Bibber connections include Daniel Boone having rescued John Van Bibber from captivity, and Daniel's sons, Nathan and Jesse, marrying into that family.

Catherine G. Welch, granddaughter of John Van Bibber, wrote to Draper in 1866 that Daniel Boone and her grandfather had served together as representatives of Kanawha County to the Virginia Legislature in 1789. Boone was appointed Lieutenant Colonel of the County Militia in 1789. DM 28C 66.

14C 62-63 Col. John Johnston. John Flinn, Mother & Sisters Captured. From Cist's Advertiser, Cincinnati, Nov. 23, 1847 from Col. John Johnston, and from History of Miami County, Ohio, 1880, Elizabeth Township, p. 563. *Col. Johnston knew John Flinn well and helped him obtain a tract of land in Ohio.*

> **[John's mother] preserved in his mind a remembrance of the English language... at which times she would give vent to her sorrow in a profusion of tears.**
>
> **John received from the Indians the kindest treatment, which he ever afterwards returned by a devotion and attachment to them**

Col. John Johnston's Correspondence

John Flinn, or Ques-tas-ke, the Man that Limped or the Lame Man, many years my Pottawattomie interpreter, was taken prisoner when a youth from Green Brier, Virginia. His father and some of the children were killed while at work in a corn field. The Indians then went to the house, took the mother and three children prisoners, plundered and burned the premises, and made their escape. The mother & John fell to the lot of the same family, and were not separated afterwards.

The two sisters were allotted to others, nor did he ever see them until he met them when they were married and settled in Virginia, having been surrendered and delivered up by the Indians under the provisions of the treaty of peace made with Gen. Wayne in 1795.

John was not surrendered, preferring to remain with the Indians. His mother died five years after their captivity. She preserved in his mind a remembrance of the English language, which he would otherwise have forgotten. Her practice was, when they were alone, to talk much with him, at which times she would give vent to her sorrow in a profusion of tears. Being advanced in years [age 29?], she was of little use to her unfeeling captors, denied a sufficiency of food and clothing. Death terminated her sufferings.

On the contrary, John received from the Indians the kindest treatment, which he ever afterwards returned by a devotion and attachment to them which suffered no abatement. He was strictly honest, and for many years he served in my department; I never knew him to utter a falsehood. He used neither tobacco nor whisky. I took good care of his money, and at a proper time, purchased in fee from the United States for him, 330 acres of prime land, in Miami County Ohio, and on which he has resided many years. He married and raised a large family.

Apparently living when this was written near the close of 1847. [LCD?]

14C 63-63(1) Flinn Captivity from History of Miami County, Ohio, 1880, Elizabeth Township, p. 563.

Benjamin Flinn, deceased, born in Miami County, April 2nd, 1822, was a son of John & Agnes (Priest) Flinn, he being born in Virginia & she in Kentucky. The father John & his mother were captured in Virginia by the Indians, and kept in captivity for fourteen years, during which Mrs. Flinn died. John gaining the confidence of the Indians, was granted many privileges to go and come as he pleased, and finally was permitted to visit his friends in Virginia, which he did, and then returned to the Indians. Becoming dissatisfied with them, he went back to Virginia, and soon after came west, and became interpreter for Col. John Johnston, the Indian Agent, during the War of 1812.

It is supposed he became a settler of Miami County prior to 1807, which would make him one of the early pioneers. Here he married Agnes Priest, by whom he had a large family of children, of whom Benjamin was the seventh child. He lived with his father, mostly, till his marriage, which occurred Nov. 20th, 1845, with Catharine, daughter of John & Rebecca Smith – he born in Maryland, and she in Virginia. By this union they had six children, of whom five are living, viz: Agnes, Rebecca, Jane, Charlotte, Franklin, and Mary. After their marriage they located upon the farm, where his widow, ___ Flinn, now resides. He died March 13, 1879. Since his death, his son Franklin, and son-in-law, Wm. Paul[?] are taking charge of the home farm, consisting of 158 acres of fine land, with good buildings and improvements, also another farm of 89 acres. Mr. Flinn was an industrious, enterprising man, &c.

14C 64-65 LCD to St. Clair Ensminger, Esq., Jan. 15, 1883

...Pray, write me as well as you can in reply to these inquiries, giving...your brother's understanding of these matters as you derived them from your grandmother or mother. I hope & entreat that you will not disappoint me.

Very Truly Yours,
Lyman C. Draper

14C 66-66(1)-62 St. Clair Ensminger, Shelbyville, Ind., Jan 30, 1883, Chloe Flinn's grandson.

My request to a note received from you not long ago concerning my grandmother I now will give you what little information I know about her capture and captivity, answering according to ___ ___ your _____ Jan 15th, 1883.
1st I have no record of her birth &c.
2nd She was seven years old when taken. I don't know what tribe captured her.
3rd Seven months in captivity. I don't know where she was taken to.
4th She was rescued by Daniel Boone. I am not certain but think by a Treaty or by a trade Boone made with the Indians.
5th [skipped]
6th Near Point Pleasant, W. Va.
7th Don't know what year
8th Age seventy-three [eighty-three. LCD]

She was captured at Point Pleasant near the mouth of the Kanawah river. Her father was shot down in the yard. After they had killed the old man [about age 30], took the mother and three children and Started with them – the old lady [about age 30] not being in condition to travel, after a short distance [they] tomahawked her and left her.

After Chloe came back She lived near the place She was captured till She was about sixteen years old when she married John Ballard.

Yours &c
St. Clair Ensminger

14C 67 LCD Memo – If Chloe Flinn was born about 1781, as Mr. Kisinger says, & married at sixteen as stated above by Mr. Ensminger – that would bring her marriage[?] in 1797 – then Chapman was born in 1798 – St. Clair in 1800, &c. If born about 1781, & captured at [age?] three, that would make 1784, but it was in 1786 when an Indian war commenced... would show that Boone was not living in W. Virginia - & she must have been brought & given up at a treaty or Boone went for her from Maysville into the Indian country.

As Alba[?] Rece, who settled in the Kanawha Valley in 1791, & died in 1878, never mentioned Chloe Finn's captivity to his family...

14C 68-68(1) St. Clair Ensminger, Shelbyville, Ind., Aug. 19, 1883

Mr. Draper I have neglected to answer your letter in regards to Grand mothers age. Not living near the old cemetery, I happened along by the old cemetery, and I got over the fence and got this information:

Grandfather died March 31, 1855, was 84 years old when he died

Grand mother died November the 9th 1863 – was 83 years old when she died.

Now that was all that was on the old slabs. Mother was Born July 12, 1807. She died March 5, 1872. I can't give any others ages for they are all so far away that I can't recollect any of their ages.

Uncle Medley lives in Missouri. I can't tell you anything about him. Grand father was born 1771. What day and month I cant tell. Grandmother was Born 1780.

Yours,
St Clair Ensminger

John F. Ballard lives up in ____ecks County.

14C 69-69(10) John W. Flinn, *son of the captive.*
Marion, Grant County, Ind., March 13, 1884.

> **[The Indians] packed all on their ponies, with the five year old crippled boy. Then set fire to the house & made for the woods, driving grandmother & the little girl before them.**

John Flinn's Captivity

My father's name was John Flinn. His father & mother with their three children – one son & two daughters -emigrated from the old country, perhaps Ireland, & settled in Greenbrier County, Virginia, about the year 1771. They built a little cabin & cleared off & fenced with poles & planted corn, & truck, perhaps an acre of ground. And when the corn got up perhaps to roasting ears, the wild animals, especially the bears, became very troublesome in throwing down the fence & destroying the crop.

So they left my father, who was then a cripple from a severe cut in his foot which rendered him a cripple during life, with his little sister. He being, he thought, only five years old & his sister perhaps seven – in the cabin. Mr. Flinn & wife and oldest daughter went to the corn patch, some distance from the house, to repair the fence. They had been there but a short time, when from the woods two guns fired. Grandfather & the girl fell at the report of the two guns, seemingly both at the same time. The girl fell on her face, seeming to be dead; but the two balls had entered the breast of her father. The Indians not knowing how each had fired, supposed that they had killed each one of their prostrate victims. Not stopping to examine, they took the mother & hurried to the house. When the Indians were out of sight, the girl (who was not hurt) got up, and escaped first to the woods, & then to a settlement.

The Indians took my grandmother & my father & sister – ransacked the house of such as they wanted, bed clothes and the scanty supply of provisions – packed all on their ponies, with the five year old crippled boy. Then set fire to the house & made for the woods, driving grandmother & her little girl before them.

My recollection now is that they stopped where Upper Sandusky now is, where they remained for some time. How long I do not remember. But during their stay there, there was a skirmish (hostility) between the whites [with the] Indians along the frontier somewhere, by which the whites took some Indian prisoners; & according to their custom, they always, so far as they had prisoners, mutually exchanged them. Thus the little girl was lucky – she being exchanged, & thus got back among her friends.

There they took father & his mother and came West to the Wabash river, near where Huntington is now. He being small, & seeing his mother fretting when she would without being detected, caused him to fret and cry, which made the Indians displeased. So they _____ed them, taking her down the Wabash to where Logansport now is, where was an Indian village called Old Town.

The trouble and grief with the hardships she endured, having to cut and carry wood, and do all kinds of hard work, soon put an end to grandmother's existence, as she only lived with the Indians about three years. Her body was buried after the Indian fashion at Old Town – Logansport.

My father was left fatherless & motherless, with the wild woods for his home, & the Indians for his protectors. As he grew up, he had all the western country from the head of the Wabash river to roam over. The Indians sold and traded him from one tribe to another, as we would a horse. My recollection is that grandmother & father were first taken by the Miamies, but father was owned successively by five or six different tribes. I do not remember the names of the Chiefs or heads of those tribes. There were Miamies, Shawnees, Chippeways, & Pottawattamies with others I do not remember.

Father use to talk five different Indian tongues, also French. His stay with them was about sixteen years - & of course, could talk but little English. He did not see bread for seven years, living entirely on wild game.

As soon as he was big enough, they provided him with a light gun, & learned him to hunt & kill small game. When bigger he got a heavier riffle, and soon he became a successful hunter. His equal as a hunter was not to be found among the Indians. Hence he was readily traded among the different Indian tribes.

He made several narrow escapes of his life. At one time, as the whites had been more successful than the Indians in some fight they had, the latter determined to kill him. They held a council as to the manner of execution and decided to burn him alive. So they directed him to gather dry fuel and build a fire. Pretty soon, however, he began to mistrust it was for his own execution, and while he was out for the last armful of sticks, the old Indian that then owned him, & thought a great deal of him, plead hard for his life. Father, only a boy, was a little slow coming in with the last armful of wood, and watching the motions of the Indians, when his old master motioned to him to go away into the woods, which he obeyed, and thus escaped a firy death.

But exposure, hardships & privations and starvation seemed to be always in sight. But his privileges increased as he approximated manhood, and he was soon permitted to do for himself. Their trade consisted entirely in peltry – skins & furs, and as he was a superior hunter, he always had considerable to trade. Vincennes was their trading point. The Indians would pack their skins and furs on ponies, and go down there twice a year to trade.

The whites from Virginia & the East came with flatboat loads of fruit, flour, bacon, powder, lead, &, of course, whisky – ran their boats down the Ohio river & there is where the commencement of a separation between him & the Indians began.

These traders noticing that he was white, began through the interpreters making inquiries, who he was, and where from. Some of the Virginia traders remembering to have heard of the circumstance of his captivity, and from the region near which he was taken – knew his folks, the sister then being married, and he almost forgotten. They prevailed on him to pay his folks a visit; but he did not at that time. As from time to time he would go down to Vincennes trading, he became more and more anxious to hear from his folks in Virginia.

About this time, Government started a store at where Fort Wayne now is under the management of one Mr. John Johnston, who was then Indian agent. As their conversation often came up between the Indians & father about his folks in Virginia, & the Indians themselves after the visit (to Virginia) was related[?], kept a record of his nativity, & as they are great for visiting each other, they persuaded him to go. But as he could not speak nor understand English, he did not know how to proceed. As he had become some acquainted with Mr. Johnston at Fort Wayne, & he learning father's desire, proposed to help him effect his purpose.

So when father got ready to start, Johnston gave him an instrument of writing to take to the Governor of Kentucky, which he presented. The Governor when receiving it gave him a paper to show to the people on his way, which requested that they should direct the bearer to a certain place in Virginia, naming it, & supply him with food, & left him pass on, & signed his name to it as Governor of Kentucky. So he prosecuted his journey, & at length reached his friends in Virginia, who received him very kindly – his sisters recognizing him more readily from his being a cripple.

They then provided him with clothing after the custom of the whites – as he went to them in his Indian garb, gun & tomahawk. They aimed to make it as pleasant for him as possible, in hopes of weaning him from a heathen life. So they took him around in society to parties and places of amusement, which seemed to do well for a while, until his company commenced breaking off – some to plowing, some to one thing, & some to another. Then he became lonesome, & thinking of his home in the woods. So between Sun-down & morning he gathered his outfit for the woods, and started for his Wabash home, which seemed to him as almost the place of his nativity. In a short time, he found himself among the camps of the Indians.

He did not seem to be satisfied with his old Indian mode of life, after having been with the whites three or four months. The Indian huts he now found were dirty, as he was not satisfied as he formerly was. So he went up to Fort Wayne, & hired to Mr. Johnston in the public store as interpreter, as he then could talk some English. Getting seven hundred dollars a year, with the privilege of hunting mornings & evenings, & thus made money selling game to the people of the garrison that were stationed there at that time by the Government.

After remaining there Seven years, he left the store, and went to Miami County, Ohio, six miles east of where Troy now stands, & entered three hundred & twenty acres of land about the year 1810. He commenced a little improvement, built a log cabin and then married a Miss Agnes Priest, and then with a view of making a living at farming, went to clearing and improving his land, which was very heavily timbered, and seemed to find plenty to occupy his time until the Indian war of 1812 broke out. Then he was employed by Government as a spy, & again visited the wilderness country up and down the Wabash river, ascertaining the numbers of Indians their localities, & plans - & so reporting to head quarters of our army.

At one time, the Indians seemed to mistrust him. The next day after a battle – it might have been at Fort Meigs – they detained him, leaving him in the hands of the squaws until the warriors would go out to visit the battle-field. If there were more Indians killed than whites, they would kill him. So after the Indians had started, he unconcernedly took his gun, as he went in Indian garb, telling the squaws that he would take a little hunt around, and would return soon. He started for the woods rather leisurely, but as soon as he got out of sight, he made for the settlement. After finding a good hiding place, he laid by in daytime, traveled after night, keeping entirely through the woods. In crossing trails or fording streams, he could see the Indians were after him by the sign of their tracks in the damp ground. But being as well up to Indian cunning & wood-craft as the Indians themselves, he made good his escape.

But he was very venturesome, & ran many narrow risks during the War of 1812. But after peace was made, he settled down to a farm life, & having some money, he hired clearing done & rails made, as he did not understand the business of farm improvement much himself. But he succeeded in opening quite a farm, on which he raised quite a large family – fourteen children, twelve boys and two girls. He continued on the same farm till his death, which occurred June 9th, 1857, in his eighty-fifth year. His companion, my mother, lived till February, 1866, when she died in her seventy-eighth year. Eleven of the children are living, three having passed away. The eldest is less than seventy-two years, and the youngest over fifty.

Thus ends of the career of my pioneer parents - & the same will soon be told of the entire family. So I will close this imperfect narrative by subscribing myself

Yours, &c.
J. W. Flinn

P.S – If there is anything omitted that I can do, inform me. I should like the history you speak of, & will thank you for it. I should like one containing this narrative for each child of this noted family. When you receive this, let me hear from you, & your opinion in reference to it - & oblige me. Couldn't I sell books on commission, 3 or 4 different kinds as I am not doing much. If anything is lacking in this narrative, write.

John W. Flinn

John Flinn. Wisconsin Historical Society

14C70-70(3) John W. Flinn, Marion [Ind.], March 27, 1884 (copy – from Pencil. LCD). John Flinn's Captivity – 1786.

> **They left in the distance that sacred spot of their dead husband & father and the flames bursting from their little cabin.**

Mr. L. C. Draper

Dear Sir:

In conversing with one of my brothers, we conclude the capture of our father must have been in 1777 – he then five years old. His stay with the Indians was 18 years, & with Mr. Johnston at Fort Wayne, 7 years. After he left there he bought land four miles east of Piqua, & improved it some, then sold it, & bought east of Troy, which we think required 8 years. Which brings it up to 1810. At this time he married, lived 47 years [more] & died.

Your second paragraph - I do not mean invasion by the whites – I mean that there was fighting along the frontiers, & prisoners taken, on both sides, & exchanges made.

Father's age at the time of his threatened burning I do not know.

I only remember of one sister being taken prisoner with father & their mother – her name was Polly. Chloe fell at the report of the guns, & after the Indians passed to the house, she got up & left. [These names should be reversed. LCD] I learn there was another girl, whose name was Nancy. I never heard of her having been captured.

There was a number of Indians with their ponies at the time of the capture – I do not know how many, but only two shots were fired.

I heard father often speak of Tecumseh – but don't know of what tribe.

Polly married a Mr. Adam Maner & Chloe [married] a Mr. James Ballard. I think I remember the name of Nancy, but never heard of her being captured. I think she married a man by the name of Miller. I know nothing of her positively.

If I learn more, I will write again.

Let me hear from you.

1772 – Father born in 1772
1777 – when captured, 5 years old
1795 - 18 years with the Indians
1802 – 7 years with Col. Johnston
1857 - 47 years after that when he died aged 85 years.

The Flinns were captured in 1786. Above dates are incorrect.

As I told you in my last, my parents raised a family of 14 children – 12 boys & 2 girls, as follows:

1. James Flinn, born June 16, 1812, P.O. Shidler, Delaware County, Indiana
2. John W. born August 1, 1813, Marion, Indiana
3. Amos born May 27, 1816, Frankfort, Marshall County, Kansas
4. Amelia born Dec.28, 1818, Muncietown, Delaware County, Indiana
5. Elizabeth born July 24, 1820, Port Jefferson, Shelby County, Ohio
6. Adam born Oct. 17, 1823, Oregon, Hott County, Missouri
7. Peter G. born July 5, 1825, Marion, Indiana
8. Obadiah born June 19, 1827, same
9. Isaac born Dec. 19, 1828, Albany, Delaware County, Indiana
10. Chapman born Aug. 15, 1830, Marion, Indiana
11. Elijah born Oct 8, 1832, South Bend, Indiana

Deceased.

12.George born July 17, 1817, died March 20, 1874
13. Jeremiah born Jan. 10, 1815, died Jan. 1882.
14. Benjamin born April 2, 1822, died Feb. 1880

Enclosed find a picture of the once little boy, who after being shot down by the Indians, with his mother & sister was compelled to submit to the fate of a prisoner, & marched to the woods – not even permitted to give vent to their sad stricken hearts, as they left in the distance that sacred spot of their dead husband & father and the flames bursting from their little cabin – their once happy home – only to be forced farther & farther into the wilds of a dense forest. And farther to drag about ___ 18 long years of hard, lonesome & miserable life, incidental to Indian usages.

This picture is a fac-simile of our father, the prisoner boy.

I would like an agency to sell the volume containing this narrative.

Yours &c.
John W. Flinn

Caption on photo sent to LCD:
John Flinn – captured by the Indians in 1786, when 5 years old in West Virginia on Cabin Creek. Died in Miami County, Ohio in 1843.

***

14C 71-72 LCD: **Daniel Boone, 1787**.
This was the year of the exchange of prisoners at Limestone. Indian prisoners who had been captured in Ohio and held at Danville, Kentucky were exchanged for captives returning to Kentucky.
1787 February – Indian camp attacked

Massey Harbison, new edition, 163
[*Draper must have referred to* "A Narrative of the Sufferings of Massey Harbison...Giving an Account of Her Captivity," *dictated in her pension application in 1835.]*

April 27 – Capt. Wolf & Shawanoes at Limestone
Pennsylvania Packet, July 12, 1787
Massey Harbison, new edition, 164-165

May - Cols. Boone & Patterson exchange prisoners:
Magazine of American History, July 1877

Life of Maj. Harbison. See 4 pages after Massey Harbison, 165-168

June – Todd's Expedition. Pennsylvania Packet, July 31, 1787. See the other references 5 pages after.

[Daniel Boone] kept a warehouse & fort at Limestone: Shane's Collections, iii, Montgomery County, p. 79[?]

After the treaty – in Summer Blue Jacket & Boone's son [Daniel M. Boone] often went hunting over the Ohio – an evidence that the Shawnees had made peace in good faith. Shane's Collections, ii, Montgomery County, p. 21

August – Col. Benjamin Logan & Captain Johnny at Limestone. Life Massey Harbison, edition 1836, pp. 165-168

1788 John Saunders' daughter killed. Shane's Collections, ii, Montgomery County p.8, 78; & Clark County, p 32

Mrs. Lamond saw Miss Elizabeth Sanders, a grand daughter of William Grant (whose wife was a sister of Daniel Boone), was killed at the same time as the Shanks family. Miss Sanders was a grand niece of Daniel Boone. Letter [of Mrs. Lamond] Aug. 23, 1845.LCD

1788 – Mrs. Shanks' Affair on Cooper's Run.
April 11th – Shane's Collections ii, Montgomery County p. 9, 30, 78. This really belongs in March 1788 – see note there. [1788?] Blue Jacket, horse stealing, Shane's Collections, ii, Montgomery County, p. 20-21.

14C 73 LCD: **Indians Exchange Prisoners at Limestone 1787.** From New Haven Gazette, July 20, 1787

> **Seven warriors of the Shawanese Nation had come in there, on the 27th of April with nine white people to exchange with the same number of Indian prisoners...**

Pittsburgh, May 26, 1787

A gentleman who arrived here from Limestone, which place he left on the 1st of May, informed us that seven warriors of the Shawanese Nation had come in there, on the 27th of April with nine white people to exchange with the same number of Indian prisoners taken by Colonel Logan. The chief of these savages, Captain Wolf, gave the gentlemen to understand, that 30[?] warriors of the Cherokee nation were then at war. Our informant adds, that as he came up the river, he saw five bark canoes and three rafts cross below the mouth of the Scioto, full of Indians.

At the Mingo Bottom, the gentleman saw a woman from Wheeling by the name of Purdy, who informed him that fourteen of the inhabitants of that place and the settlement adjoining had been killed and taken by the Indians, a short time before, and that the rest of the settlers were then forted.

Blue Jacket & Boone's son hunt over the Ohio from Limestone – Shane ii, Montgomery County, p. 21

14C 74 LCD: **Col. Daniel Boone – 1787**
Todd's Expedition -
McDonald's Sketches
Marshall's Ky, I: 271
Extracts from Pennsylvania Packet July 31, 1787

Notes Gen. Henry & Peter Lee; Shane's Collections ii, Montgomery County, 77-[?] Trip, 1860, iv: 165; Shane ii, Montgomery County 77-78.
October – Supplied Indian prisoners – Trip, 1860, V, 158.

Doubtful as he [Boone] was at Richmond Va. in Legislature, Oct 15th – On reference I see this claim of Boone's was allowed Oct. 1787. No doubt the account was for supplies the preceding spring.

Oct 15 Daniel Boone at Richmond in the Legislature [opening of Legislature October 15?] till its [close] Jan 8 – 1788[?]

Petition for aid for southwestern counties of Virginia. Trip 1860. Lee Journal p. 4, 19, 52, 55, 57, 82, 121.

14C 75-75(1) LCD: **Col. Daniel Boone – 1787.**

Letter of the Delegates from the Kentucky Counties to Governor Randolph of Virginia

Arthur Campbell, Andrew Cowan, Samuel [_____?], Daniel Boone, and Thomas Carter, to Gov. Randolph, Dec. 31, 1787

> **A stand of colors, drum and fife, would be useful for each company.**
>
> **The arms sent out in the Spring of 1787 were generally unfit for service, and not a single scabbard, belt, cartridge box or flint came with them.**

Sir:

If it is found next spring, that a war with the Indians is unavoidable, we are of opinion that two companies of Rangers, of 50 men each, will be necessary to protect the frontiers of Washington, Montgomery and Russell [Counties, Virginia]. Those allotted to range so as to be a safeguard to the inhabitants of Montgomery to be stationed on the west side of the Great Kanahawa, where the Greenbrier road across to Kentucky; and on Sandy River, where the said road crosses that river.

Those for the defence of the other two counties might be stationed: 1st a detachment at Park's Spring in Powell's Valley; another at Yoakum's Station, where the waggon road crosses Powell's River; a third in the Rye Cove; and the remainder in the neighborhood of Castle-Woods, the New G___ or Richlands. Scouts ought constantly to be passing between the Castle-Wood Station and The Fort on Sandy River.

Muskets suitable for light infantry are preferable to rifles, as buckshot may be used, and the bayonet will be excellent for night attacks and defence.

Five hundred pounds of powder, with lead equivalent, will be sufficient for Washington and Russell [Counties], and the like quantity may be necessary for Montgomery.

A stand of colors, drum and fife, would be useful for each company. *Virginia Calendar* iv, 375-376.

Jan. 5, 1788 – Delegates to Virginia Legislature:
Daniel Boone.
Bourbon County, J. Marshall;
Fayette County – J. Fowler, Jr.
Mercer County- [blank]
Madison [*County*] – Thomas Kennedy
Nelson [*County*] – C. Harrison[?]
Jefferson [*County]* – Abner Field

The Delegates from Kentucky, D. Boone, J. Marshall, & J. Fowler, Jr., inform the Executive that the number of militia necessary to defend the frontier of that District will depend upon the rigor with which the Savages may carry on the war. They, therefore, recommend that the matter be left to a meeting of the field officers of the District, to be called by the County Lieutenant. Most of the Cavalry in that country are volunteers, had elected their own officers subject to the general militia law, and they therefore decline to recommend any. The arms sent out in the Spring of 1787 were generally unfit for service, and not a single scabbard, belt, cartridge box or flint came with them. *Virginia Calendar* iv, 390-391.

14C 76-77 LCD: **Daniel Boone, 1788**
Boone &c Suggestions for defence of Ky – Trip 1860, iv, 167 &c

March about 21st – Miss Sanders killed & The Shanks Family. This is the correct date, as shown by Trip 1860, iv, 182, letter of Col. Levi Todd, says a house on frontier of Bourbon [County] was attacked in the night, five killed. Pursued & killed 2 Indians & wounded one. So reported in Bradford's Notes (furnished from memory by Joseph Ficklin as he told me – save that Ficklin's account related one Indian killed & one wounded.)

Joseph Ficklin's account of the Shanks Massacre is transcribed in *Warrior-Pioneers,* p. 340.

[LCD] Not in my Kentucky Gazette extracts.
Marshall's Kentucky I:284, gives the date correctly – "about March 21st, 1788.
Shane I, Clark County, p. 32; Shane ii, Montgomery County, p. 9?, 73?

April or Early May - Capture of Blue Jacket – see Separate Memo of Blue Jacket's career in Kenton Notes, 1788. Shane I, p. 28, Clark County
Trip 1860. Vol. iv, p. 185.
'A few days" before March 12th
Sudduth's Narrative p. 12
Shane's Collections, ii, Bath County, p. 75 & other references
Shane ii, Montgomery County, p. 20 &c.
Miss Sanders – See notes & ____ in 1787 – April 11th is wrong date
Also Shane ii, Fayette County, 59, 70, 72
Shane ii, Clark County, 32
Shane ii, Montgomery County, p. 8, 73
March-June – Condition of Kentucky – Trip 1860, iv. 182-185.
August [*1787*] The Grist Incident – see references in Kenton Notes.
Fall – [Daniel Boone] went up Ohio with Ginseng & visited Bucks County, Pennsylvania. See Nathan Boone's Notes, 173, 329 &c.

14C 77 LCD: **Daniel Boone, 1788, Kanawha Valley**
August – The Grist Incident – see references in Kenton's notes
Fall – went up Ohio with ginseng & visited Berks County, Pa. Nathan Boone's notes, 172, 329, &c.; R____ Lightfoot's recollections in Mr. Lee's Letters – Vol.1 B___ Papers. Camped near Gaddis' Fort in Fayette County: History Fayette County, 567.

14C 78-79-80 J. P. Hale, Charleston, W. Va., June 19, 1882, July 11, 1882, Oct. 12, 1882.

J. P. Hale mentioned a paper he had written and sent to Draper. Also mentioned is Mrs. Mary Ingles "who was a Miss Draper," that J. P. Hale wrote has "probably more data than any one now living relating to the captivity & escape of my great grand mother Mrs. Mary Ingles..."

LCD: Daniel Boone in Kanawha Valley – 1788 &c. Washington in West Va. – 1773.

14C 81-81(2) LCD: **Boone Survey**, 1786 [copy]

I lost my plating instruments and only have the Short field Notes

To John Overton of Lincoln County to bee left at Elijah Smith's

Lexington. July the 20th 1786
Sir the Land has been long Survayed and Not knowing when the Money would be Radey was the Reason of my note Returning the works however the [they?} may be Returned when you pleas But I must first have a Nother Copy of the Entry as I have lost that I had when I lost my plating instruments and only have the Short field Notes Just the Corse Distance and corner trees pray send me a Nother Copy that I may know how to give it the proper Bounderry a greeable to the Location and I will send the plat to the ofis amedetly if you chuse it the Expenses is as follows viz

Survayers fees 9.38
Ragester fees 7.14.07
Chanmen and Marker 11 days 8.0.0
Purvistions for the tower 2.0.0
[Total fees] 26.27.81

You Will also Send a Copy of the agreement betwixt Mr Wales overton and my Self When I Red the Warrants.

Daniel Boone

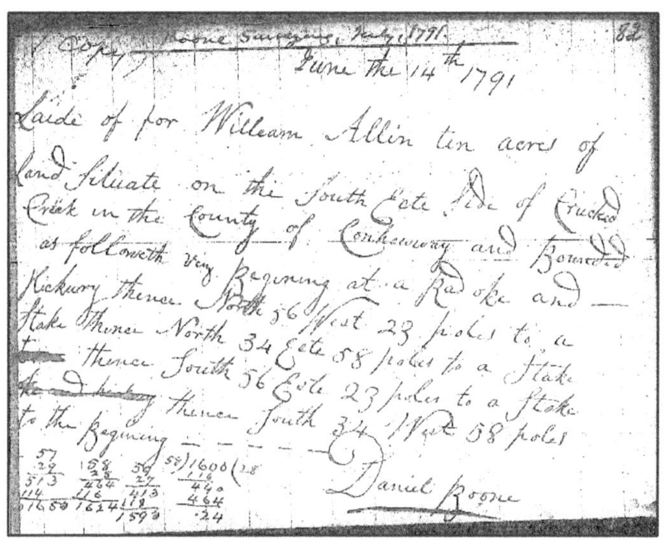

Copy / Boone Surveying, July 1791. 82

June the 14th 1791

Laide of for William Allin ten acres of land Situate on the South Este Side of Crucked Crick in the County of Conhaway and Bounded as followeth viz. Beginning at a Red oke and Hickory thence North 56 West 23 poles to a Stake thence North 34 Este 58 poles to a ~~___~~ thence South 56 Este 23 poles to a Stake ~~and hickory~~ thence South 34 West 58 poles to the Beginning

Daniel Boone

Daniel Boone Survey 1791. DM 14C 81.

14C 82 LCD: **Boone Surveying, June 14, 1791**. *The survey for William Allin in Kanawha County is in Daniel Boone's handwriting.*

Laide of for William Allin ten acres of land Situate on the South Este Side of Crucked Crick in the County of Conhaway and Bounded as followeth viz beginning at a Red oke and hickory thence North 56 West 23 poles to a ___ thence South 56 Este 23 poles to a Stake to the beginning.

Daniel Boone

14C 83-85 LCD: **Daniel Boone – Incidents about 1788-1790**

> **A large body of buffalo came dashing along, & he had to climb a tree to save himself. So large was the drove that he was kept up the tree several hours.**

From [interview] Jacob Boone, near Tone[?] City, California, March 4th & 5th. 1890 – son of Daniel Boone [not the pioneer] & grandson of Jacob Boone of Maysville, Ky. – the former Jacob Boone born in Brown County, Ohio, Aug. 11th, 1806. His father, Daniel Boone, son of Jacob Boone, was born near Reading Pa., in Sept 1784 - & was four years old when his father, Jacob Boone, moved to Maysville – hence 1788.

Jacob Boone, Sr. once went with a party after Indians who had attacked a boat between Maysville & mouth of Scioto – no particulars recollected.

Jacob Boone kept a tavern & warehouse in Maysville, near mouth of Limestone – probably succeeding Col. Daniel Boone in the business, & continued till his old age, retiring about 1815. He died at Maysville about 1825, either 74 or 76 years of age. Had kept a farm over the Ohio [River] for many years till one Campbell built a houseboat & superceded him.

Informant often heard him speak of Col. Daniel Boone, whom he well knew. Boone went a hunting with Jacob Boone – Daniel Boone seemed to have trained himself to the woods, so that his eye seemed to be on the constant alert, like a wild turkey's. Jacob Boone could discover nothing, but Daniel Boone discovered the tip of the ear of a deer lying down – flies pestering it marked its ear – slipped around, until he could get a fair shot of the Deer & shot him. Over the river in Ohio. This must have been soon after reaching Maysville.

Daniel Boone when alone was walking up a ridge, saw an Indian dodge behind a tree. 'Naturally, of course," said Boone, "I stepped behind one too." Both watching each other, fearing if he exposed himself the other would shoot him. Finally, Boone said he concluded to put his old cap on the end of his ramrod, & peer it out carefully, as if trying to get a sight, when the Indian saw the cap, shot at it, & Boone let it fall & stood to his place until the Indian came up within about ten paces of him to get his expected scalp – when Boone confronted him. when the Indian exclaimed "Yankou" [?] – that is played a trick on him. Boone shot him.

Jacob Boone. Girls taken – 1776.

There are errors in the recounting of the rescue of the Boone and Callaway girls. Not all the captors were killed, and Boone and the rescue party started back to the fort with the girls rather than pursuing the captors as stated here.

Daniel Boone said...when Indians were chasing him, he could generally out run them...

A preacher – one McBride – who attended a camp meeting in Pike County, Missouri, said he had recently seen Miss Callaway, who was one of the captured [girls], who related that when she was taken & rescued – Indians had stopped – thinks there were one more Indian than whites. Jemima Boone had dropped a string from her sun bonnet knotted with the number of Indians, so Boone knew the knots referred to the number of Indians comprising the party.

Boone said "allow me two" - & leaving each after others one Indian to encounter. Jemima Boone was looking over the head of the younger Callaway girl, when she discovered her father making a slight noise while creeping upon his breast like a snake, & he, to caution her, gave her a sign by shaking his finger to keep quiet. The whites fired, killed all the Indians but one, who fled & Boone after him & killed him. Callaway killed one; it was Flanders Callaway who afterward married Jemima Boone. When Boone returned he said he had rescued his two.

After discovering her father, Jemima said she was so excited that she could not have felt a ____ had it been as large as her thumb.

When the whites fired, Jemima & companions made a break toward her father & friends. But Boone did not tarry to meet & greet them but kept on after the fleeing Indian.

1770 – Once when Daniel Boone was at the Blue Licks, a large body of buffalo came dashing along, & he had to climb a tree to save himself. He shot several of them. So large was the drove who kept pushing on towards the salt spring, that he was kept up the tree several hours. He marked the tree, which was pointed out for many years after the settlement of the country, as Jacob Boone Sr. saw it, & spoke of it.

Daniel Boone said to Jacob Boone, Sr., when Indians were chasing him, he could generally out run them...

Anna (Boone) Nicholson was younger than Daniel Boone, son of Jacob Boone - & hence what she said about the Indian exchange of prisoners at Maysville must have been ___ hearsay.

She left 4 sons, & daughters, Mrs. Mitchell, Mrs. Ross, Mrs. _____. Sons: Strother, Harrison, Henry Clay & Thomas, who remained in the Maysville region.

Captivity of Girls, 1776. Indians took every precaution to prevent being overtaken: cut off girls' dresses nearly up to their knees, waded along the beds of shallow streams to prevent being tracked. Jemima tore a strip from her bonnet – tied in knots to the number of Indians of the party, which she felt assured her father would comprehend, as he did.

When Boone & party came up, the Indians had built a fire, & were counselling as to their further action – perhaps course of travel - while the girls were sitting on a log on the other side of the fire – south side. Girls broke off twigs [marking the trail] and the Indians threatened them.

This narrative on this & preceding page, as related by Rev. Wm.[?] McBride, is as remembered jointly by Mr. & Mrs. Jacob Boone, in all which they agree.

Hubbell's Boat, 1791. When Hubbell's boat was attacked & they[?] beat off the Indians many of the whites were wounded. They were kept until recovered enough to resume their journey, by Jacob Boone – perhaps a month.

William Boone, brother of informant, formerly of Santa Clara, now in Cowlitz, Lewis County, Washington State – about 68 years old. His sister Charlotte, born in June, 1815...

Daniel Boone, son of William B. Boone, & grandson of Jacob Boone, of Maysville, Ky., now about [age] 60 if living, at Clarksville, Mo., Pike County, may have Boone traditions.

A younger brother, William B. Boone at San Diego, also a brother Ben F. at San Diego – moved out from the Clarksville, Missouri region for health.

Mrs. Elizabeth Bradley, sister of informant, widow, lives in San Jose, California... [write her?] in care of her son, Charles Reel.

14C 86 LCD: **Rev. Stephen Ruddle and James Stark**

Stephen Ruddle was among those captured at Ruddle's Station in June 1780. He was adopted into Tecumseh's family and lived among them for a number of years before returning to Kentucky where he began preaching.

> **He was fond of rattle snakes &**
> **Pole cats, neatly prepared & cooked.**

Rev. Stephen Ruddle – Mr. and Mrs. Jacob Boone knew him well. He was a tall, heavy man, over 6 feet in height, highly regarded by all who knew him, & a very good preacher. He was fond of rattle snakes & pole cats, neatly prepared & cooked.

James Starks, of Bourbon County, Ky., was at the battle of the Thames, an officer in Johnson's Regiment – wounded & drew a pension. Moved to near Clarksville, Missouri. His son William resided in or near Clarksville. [He] may be able to tell what his father may have said about Tecumseh's death. Used to say there was [no?] mistake that Col. Johnson rode boldly up & shot the Shawnee chief. William Starks has younger brother living in the Clarksville region.

James Starks drew a pension & died since 1853.

14C 87-87(2) W. D. Boone, Cowlitz, Lewis County, Washington State. *Undated letter written in pencil was traced over in ink.*

Mr. Draper

Dear Sir:

I received your letter and was some what surprised to get a letter from an unknown person – nevertheless I will try to give all the information that I can.

My grand father's name was Jacob Boone – born in Pennsylvania near Reading, also my father and in the same house that Daniel Boone was born in. My father's name was Daniel, named for the pioneer. My grandfather moved to Kentucky in 1790; my father was 6 years old at the time he moved; he settled in Maysville. My father grew up to manhood in that town, and married Mary Wallingford[?] in that county (Mason); moved to Ohio and there all of the children were born – Jacob, Mary Ann, Indiana, Charlotte[?], Elizabeth, William D, & John W. Boone.

In 1825 my father moved back to Maysville & lived there until 1829; then he moved to Missouri. He lived there 20 years, then we moved to California. My father went back to Missouri in 1851, and crossed the plains in 1853 to California again with a drove of cattle, and he died February the first, 1855. I lived in Santa Clara County from 1849 until 1877. Then I moved to Washington Territory and have been here ever since. I have five sons and three daughters. Their names are Sarah, Anne, Daniel W., John F., James P., Martin[?], Jacob, & Nellie B. Boone. I have given you a brief sketch of the family – so you can write it out.

Yours truly,

W. D. Boone

14C 88-89 LCD: **Daniel Boone, 1789**, with Notes of Col. Durrett's Library and a letter of Daniel Boone dated May 7, 1789.

Daniel Boone referred to the "bearer" of the letter as "Mr. go." The Goe family lived in the Kanawha area and were related to the Boones.

Boone had a little store at the mouth of Kanawha: Shane's Collections, ii, Montgomery County, p. 20.

May 7, 1789 – at Goe's on Mongahela – as a News Paper published letter of his shows in Louisville Courier Journal, April 7 [below]. Just on eve of starting down the river.

Ginseng at Limestone – see newspaper copy of Boone's letter to Thomas Hart... [This letter from the newspaper is given on page 14C 97.]

... A cast of Boone's skull, taken when his body was removed from Missouri to Frankfort for reinterment – an incident that inspired Theodore O'Hara's best poem – reveals a sloping forehead, with the perceptions strongly marked, like those of a fox, and a large development behind the ear.

Some historians say that Boone couldn't write, and nearly all, from Filson to Roosevelt, persist in spelling his name without the final "e." The annexed letter [which is printed and not Boone's handwriting], which has never been published, should settle both these points:

May the 7th 1789
Dear Sir, This Instant I start Down the River. My Two Sunes Returned ameadetly from Philadelphia and Daniel Went Down with Sum goods in order to take in gensgn at Lim Stone. I hope you Will wright me By the Bearer Mr go how you Com on With my Horsis – I Hear the Indians have Killed Sum Pepel Neer Limstone and Stole a Number of horsis – Indeed I Saw one of the men Who was fired on when they killed also 5 pursons Ware Certainly killed on the head of Dunkard Crick on this River a bout Six Dayes since 30 miles from Radstone I

Likewise saw a Later yesterday frm Muskingdom to Mr. Galaspey at the old fort that 300 Indians are Certinly Sit out from Detright To Way Lay the River at Deferent placis to take Botes Sum Say 700 Sum Say 100 But the Later Cartifies of 300 this accoumpt you may Rely on I am Dear Sir With Respect your omble Sarvent

Daniel Boone

My best To Mrs Hunt, Col Rochester and Lady.
This was coppyed by the Clark and is awl Wright

Daniel Boone

A unique curiosity, showing the scarcity of paper in the backwoods, is a slip bearing on the face a note signed by the old hunter, and on the back one signed by his brother.

LCD sources for Logan's Expedition are given again here, with the addition of the following:

Aug. 31 – George Clark's Son & 2 negroes taken: Magazine of American History I, 310, 312; Solomon Clark's Notes; ___ Henry Lee's Notes; Sudduth's Narrative

14C 90 LCD: **Col. Daniel Boone at Great Kanawha – 1789.**

Dr. Christopher C. Graham, Louisville, Ky., Nov. 17, 1872. His appearance & character. Dr. Christopher C. Graham, now of Louisville, Ky. (born in Ky in 1787) writes...

Col. Boone – I have a recollection of seeing Col. Boone, Clark, Logan, Harrod & Kenton, but near 86 years have produced a forgetfulness of their particular appearance. I, however, am still impressed with

Boone's appearance. His large head, full chest, square shoulder and stout form, are still impressed upon my mind. He was (I think) about five feet ten inches in height, and his weight say 175. He was solid in mind as in body, never frivolous, thoughtless or agitated, but was always quiet, meditative and impressive, unpretentious, kind & friendly in his manners. He came very much up to the idea we have of the old Grecian philosophers, particularly Diogenes.

14C 91 C. G. Graden[?], Louisville, Ky, July 10, 1873. Letterhead is a picture of "Front View of the Public Library Building, Louisville, Ky." P. A. Towne, Librarian, and R. T. Durrett, President.

Poor old man, who ought to have owned half of Kentucky.

Lyman Draper, Esq – Inclosed you have a copy of Boone's letter... I had it copied by one of our librarians...

I was well acquainted with both Hart and Rochester. Col. Hart lived and died in Woodford County, Ky, near Versailes and left a great estate of land... Col. Rochester lived in _ Ky., and left a large body of land also. Boone wrote from Great Canawha where he was digging ginseng, and [?]. _____ _ Poor old man who ought to have owned half of Kentucky... I have Boone's old Rifle which he first brought to the Bloody land and it is in the Museum with my[?] old hunting gun (B----er) where I intend to have all the old guns that defended the early Forts in Kentucky...

In old-fashioned friendship,

C. G. Graden[?]

I would like you to have Col. William Allen's new History of Kentucky, in which my life is _____ my picture in it. It was published by Bradley and Gilbert of Louisville.

14C 92 Daniel Boone, July 30, 1789 to Cols. Hart and Rochester. *This letter was copied from the original at Louisville Public Library.*

Grate Conhonway July the 30 1789

Dear Col

After My Best Wishes to you & family also Col. Rochester I cannot help Reflecting a Litel on the Downfall of ginsang. We ware a litel unfortunet Last fall But I Doubt it will be worse this But the information Come to me in Tolerable good Time although I had took in a goodel Sir I wish to have a Later from you in Respect to my Horsis as I am a goodeel Concerned a Bout Brothers Debts pray _____ me and Direct the Later to this place. I am Sir With Respect
Your very Omble Servant

Daniel Boone

Col. Hartt & Rochester.

14C 93 LCD: Copy from original in Simon Gratz's Collection, Philadelphia, furnished by Mr. Gratz, March 1, 1879.

Copy of Daniel Boone letter dated July 30, 1789 is addressed to John Phillips and John Young, Esquire in Philadelphia. The surname McClune mentioned in the letter could be transcribed as McClure.

I sepose he thought from our Acqantance he Might make free with my name.

Daniel Boone

Mouth of grate Conhaway July the 30, 1789

Sirs

I Rec'd your Later, Dated 18th of Aperal, a few Dayes past as it had past me and Went to Cantuek and my Sun had it sent to this plass and your Request I have Complyed with as far as it is Nesescary and am Exceeding Sorry to find so much disseption in Capt. Ellis. Nothing could induse me to say what I am going to mention but that of a failing conscience and to prevent you from Laying your Selves under a Ruinous Situation. This land, Sir, had never had a chan stretched on it. Neither has Capt. Ellis ever been on this Land, he only gott me and one Nathan McClune to go and show him where this Reserved Line started from and then to follow the same to where Chapman Austen had built on a branch of Buck Crick. Your Entry begun to the Best of my Rememberance 1500 poles S. E. of this corner of Astons. Know Sr. Capt. Ellis Returned home from there with us, and I left him at Capt Whitlys and he made out the plat for your Lands that Day and told Whitly that he Survayed it and Returned that ___ plat and a few days after I saw it on the Records. My Sun and Self Satt down chan men and markers and my Sun nor Casetey was not along with us and what I Tell you you may Rely on Let him say what he will as to the Qulity of the Land he is Right as to first Second & third tho the Later contains the grater part & the first Rate the Least The Timber and Water is as good as our Country affords. The Salt Spring you may not Look for there are no such thing in all that part of the Cuntry. Where the Land Lyes there are also good ___ sites on the Tract But the Land in General is not worth more than 2/s. per acre. That is as good as could be gott at that late peroud. Know, Sirs, I would advise you to send Sum person who knows this Reserved Line and Latt them get those two men Cald for in your Paten for Markers and go and Survey the Land again to your paten and Lett it be a privet matter and Latt your old paten stand as it is and all will be well. Otherwise you will loose the whole for my ___ I shall keep it a profound Secret. Neither did I wish you to Expose Capt Ellis as I sepose he thought from our acqantance he Might make free with my name. I shall be in Philadelphia this winter – will call on you.

I am gentlemen your Most Obedient Sarvant

Daniel Boone

14C 94 William A. Lewis, St. Albans, Kanawha[?] County, W. Va., March 9, 1881

Dr. Mr. Draper

I send you herewith an extract from the records of the second day of the first Court held in Kanawha County.

You will see Daniel Boone, whose life you are looking up, was considered, at that time, a resident of Kanawha.

I found no further mention of him in the records.

You may have the same information in "Arkinstons History" for ought I know, as I have never seen that work, as I told you in a former letter.

Yours Respectfully &c

Wm. A. Lewis

14C 95 Court of Kanawha County W. Va.,

At a Court continued and held for Kanawha [County] October 6th 1789

Present: Robert Clendenin, Francis Watkins, Charles McClung, Benjamin Shotter[[?], William C. Clendenin, David Robinson, George Alderson, Leonard Morris, James Van Bibber, Gentlemen –

Ordered that George Clendenin be recommended to his Excellency the Governor for

County Lieutenant; Thomas Lewis, Colonel; Daniel Boone, Lieutenant Colonel; William Clendenin, Major; Leonard Cooper and John Morris, Captains; James VanBibber and John Young, Lieutenants; and William Owens and Alexander Clendenin, Ensigns in the Militia of this County.

14C 96 Articles of Agreement between Amos Morris and William Harbar witnessed by Daniel Boone at Point Pleasant, Dec. 16, 1789... to make a deed to one quarter of an acre of land out of a Lott formerly Mr, McClung's...said Harber is to give the said Morris... the same note that Col. Lewis Sells Lotts to other persons for cash.

Amos Morris
William Harbar

Witness: Dal. Boone

This is copied from the original, which I know to be in Col. Daniel Boone's hand-writing, save the two signatures of Morris & Harbar. The names of Col. Lewis & Morris & the date, all prove that Point Pleasant was the place. Col. D. F. B___ loaned me the original.

Lyman C. Draper. Jan. 31, 1879.

14C 97 LCD**:** The following was appended to Hon. D. Meriwether's letter – evidently by the editors – in the Louisville Courier-Journal, April 15, 1883. The letter was described:

> **The letter is written on heavy parchment, not ruled, and the folding and wafer seal show that it went without envelope.**

AN OLD LETTER

The following is a true copy of a letter written by Daniel Boone in 1789 to Thomas Hart. The original is the property of Henry Clay, of this city, and was found among the papers which have come down through several generations as heirlooms in the Clay family. The letter is written on heavy parchment, not ruled, and the folding and wafer seal show that it went without envelope. The chirography is not bad, but the orthography is, as will be seen, not the most perfect, though there will be found many Kentuckians whose education has been less neglected than was Boone's, who perchance would not greatly improve upon it. The capitals are his, and there is no punctuation. The letter is addressed to Col. Thomas Hart, Haghers Town, and is as follows:

May the 7th 1789. – Dear Sir.

This Instant I Start Down the River. My Two suns Return amediately from philadelphia and Danel Worst sum goods in order to take in Gensyn at Lime Stone I hope you Will Wright me By the Bearer Mr. Goe how you com on With my Horses – I Hear the Indians have killed sum pepel neer Limestone and Stole a Number of horses – Indeed I Saw one of min Who Was fired on When they kild also five pursons Ware Certainly killed on the hed of Dunkerd Crick on this River a bout Six Days Since Thirty miles from Rad stone I Likewise Saw a Later yesterday from Miskingdom To Mr. Galaspy at the old port that 300 Indians are certainly Sit out from Detroyt To Way Lay the river at Diferent places to Take Botes sum say 700 Som Say 100 But the Later Cantities of 300 this a coumpt You may Rely on I am Dear Sir with Respects Your Omble Servent my Best Coml'm to Mrs. Hart Col Rochester and Lady

Daniel Boone

It may be discovered that the above is written on the Monongahela River – doubtless[?] at his son-in-law Goe's father, who lived there - near Brownsville, I think. Boone had, I judge, been to Hagerstown with horses for sale, which he left with Col. Thomas Hart – a large merchant there, who bought up largely ginseng, & other western country produce. Nathan Boone's notes I took of him show something of his horse enterprise on the part of his father. LCD

Col. Marmar's [?] Manuscript papers – vol. ii, p. 48 show this: 1789 – "May 13th, Wednesday, Col. Boone left the garrison this evening in a Kentucky boat for Limestone."

The Tackett Family Captivity

Brothers Lewis and Christopher Tackett built a small fort for a few families near the Coal River in the late 1780's. In April 1790 Indians attacked the fort. In November, Col. Arthur Campbell reported the return of captive Hannah Tackett

14C 98 LCD: Daniel Boone,1789

Notes on Tackett's Fort

Hannah Tackett's escape. Tackett's Fort, at Mouth of Coal [River]

Hannah Tacket's escape. Trip, 1860, v. p. 6; N. Boone's Notes; Trip 1860, viii, 179.

14C 99 Col. Arthur Campbell to the Governor, Nov. 1, 1790. LCD copy from *Virginia Calendar*, v: 221 on the capture of Hannah Tackett.

On the 1st of October last, Hannah Tackett, one of the captives taken at the mouth of Coal [River] in Kanawha County, made her escape from an Indian who was carrying her southwardly, and said he was of the Creek nation; had gone as an express to the Northern

Indians last Spring, and was returning with a war party designed for the more southerly settlements of Virginia; but unexpectedly fell in with the defenceless people at the mouth of Cole river. The fellow, by uncommon care, passed undiscovered through the thickest settlements in this county, and had nearly reached the great mountains south of us.

A second attack was made on the fort in 1795. Both attacks were described by Keziah Tackett Young, daughter of Lewis Tackett.

14C 100-100(13) Article on Tackett's Fort from *Ladies' Repository*, Cincinnati, June, 1847, "A Historical Document" by Rev. J. G. Bruce who recorded the account of Lewis Tackett's daughter, Mrs. Young.

The writer visited Mr. and Mrs. Young and heard the story told by Mrs. Young. She was the daughter of Lewis Tackett who, with his brother Christopher, established Tackett's Fort at the mouth of Coal River in 1789. Seven families lived there; the small fort suffered Indian attacks in 1790 and 1795.

Mrs. Young's mother and her brother Lewis were captured in March 1790 and returned home the following October. The second attack occurred on August 27, 1795. Taken captive were Mrs. McElhaney, grandmother to Betsy, who was in her early 20s; John McElhaney and his wife; little boys Samuel Tackett and Samuel McElhaney; Hannah Tackett, wife of Christopher.

Those who did not survive the journey were Mrs. McElhaney and John McElhaney. Hannah returned home two years later. Betsy and Samuel returned home from Detroit. Jane McElhaney escaped; Samuel McElhaney was never heard from.

Others, hearing the gunfire, escaped down the river to Clendenin's Fort in canoes during a heavy thunderstorm. Mrs. Young, the narrator, was one of those, sheltering her infant and wondering if she would drown while escaping Indian attack.

"Time rolls his ceaseless course. The race of yore,
Who danced her infancy upon their knee,
And told our marveling boyhood legend's store
Of their strange ventures, happ'd by land or sea,
How are they blotted from things that be
How few, all weak and withered of their force,
Visit on the verge of dark eternity,
Like stranded wrecks, the tide returning hoarse,
To sweep them from our sight! Time rolls his ceaseless course"

- Scott

It was the depth of winter. The winds swept fitfully along the deep, narrow valley of Elk river, and howled mournfully, as they tossed the giant branches of the mountain oak. The light of day had faded from the highest snow-clad peak of the Alleghanies. In a small cottage, immediately upon the bank of the river, fifteen miles above its junction with the great Kanawha, blazed a bright fire, around which was gathered a happy family, in which I was a guest. Mr. and Mrs. Young had seen many a December gale. Old age, with all its attendant infirmities, was upon them. Their lives had been spent in the wilds of western Virginia, a place replete with bold adventure and hazardous enterprise. To while away a long winter night, and, if possible, snatch from oblivion facts connected with border warfare, joined to an intense but innocent curiosity to note the dangerous paths those hardy pioneers had threaded, I asked for their history. But to detail that would exhaust the patience of the reader. I select, therefore, a single event, and those immediately connected with it – the capture of Tacket's Fort.

In the month of January, 1789, the smoke of the white man's cabin arose, for the first time, amid the tall forest trees that graced the beautiful valley of the Great Kanawha, immediately below the mouth of Coal [River]. The tide of emigration had come slowly down from "Camp Union," now Lewisburg, Va., having its entire course stained with blood, until it reached "Fort Clendinson," now Charleston, where it was stayed for several years by the strong arms[?] of Indian warriors, fighting bravely and desperately to retain possession of "the beautiful river of the woods." But the mandate had gone forth...

"On to the West, dark Indian, go!" and, yielding to destiny, they slowly and sullenly retired, while in close proximity the "pale faces" followed, to spoil their temples, and desecrate the graves of their fathers.

"In January, 1789," said Mrs. Young, "my father, Lewis Tacket, and his brother Christopher, with their families, settled at the mouth of Coal [River], and built what was called "Tacket's Fort," a little in the rear of the present residence of Mr. John Capehart. This "fort" was a double log cabin inclosed by a strong stockade, which was ordinarily a sufficient protection from the Indians. They were soon joined by others as fearless as themselves. And we numbered, in fifteen months, seven families – in all, thirty one persons. The dense forest was gracefully yielding to the axe – the wilderness was becoming a fruitful field; and long exemption from Indian incursions had beguiled us into a degree of carelessness incompatible with our safety.

"On the 22nd of March, 1790, my mother and brother Lewis, being in a field some distance from the fort, were seized and carried off by a party of Indians.

Pursuit was made, but without success. They were carried to Huron, in Michigan, where my mother was purchased from her captor by a squaw who had known her when a girl, sent to Detroit, and set at liberty. The officers at Detroit interested themselves for my brother, obtained his release, and sent them down the Lake to Erie, whence they passed across the country to "Camp Union," where they arrived early in September. News of their release had been brought to us at the fort, with the further information that they would come from Erie to Pittsburg, and thence descend the Ohio river to Point Pleasant.

"My father and Charles Young left the fort on the 26th of August and descended the Kanawha river to that place, for the purpose of bringing them home; but they had gone the other route. That day I became a joyful mother. As these were the only persons that had been taken by the Indians for a long time, and their release following so close upon their captivity, it did not produce that circumspect vigilance which would have saved the fort. The people commenced building outside; and some of them (we among others) were living on Coal river, some distance from the fort. We thought the war whoop would startle us no more. Alas! "we know not what a day may bring forth."

"The 27th of August, 1795, dawned upon the fort. The sun shown from an unclouded sky. The men were busy building a house on Coal river. John McEllhany was sick in the fort, and my uncle, Christopher Tacket, was there to guard it. About four o'clock in the afternoon, some of the children were out on the bank of the Kanawha playing ball, and my uncle was keeping tally for them. Some Indians, who had approached them under cover of the banks of the river, showed themselves but a few yards from the boys, and raised the terrible war cry of their nation. Tackett and the boys fled with the utmost precipitation. He reached the gate; but waiting for the children to get in before he made it fast, the Indians rushed upon and enforced it open. He then started to the house, where he had left his gun, but was shot down and tomahawked in the yard, as were all the children.

John McEllhany, hearing the cry without, closed the door; but, in doing it, had three of his fingers shot off. Unable to defend themselves, and the Indians promising protection if they would surrender, Mrs. McEllhany prevailed with her son to open the door and admit them. There were in the fort John McEllhany, his mother, wife, Hannah Tacket (wife of Christopher), Betsy Tacket, and Samuel Tacket and Samuel McEllhany, little boys. Having secured these, the Indians bound up McEllhany's wounded hand, and taking what plunder they could, retreated on to the hill, some half a mile or more, where they stopped to divide the spoils, which being done, they left the prisoners under a strong guard, and the main party returned to the fort, to secure more prisoners. But they were disappointed, for when the people on Coal river heard the shooting at the fort, Robert McEllhany and his son Robert ran to ascertain the cause of it; and the rest of us took refuge in the house of Thomas Allsbury.

"O, it was an awful moment! We knew not at what moment the foe might be upon us, and should they come, we had no hope of deliverance. The McElhaneys finding the fort in possession of a large party of Indians, gave up all for lost, and, without returning to us, passed through the woods, crossed Coal river at the falls, and reached Clendenen's next morning at daylight. We soon ascertained that the Indians had retired from the fort, and were sufficiently acquainted with their mode of warfare, to believe that they had only retired a short distance, and would return before dark. We, therefore, took canoes instantly and started for Clendenen's.

Just after dark there came up a thunder storm. The rain fell in torrents, filling the canoe in which I was, half full of water, and it did seem that we had only escaped the fury of the savage to find a watery grave. How I shielded my child, in that long night of alarm and terror, I know not; but we all arrived safely at Clendenin's next morning about sun-rise. The Indians, finding that we had fled, killed what cattle they could find, burned all the houses, and returning to the prisoners, told them that they had killed all the people in the neighborhood. Sometime after, however, they told them the truth, that that those little rivers had saved them. And so it was; for if the rivers had not been swollen by recent rains, they would have pursued and cut us all off, or taken us prisoners.

"About sundown they were ready to move; but as a necessary preliminary, wished to bind [tie] John McEllhany. He told them it was useless; for his mother and wife being with them, he should not think about making his escape. Feigning[?] satisfaction with this answer, one of them threw down a blanket, and bade him take it up. As he stooped to execute the order, the tomahawk was buried in his head, and he rolled upon the ground a lifeless corpse! Leaving him there a prey to wild beasts and the vultures of the air, they hurried away with the mother and wife, whose apprehensions for the future were too painful to allow them to realize, to the full extent, the desolation of the present moment, or to give to the bitterness of their anguish the luxury of tears. It was one of those moments of high-wrought, intense excitement, in which the tide of feeling can only double back upon itself, and freeze the heart with horror!

"They continued their march to a late hour of the night. The elder Mrs. McEllhaney, beside being infirm from age, was very corpulent, and hence traveled with difficulty, retarding the progress of the entire company. Betsy Tacket was walking immediately behind her, the last of the sad captive train. Observing the Indians in close consultation, she guessed their fatal determination, and said, “Grandmother it is time for you to pray – they are going to kill you!” Without making any reply, she fell upon her knees and cried, “Lead me to the Rock that is higher than I!”, and, as the words tumbled upon her lips, the tomahawk of the Savage bade “The weary wheels of life stand still.” The silver cord was loosed, the golden bowl broken, and her spirit passed away to the land of the blest. She was a member of the Baptist church, and a devoted Christian. O, it is, indeed,

> “A fearful thing
> To see the human soul take wing,
> In any shape – in any mood;”

but to see it in this shape, even in the dim, shadowy distance of half a century, makes us shudder. But she was ready – her lamp was trimmed and burning. She lived in communion with God, and to her we may appropriately apply the words of [James] Montgomery:

> “Prayer is the Christians native air –
> His watchword at the gate of death.
> He enters heaven with prayer.”

Soon after her death, they encamped for the night. Next morning the Indians disagreed about something, and one of them taking Hannah Tacket, separated from the others, and turning up Guyandotte river, passed on to the Holston. He made her several times steal corn and other things necessary to their subsistence. She at length asked him if the Indians stole from each other. "No," said he, "the Great Spirit would be angry with them." "You make me steal from my people, and do you not think the Great Spirit will be angry with me for doing so?" Unable to answer her, he was content after that, to do the stealing himself. He treated her with great kindness and affection, and some eighteen months or two years after her captivity, he released her, and she returned to her friends.

"The others crossed the Ohio river and went to some of their towns on the Muskingum, where the prisoners were separated, Jane McEllhany remaining, while Betsey Tacket and the two little boys were carried to Huron.

"Jane McEllhany's captivity was short, and the manner of her escape so remarkable, as to warrant our calling it providential. The man who owned her sent her, early one morning, to a neighboring wigwam for a basket, in which he wished to wash some lye hommony. Though well acquainted with the path, she lost her way. Utterly bewildered, she could neither find the hut to which she was sent, nor any other. In this condition she wandered all day. Late in the evening she came to an Indian village, but she saw no person. She passed several huts without even an inclination to stop. At length, as she approached, some person seemed to say to her, 'Stop here!' Yielding to the suggestion she stepped to the door, and to her great joy, found the hut was occupied by a white man, whose name, as she subsequently learned, was Zanes. He asked her if she was a prisoner, where taken, and if she desired to return to her friends. Having answered her inquiries, he told her that if she would consent to be concealed for a few weeks, and assist his wife in preparing his winter clothes he would restore her to her friends. With these conditions she cheerfully complied. Taking her some distance form his house, he concealed her beneath a pile of logs, where she remained for six weeks. The hunting season at length arrived, when he conveyed [her] to Wheeling, whence she returned to Clendenen's.

"Betsy Tacket was stolen from the Indians by a Mr. McPherson, who was trading with them, and carried to Detroit, where she subsequently married Robert Johnson, who purchased Samuel Tacket and then returned with them to Kanawha.

"The fate of Samuel McEllhany is not known, but it is supposed he was killed at the time of General St. Clair's defeat, as we never heard of him afterward.

"May such scenes never recur!" said Mrs. Young, as she wiped the tears from her cheek. "I saw the dense, heavy cloud of smoke roll up from the fort, and knew full well that a sister and brother were either killed or were led away captive. Ah! Though forty nine years have passed away since that ill-fated day, its scenes are as fresh in my mind as if they had occurred yesterday."

"The clock had struck twelve – the bright fire had become dim; so, bidding my kind entertainers good night, I retired to rest, feeling grateful to God that the restless vengeance of the untutored savage would not disturb me in that quiet cottage home. And now, gentle reader, if I have beguiled thee of one care, awakened in thy heart one emotion of gratitude for the felicity of thy position, or kindled into livelier glow the sympathies of thy nature, my recompense is gained." Ladies' Repository, Cincinnati, June, 1847.

***

14C101-102 LCD: **Daniel Boone, 1791**

Living at mouth of Kanhawa - Shane's Collections, iii, Fleming (County?), p. 19

June 14 – Surveying land. Collins Ky, I, 246 &c

March[?] – Negro woman captured ____ ____, Trip 1860 v. i.

14C 103 LCD: **Daniel Boone's List,** Dec. 12, 1791 from *Virginia Calendar*, v: 410
William McMacken to the Governor, Richmond, Dec. 18, 1791 from *Virginia Calendar*, v: 413
Daniel Boone receipt for 400 weight of powder from *Virginia Calendar*, v: 416.

Daniel Boone's List – Dec. 12th

For Kenaway County, 68 privates; Leonard Cooper, Captain at Point Pleasant, 17 men; Joel Da__, Ensign at Belleville, 17 men; John Young, scout at Elk, 17 men; John Morris, Jr., Ensign at the Boat Yards, 17 men.

Two spies or scouts will be necessary at the Point to search the banks of the river at the crossing places. More would be wanting if they could be allowed. Those spies must be composed of the inhabitants who well know the woods and waters from the Point to Belleville, 60 miles – no inhabitants [between – LCD]; also from the Point to Elk, 60 miles, no inhabitants; from Elk to the Boat Yards, 20 miles, all inhabited.

William McMachen to the Governor

Richmond, Dec. 18th 1791

Sir:

I have the honor to transmit the enclosed as the form of an agreement for the transportation of the ammunition allotted for the frontier counties. The expenses attending it are[?] low, and Colonel Boones inducement to the undertaking is the payment of the consideration in advance on the determination of the Honorable the Executive in this case; the agreement will be executed, and either lodged in the Council Chamber or remain with me.

Dec. 22nd, 1791, Point of [?], Va., Daniel Boone gives receipt for 400 weight of powder and 1600 weight of lead, with one barrel of flints, for the use of the company under his command, and that under Capt. Lowther[?], which he engages to employ without charge or barter, solely in the service of the Commonwealth, &c &c.

14C 104 W. McMacken, Richmond, Dec. 22, 1791
LCD: Copied from Virginia Calendar, v: 416

Having delivered the advance stores, as required, orders Col. Daniel Boone, to deliver at Moorefield, in Hardy County, sixty of powder, 2400 weight of lead, & proportion of flints; at Morgantown, 190 weight of powder, 760 weight of lead, and proportion of flints; at the mouth of Buffalo, 150 weight of powder, 600 weight of lead, and proportion of flints, &c.

14C 105 Daniel Boone to the Governor of Virginia, Monday, Dec. 13, 1791. Original in Collection of Prof. E. H. Leffingarell[?], New Haven.

Monday 13th Decr 1792

Sir As sum purson must Carry out the a_[?] to Red Stone if your Exclency should have thought me a proper purson I would undertake it on conditions I have the appointment to pilot the Company at Kanaway so that I could take down the flower [flour] as I passe that place

I am your Excelencys most obedient omble servant

Dal Boone

To the Governor of Virginia doubtless written at Richmond, Va: see my extracts from Va. records of that period. LCD

14C 105(1) Daniel Boone to William Hord[?]

March the 3d 1791

Dear Sir

My Sun Dal Boone Wates on you for the Balance Due me for Rose and her Child Which is 32 pounds virganey money Besides the Intrust Which I hope you will not faill to pay him and Not put me to the trubel of Coming Down my Self and he will gave you a full Resete for the Same I am Sir your omble Sarvent

Daniel Boone

Mr. William Hord[?]

14C 106 Sent to LCD by A. Daly[?]. *This is the same Daniel Boone letter as 14C105(1).*

14C 107-107(2) S. G. Tucker, Richmond, [Va.] Sept. 6, 1853. *Daniel Boone was elected to the Legislature*

... I find among the returns of elections for the year 1791 that Daniel Boone was elected with George Clendenin to represent the county of Kanawha in the Legislature. The following is a copy verbatim...of the return and certificate of the Sheriff.

At an election held at the Court House of the County of Kanawha on the 4 day of April 1791 for the purpose of choseing of Delegates to represent the said County in the General Assembly for the ensuing year whereby at an open and fair election George Clendenin & Daniel Boone were

Chose...

Thos. Lewis S. K. C. [Surveyor Kanawha County?]

Boone like many of his sturdy contemporaries of the west, was a silent member of the Legislature, and his communication in the House was literally "yea, yea & nay, nay." But he seems to have been respected as a man of strong mind and was placed on two of the most important Committees in the house, the Committee of Religion and the Committee of Pro____s and Grievances.

The first note of importance on which we find his name recorded is on a resolution declaring the preemption right of Virginia to all the lands within the limits of her original charter. In May 1779 an act was passed setting forth this right and the determination of Virginia to "maintain it to the utmost of her power." See Hening's Statutes vol. 10 p. 97. In the ____ of 1791 it was found necessary to ____ this right, and accordingly a resolution was introduced for the purpose. As might well be expected Daniel Boone voted in favor of the resolution, thereby respecting[?] the sovereignty of Virginia over her soil.

The next recorded vote was in form of a subscription by the State of fifty shares to the Dismal Swamp Canal, the first work of internal improvement in which the Commonwealth was interested. The fact that Boone lived in an almost unexplored region which could never be benefited by this improvement, exhibits a liberality of feeling and enlarged views of policy, which it would be well for the more refined statesmen of the present day to imitate.

At this session of the Legislature the important subject of the glebe lands was under consideration. Prior to the revolution large bodies of land had been purchased by the State for the use of the Established Church. But after the separation of Virginia from the British Crown, and the statute of religious freedom, great discontent prevailed among the other denominations of Christians at this palpable violation of the spirit of our institutions. At the session ... a memorial was presented by the various Baptist Association of the State representing the injustice of such a policy, and its utter subversion of the principles set forth in the Bill of Rights, and praying that the lands might be sold, and the moneys applied to the ordinary purposes of government. The Committee to whom the memorial was referred, submitted a report declaring it ____ to grant the prayer of the petitioners. A motion was made to amend the report by substituting ____ a preamble setting forth the injustice of the whole glebe system and recommending the adoption of the following resolution:

"Resolved that the several acts of Assembly which rest in the Protestant Episcopal Church glebe lands which have been purchased with money arising from taxes levied on the Citizens of the Commonwealth, ought to be repealed."

For the adoption of this ____ we find the name of Daniel Boone recorded in the Journal. It was, however, rejected in a Legislature still swayed by early prejudices for the Church of England, and it was a much later day that this last footprint of tyranny was obliterated.

After careful search I have been unable to find any record of Boone having represented the District of Kentucky in the Legislature of Virginia. I sincerely wish that it was in my power to aid you further in the prosecution of your praiseworthy enterprise, and with every hope for your success, I have the honour to be very respectfully

S. G. Tucker

LCD memo: This session of the Virginia Legislature began Oct. 17, 1791 & last date of ____ is Dec 20th, 1791. See Hening's Virginia Statutes.

14C 108 LCD memo: Mr. Tucker was Clerk of the House of Delegates, & Keeper of the Rolls. Vide American Almanacs of the period.

***

15C

This volume includes Draper's notes and correspondence pertaining to the 1790s and 1800s when Daniel Boone lived in Kentucky, West Virginia and Missouri. Reports of Boone's hunting expeditions in Missouri and beyond were sent to Draper by relatives of those who had accompanied him.

In 1882, Draper asked historian Richard H. Collins to send copies of depositions from Kentucky land suits which Collins had published in his *History* several years earlier. These Draper received in April, 1883; they are included in this volume.

The deponents in the Land Suits were: Daniel Boone, Benjamin Berry, Flanders Callaway, Jesse Coffee (Cofer/Copher), William Cradlebaugh, John Curry, Levi Davis, Septimus Davis, James Guthrie, Henry Hall, Stephen Hancock, Peter Harget, Jesse Hodges, Simon Kenton, Stephen Lowry, John McCausland, John Waller [other transcriptions have this name as John Miller], Robert Patterson, John Riggs, Peter Scholl, Jacob Sodowsky, George Stockton, William Triplett, Hayden/Haydon Wells, and Thomas Young.

Events which took place in Missouri during the War of 1812 and later were reported by eyewitnesses John Gibson and Henry Dodge in accounts of Cole's Defeat, the Sink-Hole Battle, Campbell's Defeat, and the Black Hawk War.

15C 1-2 LCD: Daniel Boone, 1792

In warm weather, during the night, the grease dripped down on him from bear meat hanging overhead.

Appointed Dec. 1791 to supply provisions to soldiers on frontiers – Indian Affairs I, 223; Trip 1860 iv. 83, 84, 86; Trip 1860, ii, 119.

March 4 - Delivers powder & lead – Virginia Archives, v. 456.
1792, October – Boone's failure to provide supplies: Trip 1860, ii, 120; Trip 1860, v. 59. 60. 77.
Six Van Bibbers in militia. Trip 1860, v. 68.
Robert Sinclair killed. Trip 1860. v. 68. Nathan Boone's Notes.
May 14 – Joseph Van Bibber &c. taken [captured] – Trip 1860, viii. 183. Nathan Boone's Notes.
August – Gallipolis matters. Trip 1860, viii, 165, 167 &c, 224. Nathan Boone's Notes, 203-4 & references; Volney's Views, 326, 401.

Living at mouth of Kanhawa, Col. James Lane spent a night with him [Daniel Boone] there in warm weather, & during the night the grease dripped down on him from bear meat hanging overhead. Shane ii, Bath County, 44-45.

Ulin's[?] Leap – Shane's Collections, iii, 177, 165.

15C 3 Col. George Clendenin to the Governor, Kanawha, W. Va., March 26, 1792. Daniel Boone to supply the rangers.

LCD copied the letter from the *Virginia Calendar* vi: 561[?].

Fort Clendenin
https://secureservercdn.net/198.71.233.33/tnx.ofS.myftpupload.com p-content/uploads/2019/1O/IMG_1683-3.jpg

Sir: In the provision made for the defence and protection of the county the present year, your Excellency was so kind as to inform me that ammunition was put into the hands of Col. Daniel Boone for that purpose, and that he was also to furnish rations for Capt. Caperton's Ranging Company. I am, therefore, led to inform Your Excellency that no ammunition has yet come to hand, neither has there been a single ration furnished. A consequence naturally follows that I have been compelled to provide rations for said company as yet, otherwise let them be disbanded; & have purchased of Mr.[?] Cook for the use of said company the militia ____, gunpowder, &c. The Indians are daily committing depredations within this county. On Monday week last, they killed two very reputable men – a certain Michael Lee and Mr. Robert St. Clair. At the same time they took a white boy & a negro. Thirty of them were discovered a few days before they did the aforesaid mischief opposite to my fort across the Kanawha river in sight of the fort whose intention we suppose was to attack the fort the following night or fix themselves for that purpose. On their being discovered, they fired several guns at the fort but without doing any mischief. We daily expect to be attacked by them at one or other of our stations. The frontier counties have never experienced so desperate a summer as this appears [and] promises to be. We keep close garrison & hope for the approach of an army which may perhaps call their attention from us.

15C 4 LCD: **Daniel Boone – 1792**

LCD copied the following undated letter from the *Virginia Calendar vi: 67* and two others from the same source.

Col. George Clendenin to the Governor.

I think some 4 or 5 months after the said service – (Col. Boon to supply Capt. Caperton's Rangers with rations) ought to have commenced, Col. Boone arrived at the mouth of the Kanawha River without any means of supply for said men. When on being applied to by Col. [Thomas] Lewis if he had made any provision as required his answer was that Capt. Caperton had not done the business to his mind, or words to that effect, and therefore he had not made any provision for the reception of said men.

A few days after the arrival of the said Col. Boone, I went to the mouth of the Kanawha in company with Capt. Caperton and heard Col. Boone and him very freely (in my opinion) investigate the nature of their several trusts; where[?] agreeable to the same opinion, there appeared to have been a total non-compliance of the former, which occasioned the remission of the latter.

Received March 27, 1792 of Col. Daniel Boone, 709 lbs of lead, 190 lbs powder, a proportion of flints for the use of the men of Harrison & Monongalia counties in actual service; also a proportion of flints for Randolph County. John Evans, Co. Lt. Monongalia County

William McMachen, Ohio County, Virginia, April 5, 1792, from Moses[?] Williams on account of Col. Daniel Boone, 170 lbs powder, 568 lbs lead, one keg of flints.

15C 5 LCD: **Daniel Boone, 1792**
Hunt in Gallia County, Ohio
From Dr. John P. Hale's Facts & Incidents of Daniel Boone

In 1792, Daniel Boone and Robert Safford went on a beaver-trapping expedition on Raccoon Creek in now Gallia County, Ohio. They camped first about where the town of Adamsville now stands, and later at Beaver Dam near Vinton.

They caught over one hundred beavers. When the hunt was over and Boone returned to Kanawha, he presented to his friend Safford his tomahawk and best beaver trap which he called "Old Isaac."

The Robert Safford above mentioned was one of the first three men who, in 1790, landed on the site of, and helped to lay out and start the town of Gallipolis.

15C 6-7 A. C. Safford, Gallipolis, Ohio, June 15, 1883

They lived for 3 days, on account of snow, on a beaver tail.

Dear Sir

Your letter of Nov 3rd is at hand. I suppose you were not aware that my Father, T. C. Safford, is dead. He died in 1873. I supposed that the letters were meant for him so I got them out of the Office.

It was Col. Robert Safford, my father's grand Father and my great grand Father that was a companion of Col. Daniel Boone...

James Burford, Col. Robert Safford & Daniel Boone were the party that took the hunt. They trapped for 3 months near what is now Adamsville on Raccoon Creek & also at Vinton. They caught 100 Beavers. They lived for 3 days, on account of snow, on a beaver tail.

Col. Safford shot a panther 10 feet long.

The Life of Boone does not say anything about the beaver hunt at all. I have not found out exactly what year the hunt was but will find out [when?] possible.

Yours truly
A. C. Safford

LCD: Dr. Hale says the hunt was in 1792.

LCD comments and questions (not included here) gave names of elderly relatives to contact.

15C 8-9 A. C. Safford, July 8, 1883.

... I have been very busy harvesting or I would have answered sooner. I thank you kindly for the book. I think it is a good work.

Boone gave Col. Safford 2 of his traps one which he called "Old Isaac" – the largest one. The other one we have lost. A man who claimed to be from Portsmouth got the trap "Old Isaac" & the Tomahawk from my father. He said he wanted to write a Life of Boone and would return them but did not. I have also a small ax which cut the first tree where Gallipolis now stands...

I think the [beaver] hunt lasted 3 months.

It was not on this hunt that Col. Safford killed the Panther.

I do not know of any descendants of James Burton. He left this state and went to Indiana where he died.

Col. Safford has a son and daughter living. The son Chillis lives near to us and is over eighty years old... the daughter is visiting him from Illinois; she is 76.

I have the Life of Boone but it does not give any account of the hunt...

I will send you a sketch taken from the Gallipolis Journal but would like you to return it if you please.

P. S. I do not know how the hunters divided their beaver skins.

A. C. Safford

The clippings were not sent; Draper acquired them from the Gallipolis, Ohio *Journal* and attached them to the end of the letter. The clippings are mostly illegible and are not included here. There is no page 10 in the microfilm.

15C 11-11(1) Edgar J. Mossman, Aug. 23, 18__. ______, Gallia County, Ohio.

My Dear Sir:

Your favor of some time ago received... I send you the Mss. on the conditions you mentioned in your letter, that you would send me a copy of your book "King's Mountain" that you would have me choose a corresponding member of your historical society, and that you would send me the books issued by your society. I don't know how much of the material I send you will answer your purpose, but I send it just as written for the New Journal. It is hard to write of Boone in this county without also saying considerable of Buford[?] and Safford for whatever is the history of one is the history of the other. I am collecting material for the purpose of writing a history of this county...

Hoping to receive an early reply,

I am ever, Yours respectfully,
Edgar J. Mossman

15C 12-12(6) Edgar J. Mossman, Rodney, Ohio, undated writings titled "Reminiscences in Gallia County, Ohio of Daniel Boone and his companions, Safford and Burford."

In this account Boone is placed as a hunter in Ohio in 1802 and as returning to Kentucky in 1804. Peter Houston reported that Boone had visited him in summer of 1802 in Bourbon County, Kentucky. Boone's Missouri family said he was hunting there during these years and some said he never returned to Kentucky.

Major Burnham, with about 40 men, was sent by the Sciota Company in advance of the French emigrants to the Ohio river to lay out a town for them. Among the number were Daniel Boone, the famous Kentuckian, James Burford, the most notorious sensational yarner on the frontier, and Col. Robert Safford, a hero of revolutionary fame.

On June 8th, 1790, this party landed at the site of Gallipolis and Boone and Safford, with that spirit to take the lead which characterized them through life, sprang ashore with their axes and had the honor of not only falling [sic] the first tree but also of being the first white men on the spot. Major Burnham's men soon cleared the ground, erected log cabins, stockades and block houses for protection against the Indians. The colonists arrived in October 1790. They were obliged to suffer by practical experience before they were able to adapt themselves to the new mode of living to make much progress in rendering their situation comfortable. Daniel Boone, his companions, and other experienced American pioneers, assisted them in this. These old pioneers formed themselves into a hunting band, and supplied the colonists with provisions in the shape of wild game. Boone, Safford and Burford were the regular appointed scouts of the little band, and experienced many exciting adventures with the Indians.

These scouts always observed the Sabbath by resting from the chase, and spending the day in cleaning their guns, repairing their moccasins, and stretching and dressing their skins.

It is related of Boone, while on one of his scouting expeditions on Raccoon Creek (Gallia County) that he was pursued by the Indians to the creek bank above the Great Rapids where there was no retreat. The Indians were closing in on him with shouts of triumph when they saw him push out an old bateaux from the shore without an oar, and start down the rapids. They fired at him until he was in the thick of the rapids, and then paused to see the result. The rapids are filled with rocks looming up in every direction, with narrow channels sloping up between. Into this hell of boiling water, his eagle eye watching every chance, his hands upon either gunwale of the bateaux, that gallant old hero darted. The Indians ceased firing and with uplifted hands beheld the descent. Time after time it seemed as if the old hero would be dashed to pieces upon the rocks, but by and by he darted safely down the stream and was soon out of sight and sound.

The writer visited this rapid last spring, and is of the opinion that there are not many men in the world who would have dared the passage of those rocks, even with those howling red devils in the rear.

While on another scouting expedition up this creek, in the winter of 1790-1791, Boone discovered a cave near which were the ruins of an old log cabin almost entirely decayed with age. It was a matter of wonderment as to who the builder and occupant could have been, and it remains a mystery still.

When Boone, Safford and Burford were trapping on this creek for a livelihood, they occupied this cave for some time, and the smoke stains of their camp fires may be seen upon its roof unto this day.

The region bordering upon Raccoon Creek at this time was a wild one, abounding with wild game, thereby affording them a splendid field for their enterprise, but was infested upon all sides by Indians. The trials and adventures of these hardy pioneers constitute one of the most romantic leaves in the history of Gallia County. For over two years they were busily engaged in trapping at different points along the romantic stream.

These gentlemen were expert trappers. They were so perfectly familiar with the cunning ways and tricks of the beaver and otter that they knew just how and where to set their traps to catch them. During the time they trapped together, they caught several hundred beavers, otters, and bears. Every spring they would take many canoe loads of furs to market, exchanging them for those things they needed.

At the close of the fur season in 1802, they descended the creek with canoes loaded with furs. The Indians, who professed to be their friends, had never given them any trouble. When on their way to market, little did they dream that the Indians were plotting against them for the express purpose of robbing them of their winter's labor.

The trappers were unaware of the fact that a band of Indians were quietly pursuing them until about the middle of the afternoon, when Boone accidently saw signs of Indians. They were constantly on the alert the remainder of the afternoon, but not seeing any more signs of lurking foes they landed and made preparations for the night. They quickly lighted a fire and prepared their evening meal. They were constantly on the alert, for the sun had already disappeared and the woods were assuming a dusky hue, which reminded them that the hour the savage usually chose for his depredations was speedily drawing near. Over two hours had elapsed since they had landed, and during all of that time not a sign of an Indian had been seen, so they began to feel perfectly safe. They lit their pipes and sat down by the fire. Burford began relating some remarkable story, when all of a sudden a tremendous yell broke forth from the bushes on all sides that almost made their blood run cold. Seizing their guns, they rushed behind a projecting rock nearby, just in time to escape the...arrows that followed.

Three shots from their retreat, and as many messengers of death were on their way into the forest. These Indians fought as Indians rarely do in a close encounter, pushing on in a determined manner notwithstanding so many of their number lay dead already upon the sod. The trappers continued to fire at a terrible rate. At last the Indians gave way, scattering in every direction. Now was their time to escape while the Indians were retreating, so they hastily loaded their canoes, and were soon moving down the stream at a rapid rate. Being within a short distance of the creek's mouth, before many more minutes they were safe upon the bosom of the wide-spreading Ohio.

This little band of hunters disbanded in 1804 – Col. Boone returning to Kentucky [he was then living in Missouri]. Col. Safford [returned] to Gallipolis, and Mr. Burford was married shortly afterwards, settling on the side of their old hunting camp, where he united the pursuits of farmer and trapper.

When Boone took leave of his friend, Safford, he presented him with the largest of his traps, which he had named "Old Isaac," also a tomahawk and a small ax...

A few words about James Burford might not be entirely out of place. Mr. Burford made himself famous by relating remarkable stories in a bland, suave, and impressive manner that carried convictions with them notwithstanding their absurdity. Mr. Burford, although unquestionably an honest and truthful man in all matters pertaining to business, was, nevertheless, the most notorious sensational yarner on the frontier. He claimed the championship in this until a Yankee named Jacobs came down from "Varmount" and beat him so bad that he was forced to acknowledge it. It is said that he became completely dejected and chagrined after this defeat, and that it so worked on his feelings that it was the principle thing that prompted him to sell his farm and leave. He went to Indiana, where he died shortly afterwards. The name of Burford is familiar in nearly every part of our country.

Edgar J. Mossman

15C 13 B. Netherland to His Excellency, Isaac Shelby, Governor of Kentucky, July 5, 1799.

Letter submitted by Samuel M. Duncan of Nicholasville, Ky., who is now engaged in looking up old documents pertaining to the early history of this State for the Louisville Philotechnic Society... At that date, Nicholasville was called Mingo Tavern. The letter was published in an unnamed and undated newspaper under the title "Kentucky Ninety Years Ago." [LCD]

...three men were killed by a party of Shawneese who were pursued, overtaken and killed near the ferry at Boonesboro.

Dear Sir,

...There are but few depredations committed in this part of Fayette [County, Kentucky]. At the mouth of Marble Creek last year, it was reported three men were killed by a party of Shawneese who were pursued, overtaken and killed near the ferry at Boonesboro.

About three months past, two Indians crossed the Kentucky [River] at the mouth of Dix River and come among the few settlers, as they said, for trading. I was not pleased at seeing them and told Tom Lewis and his father to keep a watch on them. They spoke English pretty well, and were very active and pretended much friendship for our people. When they left the next day they met one of the settlers named Michael Hifner, who had been to see one Thomas Rowland and who had settled on a plantation ten miles above.

The Indians told Hifner that he must let them have his horse; this he refused to do when he heard the snap of a gun. He at once jumped from the horse and stabbed the Indian to the heart. He then turned upon the other, who shot him in the arm, and ran off into the timber. Hifner, being a brave and active young man, pursued him, and before the Indian could reload his gun, Hifner knocked his brains out with a club and threw his dead body into the river. The body of the Indian he stabbed to death was buried.

A party of Indians, supposed to be Wiandots, killed two settlers at the mouth of Jessamine last spring. Also, I have learned that at the crossing at Paint Lick, two men are reported killed by this same party of Wiandots or Shawneese. It is my impression that if fifty mounted men were employed to scour the Kentucky river cliffs during this fall, I feel sure no more of our people would be ambushed and killed. These high hills and cliffs are good hiding places for Indians to do us much injury. I must urge you to appoint Thomas Wilson Captain and Lieutenant of this end of the county. He is young and strong, and such service would be in his nature, which is wild and adventurous.

I would seek the place myself, but I have now the high and responsible duties of a husband and father which I cannot cast aside without doing injustice...

Your old friend,
B. Netherland

15C 14-15-16 LCD: **Daniel Boone, 1793**
Boone at Paris, Ky. Personal appearance.

Col. John Johnston, Cist's Advertiser, Nov. 23, 1847. Patrick Gass' letters (among Clark papers) - speaks of meeting Boone at Louisville in 1793 – had been out on Kentucky river, probably hunting.

1793 Daniel Boone: Size & personal appearance & dress: Howe's Ohio, 192; Col. John Johnston's letter March 22nd – Attack on Van Bibber – Trip 1860, vol. 58, 61; Smallpox raging - Trip 1860, v. 68, 63.

The Indians have made incursions to Kanawha County – taken two negroes belonging to William Moore – a Col. Boone and another person were killed or taken. US[?] Gazette, April 27, 1793. See notes of Nathan Boone, p. 197 June 1793 – Sherwood's capture & escape. Trip 1860, v, 68, 69, 70.

September 1793 – Andrew Lewis &c – Clendenin wounded. Philadelphia Daily Advertiser, Oct. 31, 1793

September 28th – Lewis & Burwell's[?] Adventure, Trip 1860, v, 77, 80 &c, Nathan Boone's Notes; Van Bibber kills an Indian – American Pioneer, ii, 286. Nothing of this in Col. Nathan Boone's Notes.

15C 17-18 LCD: **Daniel Boone, 1793**

Col. Thomas Lewis, Point Pleasant, April 10th, 1793

...On the 22nd day of last month, the Indians murdered a young lady and took a boy prisoner in view of the town at the mouth of the Kanawha and would most certainly have killed her father, Captain Van Bibber, & have taken a negro man had not the people of the town yielded him their immediate assistance. Previous to which being sheltered by a small cabin, he killed one of the Indians, and we expect mortally wounded two others.

The Indians have lately crossed the Ohio into our county, left the exceeding large rafts at one place, beside several other scattering ones at different places from which sign we cannot but conjecture that there is less than 100 of them in the county at the present time.

Virginia Calendar vi: 333

Col. Thomas Lewis, June 5th 1793

Just as I finished this letter, the Indians fired on a party of men going to work. John Craig was mortally wounded, & one Fleming wounded in the arm. But the whites drove off the Indians, badly wounding 3 or 4 of the Indians, whose bloody trail was followed till a fall of rain coming on obliterated the blood.

Virginia Calendar, vi: 422

Col. Rogan[?], Oct. 3rd, 1793, Harrison County, Va.

There was a spy shot by the Indians at the mouth of the Big Canhaway – one was shot through the hips, the other through the arm. The name of the latter was Andrew Lewis, the name of the other is unknown to us.

Virginia Calendar, vi: 576.

Capt. William Clendenin, of the Rangers, to the Governor of Kanawha, Oct. 9, 1793

Andrew Lewis & Joseph Burwell[?] volunteered their services to go to Point Pleasant to bring up some powder – went in a canoe. After passing down within 16 miles of Point Pleasant & discovered a canoe in the mouth of a creek, went to see what it meant.

When quite close they suddenly, in their canoe, attempted to heel to make their escape, Burwell standing up with his gun in hand, received the fire of the Indians in ambuscade, wounding Lewis in the right arm, knocking him out of the canoe. Burwell laid his gun down, took hold of Lewis & dragged him into the canoe. Then taking hold of both guns, proceeded to steer off the canoe, when the Indians shot him at the point of one of his hips & out at the groin. He succeeded in carrying off the canoe whilst the Indians repeated their shots at him. Lewis dared them to come on – about four in number. Lewis' right arm had to be amputated – no doubt he will recover. Burwell is almost well.

Virginia Calendar vi: 584-585.

15C 19-19(4) L. B. Wade, Madison, Monroe County, Mo., Oct 21, 1883

LCD: Morgan's Station Taken, April 1793. John Wade killed. Judge Richard Reid's pamphlet, History of Montgomery County Ky., pp. 5 & 43. *The first page may be in Draper's handwriting; the other pages are in L. B. Wade's hand.*

Dear Sir

I acknowledge the receipt of both your letters, and now offer an apology for not answering at once... having left my Father's at an early age, I have not an opportunity of enjoying a recital of his eventful life as a Kentucky pioneer as did my younger Brother, F. A. Wade, who lived with him until his death.

Believe me, sir, it would give me great pleasure to be able to give you an item of history that might descend to posterity. I will now take up your Questions in the order you present them.

1st what year did your father settle in Ky?

I will answer from circumstantial evidence, about the year 1791 – he was not yet a grown man.

2nd did he first locate at Boonsborough?

I think it probable he did.

3rd. Was he there when the Boone & Callaway girls were captured?

I recollect of his speaking of the two young women being captured and carried off in a south east direction to near the mouth of Red river – were followed & recaptured.

4th. What particulars did he relate about the taking of Morgan Station?

My father had lived at that Station for some time until the fear of Indians had pretty much passed away, so much so that he & a man by the name of Becraft had ventured to cultivate a patch of corn, had housed it in or near the Station. In the spring following they became more bold, thinking there was but little danger. They built a cabbin a short distance from the fort and were Batching it,..

My Father had gone into the Station to get a sack of corn. His horse was in the stable to which the [corn] Crib was attached. The Indians of a sudden opened fire on the Station which so frightened the horse that father could not catch him. He threw the door open...the horse followed and escaped. My father was swift of foot. They pursued.

Here he related an incident. An old gentleman verry corpulent whose name was Baker was just in front of him. The bullets were flying fast – he thought to gain his front would give some protection, but when near, Baker fell, wounded in the knee. They scalpt him. My father escaped.

He did serve under Gen. Wayne.

5th question I know nothing about.

6th I think my father was at the battle of Blue Licks.

7th. I know nothing of Col. Boone being in Bath County. I was born in that County & knew Harry[?] Conner on Slate.

8th. Grandfather moved [to] West Virginia – Rockingham County, I think.

9th. My father was entitled to a pension, but never applied for one.

10th. I have heard my father and Col. James Lane of Montgomery County Kentucky, who were much together in the early settlement of Kentucky and in my days the families became related by marriage. They have talked in my presence a great deal about Daniel Boon but I cannot call to my mind any particular incident.

11th My uncle's name who was killed by the Indians on Licking was John, was killed near the spot where he was wounded one year before. I have written the above with pleasure. Sorry I could say no more.

Yours respectfully

L. B. Wade

15C 20 LCD: **Col. Daniel Boone – 1794.**
February – Proposed road making: Collins', ii, 242.
April 24th, 1794 – Boone makes deposition at Point Pleasant, showing he was then there – R. H. Collins transcripts.
April 23rd – Indians attack above Belleville. Trip 1860, v. 93.
May 27 – Indians murder near Belleville. Trip 1860, v. 94.

15C 21 LCD: **Col. Daniel Boone – 1795**
In summer of 1795, Col. Boone was at Gen. James Taylor's house as Newport, Ky. Gen. Taylor in his notes does not say anything about Boone's movements.

In the spring of 1795, I think, Bailey, in his [word missing], mentions meeting Boone up Big Sandy. Settle on Brush Fork of Hinkston – Nathan Boone's Notes, 205. Spring ii, Montgomery County, 79. His place described: Col. Thomas Rogers' letter, Dec. 17th, 1862.

15C 22 LCD: **Col. Daniel Boone References** in Collins' <u>History</u>, Volumes i & ii.

1769 – John Finley, not of Washington County, Va. - ii. 412
1770 – Squire Boone's name on rock – ii, 525; 616
1773 – in Adair County – inscription – ii. 32
– Recalls Surveyors (Deposition about April 24, 1799 at Kanawha), ii, 367; i[?] 57; 238, 243
1775 – Boone's Trace – ii, 242, 525, 692
1774 – Names Streams in Madison County – ii, 493
1775 – The Warrior's Road, Finley followed – ii, 466, 494, 655
1775 – Plat of Boonesboro, ii, 514
1775 – Salt – Blue Licks, ii, 654-55

1776 – July 7 – James Cooper killed, ii, 70
1776 – July – Girls Captivity - ii, 50, 526
1776 – Scholl's Deposition – ii, 50, 526
1776 – December –... [the] powder party to Three Islands – ii, 563
1777 – Name on tree &C – ii, 341
1778 [blank]
1779-1780 – Surveying - ii, 466
1780 – July 1 – at Lexington – ii, 183
1780 – June – Bird's Expedition – ii. 72 &c.
1780 – October – Edward Boone killed, pursues Indians – ii, 63 &c.
1781 [blank]
1782 – Blue Licks Battle – ii, 600, 601
Sketch of Lewis Rose (by Robert Wickliffe?) – ii, 663;
1782 - November – Returning from Clark's Expedition – ii, 653
1783-1784 – Sheriff of Fayette County – i, 366
1785 – Trustee of Maysville – ii, 586
1786 April 26 – at Point Pleasant – ii, 362
1787-1788 – at Maysville – ii, 362
1791 – in Virginia Legislature – i, 366
1794 – Sept. 24 – Deposition – ii, 238, 243
Sept. 28 – In Northern Kentucky – deposition about escaping captivity in 1778 – ii, 362
1796 – February – on Hinkson – ii, 243-243
1795 – June – Deposition – ii, 466
1796 – Proposes to cut out road – ii, 242 -243
1799 – in Greenup, Ky. – ii ___
1817 – June – Signatures[?]
1819 – Harding painting portrait, in Ky – i, 6?
Poems on Boone – I, 572, ___
Suits in Bourbon County, Boone & Kenton, ii.
Changes of residence – ii, 24___
J. Callaway's deposition
Cofer's, Cradlebaugh's, Hancock's [*depositions?*]

Peter Scholl's deposition
John Riggs' "
R. Stockton's "
Col. Bowman's "
Patrick Henry's "
Jesse Hodges "

***

15C 24 Richard H. Collins, Louisville, Ky., April 25, 1883. Letterhead: Richard H. Collins & Co., No. 11 Courier-Journal Building, Louisville, Ky. Collins' History of Kentucky.

Richard H. Collins
www.findagrave.com.
Photograph, Todd Whitesides

Dear Sir:

At great inconvenience, but with great pleasure, I have at last completed the copy of the Depositions &c called for in your letter several months since. I found it impossible, from my notes, to give you the references which would enable you to get copies elsewhere; and so I set myself to work at intervals to copy them. It required much ingenuity and labor to find some of them, at this late day.

As you offered to pay, I could not get them elsewhere except for full pay, you may fix the value of the copy.

I have been consulting with Col. R. T. Durrett and Dr. C. Graham about George Rogers Clarke's amputated leg, &c. I suppose they have given you all the information they have.

Yours truly
Richd. H. Collins

Richard H. Collins (1824-1888) was a lawyer, newspaper editor, scholar, and writer in Maysville, Kentucky. The son of historian Lewis Collins, he had graduated from Kentucky colleges Centre and Transylvania. After his father's death in 1870, Collins visited writers and historians across the state to expand his father's *Historical Sketches of Kentucky* (1847) to a two-volume *History of Kentucky* (1874). It is one of Lyman Draper's most cited sources.

15C 25 - 25(17) Richard H. Collins

Depositions from Kentucky Land Suits 1794-1824

Copies of Depositions taken in Land Suits in Kentucky County between 1794 and 1824, gathered by Richard H. Collins while writing his *History of Kentucky.*

The Depositions

Collins collected depositions from Kentucky land suits which were taken to solve legal issues involved with the early surveys. Deponents include notable historic figures such as Daniel Boone and Simon Kenton, who were deposed several times.

At Draper's request, Collins hand copied about 40 depositions which he selected from the second volume of his *History.* They were embedded in long paragraphs with other depositions not included in those he sent to Draper.

As Collins informed Draper, the depositions were assembled "at intervals." They are in no discernible order. A narrative can be constructed by re-arranging them in rough chronological order, not by the dates they were given, but by the events and dates described by the deponents.

The Deponents

Some of the Collins' deponents were in Kentucky as independent explorers or hunters; others were in surveying companies sent out from Fincastle County, Virginia in 1773, 1774 and later.

Created in 1772, Fincastle County included all of what was to become the Commonwealth of Kentucky twenty years later. Kentucky became a separate county of Virginia when Fincastle was divided into separate counties of Kentucky, Montgomery and Washington in 1776.

The deponents were all living in Kentucky when they gave their depositions, with the exception of Missouri residents Daniel Boone and Flanders Callaway. Many deponents were in military service in Virginia during the Revolutionary War and returned to fight the last battles of the war in Kentucky where they then lived out their years.

Journal entries of surveyors who were also Collins' deponents are added to the depositions; they are not part of this original volume. These day-by-day accounts, written by their evening campfires, add details not included in depositions given in court more than twenty years later.

Note to the Reader

Collins' own notes will be found among the depositions. His list of depositions in their original order is given in the Appendix. Collins' brackets and parentheses have been retained. I have spelled out abbreviations and altered punctuation for clarity. Some depositions are divided. The reader should note that ellipses are in the original. My brief explanations are italicized within brackets. Longer explanations appear in Calibri font.

Journal entries and military correspondence which were not part of volume 15C are indented with headings in bold print. Collins' depositions are not indented. The first group as arranged here, is interspersed with journal entries of three men who were with Thomas Bullitt's company in 1773.

[1] The journalists/surveyors were Isaac Hite, James and Robert McAfee. Paragraphs from the memoir of Robert B.

---

[1] The journals of Isaac Hite and the McAfee brothers, James and Robert, are published in *Narratives of Pioneer Life and Border Warfare,* self-published by Dale Payne in 2004. Robert and James McAfee's journals are also found in DM 4CC 40-53; Robert McAfee's son, Robert B. McAfee, wrote of the 1773 expedition in his "Life and "Times of Robert B. McAfee" [*Register of the Kentucky Historical*

McAfee are interspersed among the depositions. Collins' depositions begin after the Thomas Bullitt Notice.

For information on the Fincastle Surveyors, see Neal O. Hammon, "Pioneers in Kentucky 1773-1775," *Filson History Quarterly,* vol. 55: 268-9, and Hammon, *Early Kentucky Land Records 1773-1780*, Filson Club, 1992.

Fincastle Surveying Expedition, 1773

> **... survey the Lands claimed under his Majesty's Proclamation...**
> Capt. Thomas Bullitt

In 1773, Virginia's British Governor, Lord Dunmore, sent surveyors to Kentucky in order to award land to veterans of the French and Indian War. Captain Thomas Bullitt, age 42, a man of considerable military experience and a noted woodsman, was appointed the leader of the expedition.

Bullitt advertised in the Virginia Gazette that he and his assistant, James Douglas, were recruiting men for an expedition to begin in spring of 1773:

> I hereby give notice that I shall attend, with Mr. Douglas, and such other Assistant Surveyors as it may be thought necessary to appoint. By the 15th of April...in order to survey the Lands

---

Society, January 1927, vol. 25, no. 73, and published in Dale Payne's work cited above]. A video re-enactment, "The Thomas Bullitt Survey Expedition, 1773" by Dennis Medley and presented at the Filson Historical Society can be seen on youtube.

claimed under his Majesty's Proclamation, also any other claims... Officers and soldiers that do not personally attend their Surveys to appoint Agents to see it done and receive their lands.

I HEREBY give Notice that I ſhall attend, with Mr. *Douglas*, and ſuch other Aſſiſtant Surveyors as it may be thought neceſſary to appoint, by the 15th of *April*, on the *Ohio*, oppoſite to the Mouth of the *Sioto* River, in Order to ſurvey the Lands claimed under his Majeſty's Proclamation, alſo any other Claims that I may be directed to ſurvey; therefore recommend it to the Officers and Soldiers that do not perſonally attend their Surveys to appoint Agents to ſee it done, and receive their Lands. THOMAS BULLITT, Surveyor.

Thomas Bullitt's Notice
https://bullittcountyhistory.org/bchistory/thomasbullitt2.html

The Fincastle surveyors started on horseback until they could embark on their river journey in their canoes, the horses being sent back by one of their company. They slept in the canoes at times and, without horses, surveyed on foot.

In addition to the military surveys, they marked land for themselves, and for well-known land speculators: Lord Dunmore and his associates, Patrick Henry, George Washington, William Preston and others.

One of Collins' deponents, Capt. Thomas Young, was a member of this surveying company.

Capt. Thomas Young deposed, Nov. 24, 1804: He descended the Ohio river in company with several others in 1773, and encamped several days at mouth of Limestone creek where town of Maysville now stands. At that time, Capt. John Hedges, one of the company, named it Limestone creek, by which name it has been notoriously known ever since. So, Lawrence creek was called after Lawrence Darnell, another of the company who was there with deponent that same year...

Simon Kenton deposed, Aug. 15, 1814. I knew Lawrence creek (in Mason County, Ky. 3 miles south & west of Maysville) in 1775 and ever since. I was at its mouth in 1775, with John Fitzpatrick and Thomas Williams. The former told me he was with Thomas Bullitt in 1773, and that this creek was named Lawrence creek after Lawrence Darnell.

William Triplett deposed, Aug. 11, 1798: We was in Kentucky in 1775, and again in July, 1776, with Samuel Wells and others. In 1775, he left the camp and was out improving only once with the company.

Capt. Thomas Young deposed, August 18, 1810, that in 1773 he came down the Ohio, with nine others, from Pittsburgh, but some left the company near the Sandy river. He came again in 1775, with nine others.

Richard H. Collins. This is all of this deposition which I abstracted being all that I had obtained from others of his depositions.

In another deposition in a suit tried in 1819, he says...

Thomas Young. During both trips [*1773 and 1774*], we _____ the Three Islands [about 10 miles or 11 miles above Maysville], which appeared to be a point of considerable _____ for we had been informed of it at Pittsburgh.

In 1773 opposite the upper point of the Three Islands, we found William Kennedy and his company encamped. We went ashore and were surveying the bottom between what is now (1817?) called Salt Lick Creek, then Big Buffalo Creek, and the Sciota river; where two men came up the Ohio and told us that Kennedy & company was encamped opposite Three Islands, where we afterwards found them.

Of the Three Islands, the upper one is nearly opposite to Brush (then Indian) Creek. It is the first below Salt Lick Creek, and about 12 miles above Limestone. Salt Lick Creek ____ Big Buffalo Creek, and the Scioto river where two men came up the Ohio and told us that Kennedy ___ were encamped opposite the 3 ____ where we afterwards found them.

The first bottom below the Three Islands was at Crooked Creek, the second at Limestone, the third at Lawrence Creek. The "narrows" was those points[?] where rivers and hills met, or where the hills put into the rivers.

In late May, the McAfee brothers (James, age 37; George, age 33, and Robert, age 28) joined Bullitt's men at the mouth of the Kanawha River. With them was Robert's brother-in-law, James McCoun, and Samuel Adams, a single man, age 19.

Robert McAfee's son, Robert B. McAfee, having heard accounts of his father and uncles, described preparations made for the months-long journey, including the making of their own canoes.

Robert B. McAfee memoir

...the prospects of making future fortunes, and the honor of being among the first adventurers in the western wilderness consoled and supported them...

They spent about a week in selecting suitable trees and dug out and prepared two canoes to carry their baggage and clothes, the former consisting of their rifles, ammunition, tomahawks, butcher knives, blankets and ...a few fish gigs, etc.

They met Capt. Thomas Bullitt, [James] Douglas and Hancock Taylor, surveyors and their company, who were going down to the falls of the Ohio to survey Proclamation rights of 1763.

In the following deposition, recorded in the *Virginia Calendar of State Papers*, James Douglas told of a separate excursion made by Thomas Bullitt in June 1773. Douglas left the surveyors to visit the Shawnee in their towns to discuss his plans for traveling on the Ohio River. With the help of an interpreter, an agreement was made. Following Douglas's deposition is a journal entry from one of Bullitt's surveyors, who must have heard the news from Bullitt himself.

James Douglas, statement in 1778:
In Spring of 1773, going down the Ohio River from Pittsburgh with Thomas Bullitt as his guide, that Bullitt left the group and visited the Shawnee towns to acquaint the Indians with his plan of going down the river.

Bullitt returned to the group opposite the Scioto with 15 or 20 Shawnee

Indians who had been informed of Bullitt's plan to go down the Ohio River. The group continued...to mouth of Kentucky River where they met a group of Delawares who were hunting. Bullitt asked them to have a council to discuss his plans, which they did. He proceeded to Falls of Ohio where they met Two other groups of Indians who knew of his plan. All of these tribes, according to Douglas, knew of the Treaty of Stanwix and accorded the explorers the right to the territory.

James McAfee, journal entry in mid-June: Captain Bullitt, three white men and Three Delaware Indians got to the [Indian] nation undiscovered, which the Indians thought very strange.

They were obliged to stay at a Wigwam ... Captain Bullitt and the white men were ordered to the town where 115 warriors, [with] spears and fixed bows and arrows...one of them running up with a tomahawk drawn. Some of them shook hands... to make peace with them. Captain Bullitt stayed five days ...before he got his business settled with them.

Thomas Bullitt returned to the surveyors on June 13; later that month, Isaac Hite, age 20, with several men joined the surveyors. The company went on to Big Bone Lick.

James McAfee, June 28
Mr. Hite and 6 men in 2 canoes came

to us from Pittsburg. Mr. Hite, surveyor
in that company.

Robert McAfee, early July
We went to see the Big Bone, which
is a wonder to see the large bones
that lie there, which have been of
several large big creatures...

Robert B. McAfee
...making use of the short joints of
the Back bones for stools and seats
& their ribs for tent poles to streach
their blanketts on.

The number of Buffaloes, Elk, Deer,
Beaver and wolves at this lick
was astonishing. The roads round
were much beaten as in the neighborhood
of a populous city.

Robert McAfee, July 7th
In the evening we left Capt. Bullitt ...
to get our lands surveyed... We went
till 8 o'clock at night & put to shore
and lay in our canoes all night.

The depositions of **Simon Kenton**, **Thomas Young** and **William Triplett** were taken by *[Land]* Commissioners, Aug. 23, 1796 - from which it appeared that in 1773 John Fitzpatrick was here with Col. Thomas Bullitt (below Augusta, in now Bracken Co.) and then called this Turtle Creek; that it was so called by Patrick Doran in 1774; that in 1775, John Hedges, for and by whom the land was surveyed in 1773, was still on his improvement; and that the creek was called

Turtle Creek until 1782, then changed to Locust Creek. Thomas Young was chain carrier in 1773 for that and several other surveys in that neighborhood.

Richard H. Collins, Nov. 9, 1882
Thomas Young lived in Maysville until his death about 1837 or '38, in the home of Mrs. Elizabeth B. Langhorn, who died in Louisville in 1878, & whose daughter & son-in-law, Henry Waller and wife, now live on Ashland Avenue in Chicago, aged 72 & 62 respectively. I do not know that they could tell you anything of value, except of Capt. Young's personal appearance, habits, &c. I was a boy of 13 or 14, & knew him slightly.

The Fincastle Surveyors returned from their journey in October 1773. Thomas Bullitt submitted surveys to Colonel William Preston, surveyor of Fincastle County, only to have most of them invalidated.

The Second Survey Expedition, 1774

> **We called our canoe the Good-Hope, imbarked on board of her, sailed 9 miles down the river...**
>
> Thomas Hanson, April 1774

Colonel William Preston sent out surveyors from Fincastle County in the spring of 1774. They were headed by John Floyd, already distinguished by his early 20s as a surveyor and scholar.

Preston's company included some experienced surveyors, given that a number of Bullitt's men signed up again. Hancock Taylor and Abraham Haptonstall joined the group en route, making their third journey to Kentucky. James Douglas and Lawrence Darnell were on their second journeys, with two of Collins' deponents from the 1773 expedition, James and Jacob Sodowski.

Alexander Spottswood Dandridge started out with the company but returned with others of the company to Virginia. James Harrod and James Knox, hunters in Kentucky before 1773, may have been pilots for this 16-man company and definitely did meet with them in Kentucky.

Many hunters and explorers were in Kentucky at that time, and Floyd's men were joined by another 20 or so en route. Thomas Hanson and William Nash were chainmen for Floyd. Thomas Hanson kept a journal along the way. [2]

In Virginia, the 1774 surveyors' journey was monitored in correspondence of Colonel William Preston, Lord Dunmore, George Washington and other military personnel. They heard from the surveyors themselves only when some members of the company returned to Virginia bringing messages.

The 1774 Fincastle surveyors would encounter more danger from Indians than the previous group, and some would not return. Thomas Hanson, naming his fellow travelers,

---

2 Hanson's Journal is published in *Narratives of Pioneer Life and Border Warfare,* Volume II, self-published, Dale Payne, 2005. Draper had obtained a copy of it in DM 24CC 1-40. The journal was annotated in *John Floyd, The Life and Letters of a Frontier Surveyor,* Neal O. Hammon, ed., 2013, Louisville, Butler Books. Other depositions and newspaper notices are from Hattie Marshall Scott, *Kentucky Court and Other Records,* Kentucky Historical Society, Frankfort, 1953; Draper Manuscripts letters and interviews as noted; *Preston and Virginia Papers* of Draper's Collection; the *Virginia Gazette* as noted.

reported that they started off on horseback escorted by Colonel Preston.

> **Thomas Hanson**, April 7 - 8
> We left Col. William Preston's in
> Fincastle County at one o'clock
> in high spirits, escorted by the
> Colonel three miles, eight of
> us being in company, viz. Mr.
> John Floyd, surveyor, Mr. [James]
> Douglas, assistant surveyor, Mr.
> [Isaac] Hite, Mr. [Spottswood]
> Dandridge, Thomas Hanson,
> James Knocks [Knox], Roderick
> McCra & Mordecai Batson.

Between April 9 and April 13, 1774, Hanson recorded they had traveled about 69 miles. Before leaving western Virginia, they made surveys for George Washington and Patrick Henry.

On April 13, Hanson wrote that they were joined by Hancock Taylor and his company of seven men. They proceeded on their journey, being informed that Indians were placed on both sides of the river and intended war.

> **Thomas Hanson,** April 14 – 17
> ...at New River where we expected
> to have got a canoe... Taylor likewise
> stopped to make a Canoe, and
> Mr. Floyd hearing there was one
> at Elk River unfinished hired a man
> at 3s per day to go & finish it.
>
> We proceeded 14 miles down the
> river passing by the burning springs

which is one of the wonders of the world. We called our canoe the Good-Hope, imbarked on board of her, sailed 9 miles down the river...

Thomas Hanson, April 18 – 20
We surveyed 2000 acres for Col. Washington bordered by Coal River & the Canawagh. Mr. Dandridge... lost himself which put Mr. Floyd to a great deal of trouble to find Him in the night.

Mr. [Hancock] Taylor and his company joined us. We catched a Cat fish that weighed 40 pounds.

We proceeded to the mouth of the Kanawha, 26 miles...found 26 people ... One of them could speak Indian language...told us to take care of our scalps.

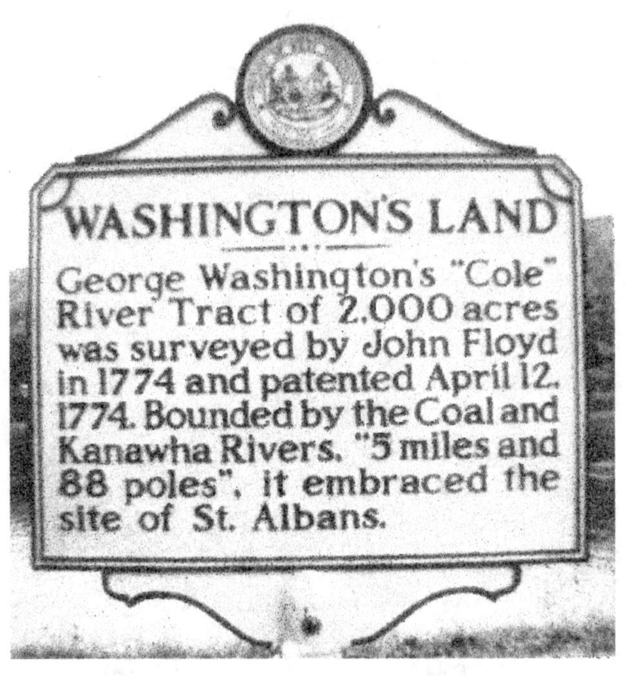

George Washington's Cole Survey, 1774
Historical Marker Database. Photo by Forrest McDermott.

Alexander Spottswood Dandridge, satisfied that his survey (and George Washington's) would be completed, turned back with some others, informing Colonel Preston:

> **Alexander Spottswood Dandridge**
> You'll be much surprised at the News of my Speedy return from the Ohio, the cause of which was the meeting of one Lawrence Darnold [Darnell], an experienced woodsman ...extremely well acquainted with the Lands upon the Ohio. Him I thought a proper person to entrust the locating of my Lands...

I left the whole company under great apprehensions of danger from the Indians...

According to your instructions Mr. Floyd surveyed for Colo. Washington 2000 Acres of Land....

In the meanwhile please enter for me 1000 acres of land upon Lawrence's Creek about five miles from the Ohio beginning at a large Limestone creek...

DM 3QQ 26

On April 26, John Floyd wrote to Col. Preston that three men had come to their camp after being ordered off the river by a party of Shawnees. The Shawnees sent the men away threatening to kill all the Virginians they could find.

Floyd wrote that he was sending George Washington's plat by the men who were returning to Virginia.

Thomas Hanson reported that his 200 acres were surveyed and that their number of surveyors was increasing.

Thomas Hanson, April 26 – May 1
3 men came to our Camp...alarmed by Indians & made their escapes. 2 of them joined Mr. Floyd, viz [William] Nash & Mr. Glen, and Lawrence Darnell joined Mr. Taylor.

Mr. Douglas & Mr. Hite joined us with 13 men, which makes us 37 strong... 4 [turned] back...embarked in our Canoes, and floated all night.

In the morning we discovered that we had floated 25 miles. It being Sunday we took our rest.

Thomas Hanson, May 2 – 3
We made a survey...for Paterick Henry... 400 or 500 acres of very good land. The land is excessive good. There is a Sycamore tree 37 feet in Circumference.

Thomas Hanson, May 7
We rose early and searched the woods for Indians...Surveyed 200 acres on Brackin's Creek for Thos. Hanson, good land with a high Ridge... Rain and Thunder.

Jacob Sodowsky deposed, April 27, 1818, at his own house in Jessamine County, that he first became acquainted with the mouth of Cabin creek in 1774 a-coming down the Ohio river... The number and signs of the Indians was so great...

Cabin Creek. named for the few cabins built there by surveyors and explorers, was the entry point from the Ohio River into Kentucky. About five miles from Limestone / Maysville, it was a War Road used by Indians as well.

In mid-May the surveying company of 1774 reached Big Bone Lick in Kentucky.

Thomas Hanson, May 12 – 14
There is a number of large Teeth to [be] seen about this Lick, which the People imagined to be Elephants. There is one Seven Feet 7 three Inches long. It is nine inches in Diameter at one End and five inches at the other.

Our company divided, eleven men went up to Harrod's Company one hundred miles up the Kentucky on Louisa River (n.b. Capt. Harrod has been there many months building a kind of Town &c).

This day a quarrel arose between Mr. Lee and Mr. Hyte. Lee cut a stick and gave Hite a whipping upon which Mr. Floyd demanded the Kings Peace.

In late May surveying began at Falls of the Ohio, the area of present-day Louisville, Kentucky. The men divided into small groups, planning to meet later at Harrod's cabin.

In early June, Abraham Hite wrote expressing concern for his brother Isaac:

Abraham Hite, Jr to Col. Preston:
There is ...a Lad, who is just come in that says he was at the Mouth of the big Connowa...that my Brother & the other surveyors were there with about thirty men besides, but then were in great doubt what to do, whether to proceed down the river,...
DM 3QQ 35

Thomas Hanson, June 26
...saw a canoe coming down the river with a Red flag flying. We hailed them... found them to be 2 Indians... [going] down the River to collect their Hunters and cause them to go home, as they expected a war between the white people & the Shawnese... We parted with them but were afraid that they would follow us...

Mr. Floyd and the rest of the surveyors were determined to do the business they came on, if not repulsed by a greater force than themselves. We proceeded to Otter Creek... Good Land.

Captain Russell wrote to William Preston that he had engaged Daniel Boone and Michael Stoner to recall the surveyors because of increasing Indian attacks.

Capt. William Russell to Col. Preston
Sunday, June 26, 1774 from Clynch

I have engaged to start immediately two of the best hands I could think of, Daniel Boone and Michael Stoner... I hope the Gentlemen will be apprised of the eminent Danger they are in.

DM 3QQ 46

W. D. Hixon sent Draper an undated deposition of Daniel Boone. Boone told of the instructions given him for this undertaking:

Daniel Boone
In the year 1774 I was requested by Governor Dunmore to go to Kentucky and bring in the surveyors. I was at General Lewis's own house a few days before I started, and he undertook to give directions how to travel and where to find the surveyors.

General Lewis directed me to cross the Cumberland mountains at Sounding Gap an old war road... Governor Dunmore, however, changed the route and ordered me after I crossed the mountains to take the Kentucky and meander to the south.

DM 6C 102, 104

The following is one of Collins' depositions in which Daniel Boone told of choosing Michael Stoner, a noted woodsman, to accompany him to Kentucky. Stoner made his own statement and his son told Draper about their journey to recall the surveyors.

Daniel Boone deposed, April 24, 1794 at Point Pleasant, On June 26, 1774, I was employed by Gov. Dunmore to go out to that country and give the surveyors notice of the out breaking of the Indian's war. I took with me Michael Stoner, and on the creek that goes by the name of Hickman's creek, about 2 or 3 miles below Col. Levi Todd's, I cut the first two letters of said *[James]* Hickman's name on a large water oak, with a large stone grown past in said tree, in presence of said Stoner. And finding the surveyors (were alarmed by, or were posted about) the Indians, I returned home, and wrote to Col. Preston to make the entry for Mr. Hickman at that tree and agreeably to my instructions.

Michael Stoner
In the year 1774 and in the summer
Boone and myself came out...

DM 6C 104

George W. Stoner, son of Michael Stoner
Boone was seeking for someone to
go with him to Kentucky to notify
the surveyors there of the Indian war
just broken out. Stoner said he would go,
if he only had a gun. Boone replied
"Well, Mike, you shall have mine & I'll
get another – your the man for me."

When they would stop to eat their
morning or noon meal, & sitting upon
a log, one would face one way upon
their back track, & the other in the
opposite direction, to see that no
lurking enemy crept upon them.

Of nights, would camp in some secluded
& deep ravine, strike their fire, cook
their meat - & then hide away for the night.

LCD interview, 1868.
DM 24C 55

Thomas Hanson, July 1- July 8
All the land that we passed over
today is like a Paradise it is so
good & beautiful.

Mr. Floyd, Nash, McCra & Hanson
left the rest of the company
with an agreement to meet at Mr
Harrod's Cabbin 20 miles off, higher
on the Kentucky...

> We had to swim the Creek with our Guns,
> & Packs on our heads. Our surveys
> begin on the North branch of the Elk
> Horn Creek... The land is so good
> that I cannot give it its due praise.

The Sodowski brothers were deposed in Kentucky, Jacob in 1804 and James in 1805; their statements were recorded in Fayette County, Kentucky.

> [3] **Jacob Sodowski** at the house of Benjamin Netherland, Jessamine County, Ky., Feb. 8, 1804.
> Douglas surveyed about 40,000 acres on Hickman, Jessamine and Elkhorn Creeks and others... I made one entry in name of Jonathan Sadowski... Cogar's big spring from 1774 [was] renamed Jessamine by Douglas after his daughter... I was chain carrier for Douglas in 1774.
>
> **James Sadowski**, Bourbon County, Ky., Aug. 27, 1805.
> In spring 1774, came to mouth of [3]Kentucky River with James Douglas and about 30 men. Some went to Falls of Ohio, eleven men came up the Kentucky River after Harrod's party.

On the 8th of July Indians killed two of our own company...the balance of us started off from the country

[3] The depositions of James and Jacob Sadowski are found in "History in Circuit Court Records of Fayette County, Kentucky," Charles R. Staples, *Register of the Kentucky Historical Society*, vol. 31, 1933: 110 ff.

the second day afterwards in company with Harrod's party, amounting in all to about forty three men.

While Hanson's group were on their way to Harrod's cabin, James Knox and nine others were at their camp drying papers in the sun when twenty Indians fired on them. James Cowan, who was from Pennsylvania, was killed; James Hamilton, also killed, was from Fredericksburg, Virginia.

Draper's Notes
DM 3B 125

Floyd's men met as agreed at Harrod's cabin to find it deserted with the camp fires still burning and a note explaining the departure of the other surveyors.

> **Thomas Hanson,** July 23 - 24
> We crossed the river, some of us on a Raft with our packs & Guns, & others of us Swam over... proceeded to [Harrod's] Cabin.
>
> At our arrival we were surprised to find everything squandered upon the ground & two fires burning. Mr. Floyd, [and] Nash went down to the landing place & found these words wrote on a tree:
>
> "Alarmed by finding some people killed we are gone down this way" [from] Mr. Hite's & Mr. Douglas's party that arrived here 2 days before us...
>
> We made search for Floyd's saddle bags but could not find them.

John Floyd and his men departed for home immediately. Thomas Hanson made his last journal entries.

> **Thomas Hanson**, July 27
> We were in a very bad plight for
> traveling home, but about 15 rounds
> of powder, and none of us knew the way.
>
> **Thomas Hanson**, August 8 – 9
> The mountains here so steep that
> we were obliged to throw all away
> except our knit leggings and moccasins.
>
> We had a blazed road which took
> us through the gap of a large
> mountain ...we traveled this day
> 30 miles.
>
> ...we came to Clinch river...where
> we found them forted in, preparing
> for war with the Shawnees.

Also on July 27, Hancock Taylor, James Strother and Abraham Haptonstall were in a canoe bringing in provisions when they were shot by Indians. Strother was killed and Taylor and Haptonstall wounded. Haptonstall was able to make the return journey, but Taylor was able to walk only the first 2 or 3 days, and then had to be transported.

Reaching present-day Madison County, Kentucky, Taylor could go no further. John Geen found unsigned surveys in Hancock Taylor's Survey Book and had him sign them. Green and John Bell witnessed Taylor's will. He was buried on August 1st near present-day Richmond, Kentucky. The company made their way through the mountains, reaching their Virginia homes in late August.

Floyd's men, who started back earlier, had already reached Clinch River on August 13. On August 15, there was concern for the surveyors who had not yet returned:

> **Col. Preston to George Washington:**
> John Floyd and three others came in last Saturday. The other surveyors are still out but there is some reason to hope they are safe.
>
> ...I began yesterday to build a fort around my house for the defence of my family.
>
> DM 15S 80

On August 28, four of Hancock Taylor's men arrived bringing Taylor's will and his survey book.

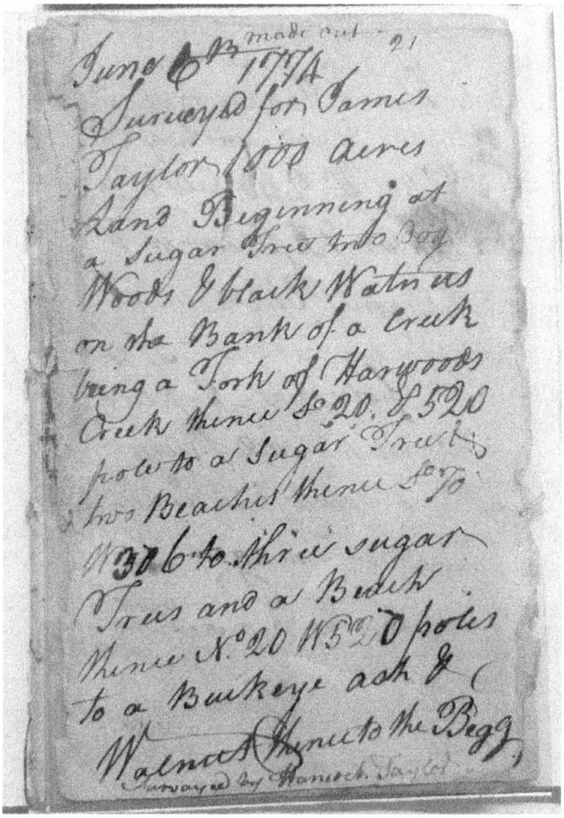
June 6th 1774 made out 21
Surveyed for James
Taylor 1000 acres
Land Beginning at
a Sugar Tree two Dog
Woods & black Walnuts
on the Bank of a Creek
being a Fork of Harwoods
Creek thence So 20. E 520
poles to a Sugar Tree &
two Beaches thence So 70
W 306 to three sugar
Trees and a Beech
thence No 20 W 520 poles
to a Buckeye ash &
Walnut thence to the Begg,
Surveyed by Hancock Taylor

Hancock Taylor Survey Book, 1774
Clements Library, University of Michigan

Daniel Boone sent word that he was ready for the next expedition.

Capt. William Russell to Col. Preston
Mr. Jno. Green and three others
of Mr. Taylor's Company have arrived
on Clinch...

Mr. Taylor traveled two or three days,

and his Company carried him two more before his death.

The Company buried him on the first of this Instant [August 1st]. One more of the Company was shot in the canoe but the works are brought in, except for one survey.

This day an Express from Mr. Boone overtook me to inform me of his return and desire to go on the expedition.

DM 3QQ 84

By "the works" Capt. Russell meant Taylor's surveying notes. One page of Hancock Taylor's Surveyor's Notebook (26 pages) is missing.

Boone and Stoner probably led this group as they all returned on August 26 or August 28. Some surveyors were still not heard from by mid-September, as reported in the *Virginia Gazette:*

September 14. 1774:
...we have advice, by one Bell who is just arrived in this Town from Kentucky, that Hancock Taylor and James Strother were both killed as they were returning from the mouth of that River, where they had been to survey some land...

Hempenstall, who was missing when Colonel Preston wrote to you, is since come in; he was with Taylor and Strother when they were fired upon by the Indians. Taylor lived several days after he received his wounds, and came with Hempenstall and Bell at least a Hundred Miles towards the settlements.

John Willis, John Ashby, and several others, are still missing; but they are gone down the river, it is believed.*

*https://www.wikitree.com/wiki/Taylor-21695

Hancock Taylor historical marker
https://commons.wikimedia.org/wiki/File:2021-09-19_Hancock_Taylor_Marker_Richmond_KY.jpg

The missing men were on their long journey from New Orleans by water, bringing the saddle bags containing Floyd's surveying instruments. Among those were Isaac Hite, James Douglas, Jacob Sodowski and perhaps John Ashby and John Willis. In the deposition he gave in 1805, previously cited, James Sodowski stated that he and his brother Jacob did not return to Virginia together in 1774, that he did not see Jacob until early that winter when the last of the surveyors got back.

On December 14, 1774, William Preston learned of their return.

> **James Douglas**
> Sir, This day being the 14 of December
> I safely arrived in Williamsburg after a
> long, tedious and fatiguing Jurney.
> And am extremely glad to hear that
> your... Famly are well, and likewise
> of Mr Floids safe return.
>
> I promise myself the pleasure of seeing
> yew all in a few weeks. I intend to rest
> my Self, and in doing of which to make
> out my Plots.
>
> Inform Capt. Floid that I have
> his Instruments, and that all those
> who was in our party is safe arrived
> and well.
>
> I was so Fortunate as to get my
> Business done before we took
> our departure. The short time I tend
> to stay here, and the Bearer
> being immediately to set off, will

sufficiently apologize for my short epistle, although I have a great deal to say.

I remain at your Comand

Jas Douglas

DM 5QQ 137

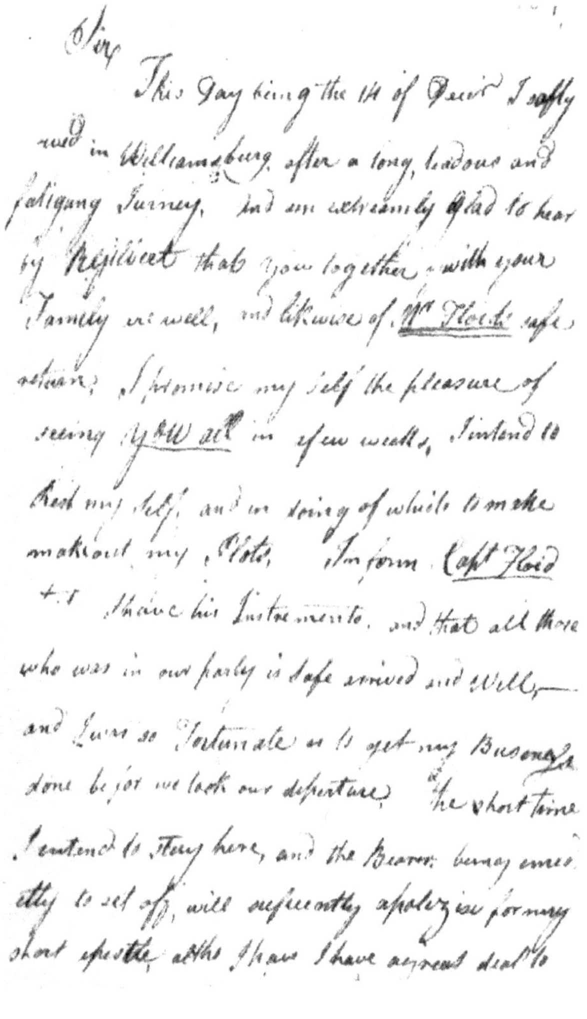

James Douglas letter, 1774. DM 5QQ 137

The Fincastle Surveyors were exploring and surveying in Kentucky in 1775 and later. Thomas Young came back to Kentucky several times while also in Revolutionary War service in Virginia. He came to Kentucky to stay in 1791, as he stated in his deposition of 1810. Other Collins deponents reported encountering him during their surveying and cabin-building

The Sodowski brothers and the McAfee brothers established their stations near Harrodsburg during the late 1770's. Fellow surveyors John Floyd, Alexander Spottswood Dandridge, James Douglas and Isaac Hite were all in Kentucky in 1775. John Floyd was on his way to Kentucky that year:

> **John Floyd to William Preston:**
> When I consider that the settlement
> of that land will ruin the hunting ground
> of the Tawas, Kickapoos and some
> other nations, I a little dread
> the consequences.
>
> DM 17CC 169

John Floyd had lived in Kentucky only a few years when he was killed by Indians in 1783. His family was left at their station on Beargrass Creek: two young children and his wife Jane Buchanan Floyd, who was expecting their third child.

Collins' Depositions, continued: Surveyors and Settlers of 1775 and Later

The next depositions are arranged by events which took place in Kentucky before statehood. In 1775, Boonesborough and Harrodsburg were settled; there were few Indian attacks. In 1776, the Boone and Callaway girls were captured at Boonesborough and rescued by Daniel Boone. In December that year, Indians attacked McClelland's Station; some of the Fincastle surveyors were present and helped move the fort residents to Harrodsburg. In early 1777, the same surveyors went with a company led by James Harrod to retrieve gunpowder hidden at Three Islands.

In winter of 1778, Daniel Boone and his saltmakers were captured. Boone escaped in June, and in August led the Paint Creek Expedition just before the Siege of Boonesborough in September.

One of Collins' deponents was with militia who escorted British Governor Henry Hamilton from Falls of Ohio to Williamsburg, Virginia in 1779. Several deponents discussed their participation in Bowman's Expedition that year.

Daniel Boone's brother Edward was killed by Indians in 1780. Colonel Richard Callaway was killed by Indians near Fort Boonesborough the same year. George Rogers Clark's expeditions took place during this time, and the Battle of Blue Licks was fought in August 1782.

The arrangement of Collins' depositions continues in rough chronological order which took place in Kentucky during the settlement years. One of the most often mentioned place names is Cabin Creek, not to be confused with Cabin Creek on the Kanawha River in western Viriginia which was the site of Indian attacks. Explorers and settlers coming to Kentucky down the Ohio River would land at Cabin Creek just north of

Limestone/Maysville. Joseph Scholl (in 1818 in DM 7C 87) stated that it was a "great crossing place for the Indians."

Collins' Depositions: Landing, Surveying, Settling Near Cabin Creek

Hayden Wells deposed, March 14, 1797, at Gen. Henry Lee's residence near Maysville (about 1 mile north of Washington). In June, 1775, he and Thomas Young and others landed at the mouth of Limestone creek (now Maysville) for the purpose of improving lands... they built a cabin for said Young...

Simon Kenton deposed, August 24, 1796. In 1775, he built a cabin on what is now known as Richard Wade's improvement on waters of Lee's Creek in now Mason County. In 1778 he became acquainted with said Wade at Fort Detroit, where he left him in 1779. [*Richard Wade, one of Daniel Boone's saltmakers captured in 1778, was still in captivity when Kenton saw him in Detroit.*]

After his return to Kentucky, he (Kenton) proposed to James Estill that he (Kenton) would furnish him with a location for said Wade, if he (Estill) would do the other business necessary to secure it before the Commissioners for granting rights of settlement & preemption in the District of Kentucky. He did furnish this location, where he had built a cabin 5 or 6 rounds high, with ribs & ridge poles & joists.

I built 3 cabins on the same branch near that cabin, one above & one below it, and several on a branch more northwardly that empties into the main [North Fork] creek lower down; and some towards the dividing ridge between Lee's creek and Shawnee's Run, on the drains of Lee's Creek; and a number on easterly side of Lee's Creek, some of which on the branch went[?] below the

Big Spring branch. Thomas Williams was with me when I made the improvements.

Daniel Boone, April 24, 1794 at Point Pleasant. In March, 1775, I went out [*to Kentucky*] again, where I met Mr. [James] Douglas, who surveyed [during] the year before on Hickman's creek, and applied to him to make Hickman's survey. He told me he had surveyed that land in 1774, and that I had better move the entry. Some time that summer, I went over to Col. Floyd's on Boone creek . . .

The following is a copy of the certificate filed with Boone's deposition: "I do hereby certify that Capt. Daniel Boone attended, assisted and directed me in the surveying of 4,000 acres of land for Mr. James Hickman. Given "under my hand this 29th May, 1775. John Floyd, Asst. Surveyor."

Flanders Callaway, aged 63,.. Sept. 22, 1817 at the dwelling house of John B. Callaway, in the St. Charles Missouri Territory where Daniel Boone deposed (see p. 6 hereof), deposed that he came to Kentucky in 1775, settled at Boonesborough, & continued there about 7 or 8 years; then returned to Virginia; & back again the same Fall. I became acquainted in 1775 with the Upper Blue Licks, and for 6 or 7 years hunted about there, and between there and Boonesborough in company with others...

Simon Kenton deposed, Sept. 12, 1797: In summer of 1775, he and Thomas Williams came here [on Jacob Lockhart's entry in Mason county] and deadened trees; & in 1776 put up a cabin, and sold the improvement to Scott. He and Scott afterwards "recanted that bargain," and Kenton sold to Lockhart.

Colonel Robert Patterson (1753-1827) came to Kentucky in 1775 via the Ohio River from Fort Pitt. He served in military campaigns of George Rogers Clark, and survived the Battle of Blue Licks. He was involved in founding the cities of Lexington, Kentucky and Cincinnati, Ohio.

Col. Robert Patterson at his own house, Oct. 19, 1818, deposed that in November 1775 we reached Salt Lick Creek (where Vanceburg, Lewis County on Ohio river, now is) from Fort Pitt, in company with David Perry, William McConnell, and Stephen Lowry. Thence Perry - who had been in [*Kentucky*] the Spring before, undertook to pilot us on to Leastown, on the Kentucky River. We kept up Salt Lick creek westwardly; then continued westwardly, crossing Cabin Creek, until we came to the Stone Lick; then kept going about the same course, until we struck the buffalo trace, leading from Limestone to the Lower Blue Licks, at Mayslick; crossing that trace, we came to the middle trace - which we kept to the Lower Blue Licks; thence on to Hinkston, and to Leestown.

Stone Lick was not then called by that name; but it is the same place where Francis McDermid's settlement and preemption was afterwards laid, and was called Stone Lick from the time McDermid's was surveyed; it is where Williamsburg (now called Orangeburg) is placed, or near it . . . We had 9 horses and 14 head of cattle with us, when we went from Stone Lick to Mays lick in 1775.

Simon Kenton deposed, June 5, 1824: In 1775, 1776, May 1780, & 1784, he was well acquainted with the mouth of Cabin Creek, the North Fork of Licking, and the Upper Blue Licks or Springs. By those names, then and ever since, they were well known - except that, prior to 1780, some called the North Fork the East Fork. Fleming Creek, in 1776 & before, was called the Dry Fork of Licking. Two roads led from the mouth of Cabin Creek to the Upper Blue Licks - one called the war road or upper war road, the other called the buffalo road or trace & sometimes called the lower war road; the former was best known.

Simon Kenton deposed, Aug. 23, 1821: He first became acquainted in 1775 with the "middle trace" or road from Lower Blue Lick to the head of Lawrence's creek (now Washington).

In 1776, he traveled it with Robert Patterson, Samuel Arrowsmith, Jacob Drennon, Samuel Percy, & others who then called it the "middle trace." In 1778, he traveled it again with Col. Daniel Boone, Alex Barnett, & others, 18 in number [*the Paint Creek Expedition*]. In 1780, he assisted to make . . . (certain) entries - all intended to lay on or near said trace . . ..

Gen. Simon Kenton deposed, May 11, 1821, at the prison of Mason County [in the town of Washington, Kentucky]. He was now 66 or 67 years old. In 1780, he undertook to locate 3,000 acres of land warrants for Edward Byne, his pay to be 1/2 thereof. He located 1,000 acres where the town of Washington now stands; 1,000 acres at Lewis' Station, formerly called Clark's Station, on north side of North Fork of Licking river, &c.

In the division, he got the 1,000 acres where Washington now is, and the east half of the 1,000 acres at Lewis.' He made his own entry of 2,000 acres at the mouth of Wells' creek, & afterwards sold it (part of a very large sale of land) to William Wood & Arthur Fox who well knew of its interference with Byne's Station survey on North Fork. [*This may have been the tract where the town of Washington was founded in 1786.*]

Simon Kenton deposed, Aug. 15, 1814. I was there in [*Mason County*] *in* 1778 with old Daniel Boone and 16 other men; and in 1779, with Capt. Gatliff and Leaper, R. McKinney, and Marshall.

I was on said creek [*Lawrence Creek*] in the fall of 1783; landed at Limestone, with the intention of settling on the waters of Lawrence creek, about 1 mile north of Washington; and in company with William Kenton and John Metcalfe, we came out from Limestone to the spring on said creek, and we called it Lawrence Creek.

I settled at said spring in the fall of 1784. In 1776, I saw Ignatius Mitchell, Daniel Boone, & __ Hunter on said creek; and in same year it was known by Jacob Drennon, Samuel Arrowsmith, John Mills, and Col. Robert Patterson.

Thomas Young, 1810. I was here with the [?] party in 1775, again in 1784, in 1785, and since till 1790 occasionally, and in 1791 removed and have lived here ever since. I had a cabin on the Ohio below this, but never laid any claim to that after the passage of the law giving the right of preemption.

I was in the Revolutionary War, in Col. Crockett's regiment called the "Regiment of Guards to the Convention," and stationed at Charlottesville.

The Governor of Virginia Subscribed my commission as Captain. My commanding officer was Col. James Wood, a "continental" officer, from January 1, 1780 to March 1781. I located my military land warrants, a part on Green River, part on Russell's creek, and part on Price's Meadow creek. The surveys are countersigned by William Croghan. I got 4,000 acres, which I believe was what the captains got.

John McCausland deposed, August 11, 1798: Early in April, 1776, he and William Biggs, George Deakins and James Duncan came down the Ohio and landing at Limestone, were met by a man who called himself Simon Butler (the same man now called Kenton). Kenton, Biggs, Deakins & myself traveled out from the Ohio, along a war path for some distance, then turned off to a camp which Kenton had on Lawrence creek, & stayed there some time. Thence Kenton conducted us to a canebrake (now the town of Washington). At different places we made improvements, built cabins, &c. None of us except Kenton had ever seen Kentucky before. In about ten days, Biggs and I left this neighborhood. I have never been back until now.

William Triplett deposed, same day & at same time and place *[March 14, 1797, at Gen. Henry Lee's residence about 1 mile north of Washington].* He and nine others built 10 cabins [in now Mason County] one each for Samuel Wells, Haydon Wells, William Triplett (himself), Thomas Tebbs, John Tebbs, Thomas Young, John Rust, Matthew Rust, Richard Master and John Heggis [*in 1775*].

John and Thomas Tebbs left their axes in Thomas Tebbs' cabin, where I got them in 1776. They also made some improvements near the Ohio river below the mouth of Stepstone creek for Samuel Wells and Thomas Young [in now Bracken County below Augusta]. He was in the neighborhood of these improvements in 1775, 1776, 1780, 1783, and 1784, and has lived in Kentucky ever since.

Maj. George Stockton deposed, February 26, 1805, at Flemingsburg, that early in April, 1776, for purposes of improving land, he and Samuel Strode, William McClary and John Fleming descended the Ohio River and landed at mouth of Salt Lick Creek (Vanceburg). Proceeded into the country towards the Upper Blue Licks and made improvements on North Fork of Licking and on Fleming Creek, then recrossed the North Fork, fell in with John Boggs and others, and went with them to their camp on Well's Creek, near what is now Bailey's Station (in Mason County) where we saw Simon Kenton, then called Simon Butler. Three companies were thus met at Boggs' camp - ours, Boggs, Isaac Pearce, John Virgin, and others, 14 or 15 in all...

In the next deposition, Daniel Boone mentioned the route taken during the rescue of his and Richard Callaway's daughters after they were captured by Indians near Fort Boonesborough in July 1776. He continued by describing war roads, buffalo paths, noted places and the distances between them. Daniel Boone was deposed at the home of his grandson, John B. Callaway, the son of Flanders Callaway and Jemima Boone Callaway.

Daniel Boone deposed, June 10, 1817, at the dwelling house of John B. Callaway in St. Charles Co., Missouri Territory (and because of some technical oversight, it was taken again Sept. 22, 1817) that he is about 84 years old.

In June or July, 1776, we followed the Indians almost to the North Fork of Licking, along the upper war road which leads from the Upper Blue Licks to the mouth of Cabin Creek (on the Ohio river, 6 miles above Maysville); but never heard either of the roads called the Upper or Lower war roads until Oct. 1780, when we pursued the Indians past the Upper Blue Licks to the mouth of Cabin Creek, after they had killed my brother Edward Boone.

On May 15, 1780 the nearest station to the Stone Lick [now Orangeburg, in Mason County, 9 miles east southeast of Maysville] were Ruddle's and Martin's, about 45 miles distant; Bryan's, about 60 miles; Lexington, 64 miles; Boonesborough, 64 miles; and Stroud's [Strode's], near 42 miles . . .

In February 1778 I was first at Stone Lick. I sent Simon Kenton to the mouth of Cabin Creek to spy in August or September 1777. I first heard Stone Lick so called in 1781. Those who had the best opportunity to know the roads in that region were Simon Kenton, John Martin, John Haggins, Jared Townsend...

In October 1780, I knew the Indians had come along this [Upper] war road, for in muddy places I saw their horse tracks which enabled us to follow them. The whole of our company did not pursue them all the way to the mouth of Cabin Creek. Charles Gatliff, my son Israel (who went to see it), Jacob Stucker, and 8 or 9 others went with us to the Ohio River. The balance stopped at the junction of the Stone Lick road . . .

I never knew, but heard, that there was an Indian crossing at the Three Islands. The mouth of Cabin Creek, the North Fork of Licking, and the Upper Blue Licks were places of general notoriety in the Spring of 1780 and before. Simon Kenton told me that in 1776 and 1777 he traveled the road from the mouth of Cabin Creek past the Stone Lick and Lower Blue Licks; and of my own knowledge, he returned home by the Lower Blue Licks in those two years from his Spring trips, at which time he lived at Boonesborough. The men with me in October 1778 [*just after the Siege of Boonesborough*], pursuing the Indians, were from Strode's, McGee's, Bryan's, Lexington and Boone's Stations.

War roads in early times, were distinguished from roads made by game, by choppings, blazings, paintings, &c; otherwise they could not have been distinguished from the small buffalo roads.

The left hand road - after leaving Stone Lick, to Stockton's Spring - in Oct. 1780, was marked as an ancient Indian road, was pretty well blazed, and had bushes cut, upon both sides of the road. Our company gave it the name of the Upper War road.

... In 1777, I traveled and I have heard both Haggin and Townsend say that they traveled, in 1776 or 1777, out from the mouth of Cabin Creek, past Stone Lick and May's lick, to the Lower Blue Licks.

Collins Depositions: Gunpowder at Three Islands 1776-1777

In late fall of 1776, George Rogers Clark and his men came down the Ohio River to bring gunpowder to Kentucky. They hid the powder at Three Islands on the Ohio River.

In December, when Indians attacked McClelland's Station and the survivors moved to Harrodsburg. Fincastle surveyor Jacob Sodowski was with them. Other men from Bullitt's company were back in Kentucky; those said to have been at McClelland's were John Fitzpatrick, Roderick McCrae, and Thomas Hanson.

A week or so after the attack at McClellands, in early January 1777, a company from Harrodsburg went to retrieve the gunpowder.

Jacob Sodowsky deposed, April 27, 1818, at his own house in Jessamine County... I was in this country in 1776, and there was some powder came down the Ohio with George Rogers Clark and others, which was deposited at the Three Islands, late in the fall or early in the winter of 1776.

On Jan. 2, 1777, James Harrod raised a company of which I was one, to go after the powder. We went by McClelland's fort (now Georgetown), by the Lower Blue Licks and Mayslick; thence turned to the right a little, and struck the Ohio at or near the mouth of Cabin creek.

There were about 25 or 30 men in the company. They were: James Harrod, who had the ordering of the company, Joseph Blackford, David Glenn, Benjamin Linn, Silas Harlan, Henry Higgins, James Elliott, Simon Kenton, Isaac Hite, Elisha Bathi [*Baythe/Beath*], Samuel Moore, Leonard ____, Jonathan Ingram, Nathaniel Randolph, two or three of the McConnells and myself...

Two of our company went out hunting and got lost, and found their way to the Upper Blue Licks, then turned & fell in with us...

Simon Kenton, June 5, 1824. In 1777, a company of about 30 men carried a quantity of powder from the Three Islands [9 to 12 miles above Maysville] to Harrodsburg. They went down the Ohio to mouth of Cabin Creek, then by my advice struck across to the buffalo trace leading from Limestone to Lower Blue Licks...

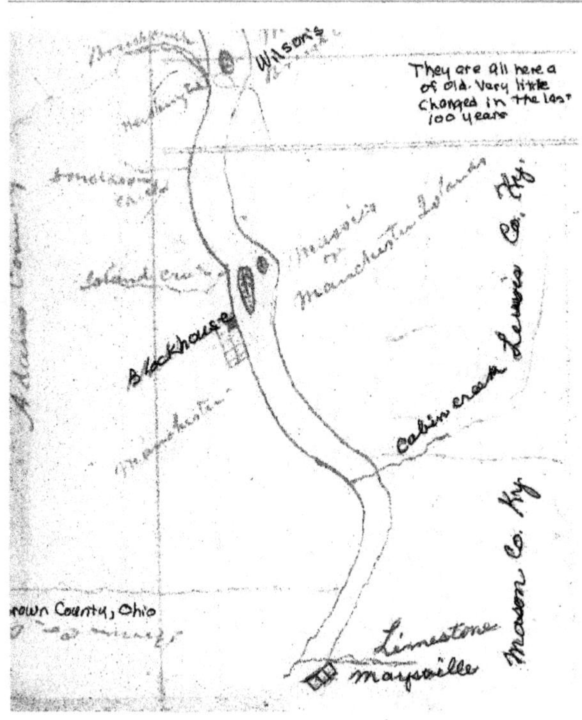

Three Islands on Ohio River
David Pennywitt, 1888. DM 16J 79

Collins' Depositions: Daniel Boone's Saltmakers and Boone's Escape, 1778

Jesse Coffee (Cofer/Copher) deposed, May 15, 1805, that he lived at Boonesborough in 1777 and about the last of December of that year, or 1st January 1778, he & about 28 others went with Col. Daniel Boone to the Lower Salt Lick on Main Licking (i.e. Lower Blue Licks), to make salt. We made a few bushels of salt; and the Indians tuck Col. Boone, myself, and the greater part of his company prisoners. [*Jesse Copher and Richard Wade with others, were captured with Daniel Boone and his saltmakers on February 8, 1778.*]

Stephen Hancock deposed, May 23, 1808, at Madison Court House [now Richmond], that he moved his family to Boonesborough in October 1777; and about 1st February 1778, went with Daniel Boone and about 30 men to the Lower Blue Lick to make salt. Col. Boone and his company that staid with him was taken prisoners by the Indians.

The Indians captured Daniel Boone while he was out hunting; there was a deep snow. They took him back to the saltmakers' camp and made captives of those who were present. Some men had taken salt back to Boonesborough or were out hunting and escaped captivity.

Boone escaped about August [*June*] following, & came home. After Boone's return, he and deponent & Col. John [*Benjamin?*] Logan & John Kennedy & others (about 28 men in all) went over same road to Blue Licks in search of Indians.

In fall of 1780, I went from Strode's Station, with Capt. Charles Gatliff and others, about 70 men in all, to the Upper Blue Lick & returned home by the Flat Lick and Round Lick, &c.

William Cradlebaugh deposed [1808] same day and place, that he lived at Boonesborough with Col. Daniel Boone in 1776 and for several years after.

About Feb. 1, 1778, I [was] sent with Boone & others, about 30 men in all, to Lower Blue Lick. "A few of the men came home, and left Col. Boone and the rest of the company at the Blue Licks to make salt; and Col. Boone and his company was taken by the Indians." Col. Boone returned home in July or August *[June]* following. Shortly after, myself & others, about 20 men in all, went (over this road) to Blue Licks, to hide the [salt] kettles.

In the summer of same year, myself and about 20 men in all went to the Lower Blue Licks to bring home said kettles; and encamped one night at Flat Lick.

In the next two depositions, Daniel Boone said he was on his return to Boonesborough after escaping from captivity in June 1778.

Daniel Boone deposed, July 3, 1797, in regard to James Peake's settlement on the waters of Flat Fork on Johnson, that on June 19, 1778, being on my way from the Indians (in captivity), came to this place, being a large open place of ground at a buffalo road and the forks of three branches of the waters of Johnston's Fork, which said land he entered, Jan. 11, 1780, for James Peake.

"On the 19th day of June, 1778, I roasted some meat, and got some ____ on the mouth of three branches."

"Peak furnished me the money to clear out the same (his preemption), and I only sold him my chance without recourse to new. George Stockton, James Bailey, & Michael Cassidy were present at the taking of the deposition, which was taken by David Morris and John Porter as Justice of the Peace. "

Daniel Boone deposed, Sept. 28, 1795, on the spot, in now Fleming co, Ky., that "on June 19, 1778, being on ___ from the Indians who had me lately before in captivity, I came to a large open place of ground at the forks of three branches, a buffalo road, waters of Johnston's Fork (of Licking), which land I entered for James Peake on Jan. 11, 1780, on the Commissioners' Books; also, on the same day, entered for David Birney a settlement and preemption adjoining on the south, which Robert Wallace claims as assignee."

Collins' Depositions: The Paint Creek Expedition, August 1778

Jesse Hodges described going on an expedition with Daniel Boone and others to find out if the Indians were on their way to attack Fort Boonesborough. They crossed the Ohio River a few miles above Cabin Creek, re-crossed the Ohio and then crossed the Licking River to return just before the siege began.

Jesse Hodges, aged 57, deposed, November 20, 1817, that in 1778 he started from Boonesborough to take an Indian town on Paint Creek, in a company of 18 men, viz. Daniel Boone, Simon Canton (Kenton), then called Simon Butler, John Cannady (Kennedy), John Logan, John Holder, Pemberton Rollins, John Callaway,

Edmond Fear, Alexander Montgomery, John Stapleton, and the others not recollected.

They passed the Lower Blue Licks, leaving the road thence to Limestone at a point between Johnson's Fork and Mayslick, and going to the right. We crossed the Ohio river near the mouth of Cabin Creek. Simon Canton was our best pilot; the company depended on him to show the way; he was a good woodsman. He talked of the Upper Blue Licks then (1778) as if he was well acquainted with them. Strode's Station was 30 or 35 miles from the Blue Licks - 9 or 10 miles nearer than Boonesborough.

Jesse Hodges, March 4, 1818, deposed . . . that the (above) expedition was in August 1778; they crossed Cabin Creek, going 3 or 4 miles above its mouth, and, returning, crossed the Ohio below Limestone, and the Licking below the Lower Blue Licks - being hard pressed by the pursuing Indians.

Collins' Depositions: Edward Boone Killed, 1780

Peter Shull *[Scholl],* age 63 [son-in -law of Edward Boone], deposed April 17, 1818, that he was one of the company that pursued the Indians at the time they killed Edward Boone, his [*Scholl's*] wife's father, in October 1780. After burying said Boone, we followed the Indians to the Upper Blue Licks; thence . . . to the North Fork of Licking... thence to the waters of Cabin Creek. There I asked Col. Daniel Boone where he thought the Indians would cross the Ohio. He said at the mouth of Cabin Creek.

Along our route were many trees peeled, and on one the picture of a turtle and, I think, that of a deer. Capt.

Charles Gatliff asked Col. Daniel Boone to send spies forward to see if the Indians had crossed the Ohio. The spies on their return met us 1 ½ *[miles]* south of the Ohio & reported that the Indians had crossed the Ohio below the mouth of Cabin Creek. We turned back, then held a council & changed our route so as to go by the Lower Blue Licks.

At Stone Lick creek we rested an hour & cracked hickory nuts. Two or three miles south of the North Fork where the land was rich, Colonel Boone proposed that he and I, & his son Israel, and Israel Grant should turn off to the left & hunt. We killed a buffalo, hurried on across Licking *[River]* at Lower Blue Licks & caught up with our party at Big Flat Creek.

Thence parting, Gatliff & his company went to Bryan's Station, & Col. Boone, myself, & others went to Boone's Station. There I found Bartlett Searcy, whom I told of the route we took. He was well acquainted with it, & believed it the same the Indians were aiming to take when they captured two of Col. Callaway's & one of Col. Boone's daughters *[in 1776]*, who were retaken 2 or 3 miles south of Upper Blue Licks . . .

I came to Kentucky in fall of 1779 via the Wilderness. I was to hunt for 4 families, & they were to raise 4 acres of corn. Bartlett Searcy hunted with me, chiefly between mouth of Cabin Creek [at the Ohio River 6 miles above Maysville] and the Upper and Lower Blue Licks, in 1780-1-2-3 & 4.

Collins' Depositions: Bowman's Expedition – May 1779

Henry Hall was in a company of militia waiting at Falls of the Ohio to escort the British Governor of Detroit, Henry Hamilton, to prison in Williamsburg, Virginia. Hamilton had been captured by George Rogers Clark's men at Vincennes. Bowman's Camp is mentioned.

Henry Hall deposed, March 10, 1804, that in February 1779 he was at the Falls of the Ohio when Capt. William Harrod's guard conveyed Governor Hamilton and party from the Falls to Harrodsburg, where he staid several days. I learned there that an expedition was on foot against the Chillicothe towns on the Miami, and agreed to go. We returned to the Falls and Capt. Harrod raised 50 or 60 men. We proceeded up to the mouth of Licking, where we were met by the volunteers from Harrodsburg and the other settled places. We proceeded, and had a fight at the town.

On our return, we dispersed at the mouth of Licking; "some went up the river and others came back to this country. I was solicited by Capt. Isaac Ruddle to come over to the north side of the Kentucky River, to settle a station on the Licking waters, in a fine country unsettled. Col. Bowman commanded the troops after we met at mouth of Licking. Became acquainted with the west branch of Licking called Mill creek. I saw a camp on it, called "Bowman's Camp." Besides this camp, Lee's Lick, McFall's Lick, and Logan's Lick were on Mill Creek. All four were notorious places.

William McGee deposed, March 10, 1804, that in the last of May or June in 1779 (I believe), myself and several others...came from Boonesborough under

Daniel Boone,* on an expedition against the Indians. Thence "we came to the place now called Lexington, though not called by that name then - where there was but one house." Thence we went to the mouth of Licking, the point of rendezvous. Capt. John Holder also marched with a Company from Boonesborough, in company with Boone and his command. Holder did not encamp with his men at Lexington, but went beyond that and encamped. I do not remember to have seen Col Bowman until after we arrived at the mouth of Licking. We went on to the Indian towns, and were under his command until our return to the mouth of the Little Miami, where ___ men dispersed to the different parts of Kentucky and elsewhere. Col. Bowman was County Lieutenant of Kentucky and as such, it appeared to me, he issued the instructions or directions.

* A mistake. - Boone had not then returned from North Carolina to Ky. LCD

Richard H. Collins. The last two foregoing, & several following, depositions were taken by Commissioners to perpetuate testimony as to the point where Col. Bowman encamped the second night, when marching to the Shawnee towns. It was an important point in numerous land surveys.

Josiah Collins (aged 47) deposed, same day and place, that he marched from Lexington in Holder's Company in May, 1779. My residence at that time was at Lexington, having moved there in April from Harrodsburg. While at Harrodsburg I drew rations; but after I moved to Lexington, meat was plenty... Holder's, Todd's, & Logan's Companies encamped on Mill creek. I was a volunteer...in the Expedition... We were discharged on the south side of the Ohio, nearly opposite the mouth of the Little Miami . . . I don't know that Lexington was a place of note before Col. Bowman's Expedition was set on foot.

Benjamin Berry deposed, May 18, 1804, on Mill Creek ...that he came the first time he was in the country to Logan's Station [on] April 17, 1779, and to Harrodsburg on April 20, 1779. Shortly after, Col. Bowman and other officers prepared an expedition against the Shawnee Indians, and he requested people to plant their corn and be in readiness to rendezvous at Lexington in May.

We accordingly met there the militia from other Stations - from Harrodsburg, Wilson's, McAfee's, Logan's, Boonesborough, Lexington, and Bryan's. Col. Bowman, County Lieutenant, then directed our march to the mouth of Licking. On our way, we encamped here (Mills Creek), the second night from Lexington ... I heard Col. Bowman give Ruddle orders to direct the men in his Station to be in readiness when called on... After our return to this side of the Ohio, and after the sale of the property was over, every company took their own course homeward, as they pleased.

The men from the Falls had been directed to meet us at the mouth of Licking, with boats to enable us to cross... I was in Capt. Levi Todd's Company. We were all volunteers... [*Benjamin Berry took part in Bowman's Expedition soon after he came to Kentucky. By "sale of the property" he meant sale of horses and booty from the battle.*]

James Guthrie deposed, May 25, 1804, that "on April 6, 1779, he landed at the Rapids of the Ohio. Immediately afterwards there was an expedition set on foot against the Indians. [*Bowman's Expedition.*] A certain William Harrod who, this deponent conceives, commanded them at the Falls of Ohio, harangued the people then there - showing the necessity of the expedition, & that the settlements from the other parts of Kentucky were desirous of having the expedition carried into effect.

In consequence, this deponent on the 13th of May marched from Louisville, with others to the number of 70, destined for the expedition aforesaid. They ascended the Ohio to the mouth of Licking, when they joined the volunteers from the different parts of Kentucky. After they had thus met, they by an election or joint voice of the respectable characters choosed a gentleman of the name of Bowman to command said expedition, and proceeded accordingly to the Shawanese town on the Little Miami, where we attacked the Chillicothe town; and success in the attack is well known.

The army returned, and recrossed the Ohio at the mouth of the Little Miami where the army was discharged. I then repaired to the place where Lexington now is, and resided there until about the last of March 1780. About 190 men met us at the mouth of the Licking. I believe it was on the other side of the river that the volunteers were organized, and formed the line of march.

Collins' Depositions: Kentucky - 1780s

Capt. John Waller deposed July 16, 1797, that in July or August 178_[?] he assisted Simon Kenton to form a settlement and built a blockhouse at a spring then called Drennon's Spring where Kenton has since lived & where was called Kenton's Station. He had employed me as surveyor for him. *The surname name Waller has been sometimes been transcribed as Miller. John Waller is known to have assisted Simon Kenton in the building of his cabins.*

Levi Davis, in 1801, deposed that he and Daniel Boone, Robert Forbes, John Gray, and John Angus McDonald were together at Maysville and on Johnson's Fork, on our return by the Lower Blue Licks in 1782.

Daniel Boone deposed March 18, 1799, that he was then "about sixty-six years;" that in spring of 1782 he located, about six miles south of Lower Blue Licks, 4,000 acres of land for Henry Miller, of Augusta; he made no charge for it, did it for friendship. "Miller lived eight years with me in my father's house."

Septimus Davis deposed, in same suit, that he was chain-carrier for Col. Daniel Boone, when marking this (Miller) survey.

John Curry deposed, in same suit, that he got information of an ash tree (in this Miller survey) from Col. Daniel Boone in 1795, he thinks, after Col. Boone had arrived back to Kentucky from the Big Kanawha.

Peter Harget deposed, April 30, 1814, that he came to Kentucky in 177_ and was in the battle of Blue Licks in 1782.

In October or November 178_, I was at Limestone in company with old Daniel Boone, William Hays, Flanders Callaway, William Cradlebaugh, and some others. We went a westerly ____, to Lawrence Creek as Boone called it - who was our pilot and was taken sick there. Our company lay about two days on said creek, hunting &c. Boone wanted to examine the land about the mouth of Limestone, and then talked of settling there & did settle there about 1785.

When we left our camp on Lawrence creek, Boone conducted us to a lick on Bracken creek, and showed us a tree marked with his name and dated about 1776.

I was at Limestone about 1786, as a guard, with others.

Richard H. Collins, Nov.[?] 21, 1882. Some of Harget's descendants are now living near Minerva, Mason County, about 11 miles west of Maysville, and near the land he passed over with Daniel Boone in 1782, now just a hundred years ago.

Daniel Boone, on June 2, 1796, at a point on a branch of the North Fork of Licking, on the path from Keith's Mill to the Salt Works at Salt Lick Creek...near Vanceburg, in now Lewis County ...made oath that in 1779 he was at this spot, and that there was an Indian camp there at the time; and that in 1780 he surveyed and located 3,000 acres land for Nathaniel Hart, to include the place where he now is, and to have the Indian camp in the center.

Simon Kenton lived most of the time at Col. Ben. Logan's and the forepart of 1780 he lived at Martin's and Ruddell's Stations. I was not a locater of land . . . In 1775 met[?] at Upper Blue Licks with a party of Indians, five men, five squaws, & some children. I did not know of any road leading from the Upper Blue Licks to the Ohio river, as early as 1780.

Patrick Henry's deposition, June 4, 1777, have[?] _____ tax[?] is in some book in my library, but I cannot now trace it up. ___ looked for it patiently, but fail to find it.

Richard H. Collins. ...several depositions were taken by the *[Land]* Commissioners to perpetuate testimony as to the point where Col. Bowman encamped the second night, when marching to the Shawnee towns. It was an important point in numerous land surveys.

David Mitchell (aged 67) deposed, May 18, 1804, on Mill Creek, that he was not in Bowman's Expedition in 1779, but a residenter in Lexington at the time (in May). I recollect of 14 citizens coming over to settle in Lexington about the 14th of April in that year. Robert Patterson and John Morrison were two of them. I killed meat for the garrison while the army was out.

Josiah Collins (aged 47) deposed, same day and place, [*May 18, 1804, on Mill Creek*], that he marched from Lexington in Holder's Company in May, 1779. My residence at that time was at Lexington, having moved there in April from Harrodsburg. While at Harrodsburg I drew rations; but after I moved to Lexington, meat was plenty... Holder's, Todd's, & Logan's Companies encamped on Mill creek. I was a volunteer...in the Expedition... We were discharged on the south side of the Ohio, nearly opposite the mouth of the Little Miami . . . I don't know that Lexington was a place of note before Col. Bowman's Expedition was set on foot.

John Riggs deposed, October 1797, that in May 1783, he and Jacob Drennon, Thomas Mills, Lot Mathews, and George Mefford came down the Ohio river to the District of Kentucky in order to locate land, and landed at or near the mouth of what is now called Crooked or Cabin creek and then along a buffalo trace to waters of the North Fork of Licking. We made some locations, at one place cutting George Mefford's initials on a honey locust on the east fork of Cabin Creek.

Richard H. Collins concluded his depositions with notes on other topics.

Richard H. Collins. You ask "Who wrote this account of the battle of the Blue Licks?" I transferred this, bodily, from my Father's "Historical Sketches of Ky." It was Gen. Robert B McAfee (which, from some earmarks, is doubtful, if not improbable), I cannot tell, & no one living can.

I cannot now find the letter of Rev. Aaron A Hogue; & returned to him the Central Watchtower of Feb. 28, 1829. He is still living, at Salvisa, Mercer County, Kentucky. Address him there. Richard H. Collins

Dr. Matthew L. Dixon's letter was first published, anonymously, some time in 1835 in the National Intelligencer, but some circumstances enabled me to locate and identify the author. He wrote it to some gentleman, who furnished it for publication.

1775 ___. "So soon as thc [Watauga] treaty was completed, Col. Boone with a company set out to take possession. They fixed themselves on Kentucky river, south side, a little below the mouth of Otter Creek. Shortly after the founding of Boonesborough, difficulties took place with the Indians, and the fort became the principal place of security to the inhabitants. Among this little band were Col. Callaway and his two daughters, Elizabeth and Frances, Boone's daughter Jemima, and a Mrs. Holder. *[This is Frances (Fanny) Callaway who later married John Holder; Holder was not at Boonesborough when the girls were captured.]* Samuel Henderson was the lover of Elizabeth Callaway, & had left his peaceful house in North Carolina on her account. Flanders Callaway was the lover of Jemima Boone, and John Holder of Frances Callaway.

"In the afternoon of a beautiful Sunday in the month of June *July*, 1776, Elizabeth Callaway (afterwards, Mrs. Henderson, & mother of my wife), then about sixteen years of age, her sister Frances, younger, and Jemima Boone about the age of the latter, procured a canoe and left the fort, paddling to an island in Kentucky river to amuse themselves in gathering blossoms and wild onions.

"After they had satisfied themselves on the island, they carelessly paddled the canoe to the opposite shore of the river, from whence they started and from the fort. They were not apprehensive of any present danger; but as the canoe drifted opposite to a honey canebrake, which came down to the water's edge, five Indians rushed furiously there, and soon made them captives. Elizabeth Callaway, however, raised her voice to the highest pitch and fought heroically with her paddle, and laid open the integuments of the head of one Indian to the bone; but all this availed them nothing, and they soon found themselves hurried off, they knew not where or to what fate.

"Fortitude and presence of mind never forsook Elizabeth Callaway. As soon as the Indians commenced their march with their little captives, this admirable female pioneer bent or broke every twig she passed, if she possibly could. The Indians discovered the stratagem, and one of them gathered the hair of her head, held it up, & at the same time brandishing his tomahawk over her or drawing his scalping knife round the tuft of hair, in indication of what would be her fate if she did not desist. But her daring spirit was not to be thus subdued, as she then would tear small pieces from the most flimsy part of her clothing and strew them along the way. The Indians gave them some buffalo meat; this in part they also crumbled in the path, but birds or something else picked up the pieces, as the pursuers saw nothing of them.

"Owing to the situation of the canoe, it was late in the evening after the girls were missed before the whites could cross the river. Eighteen at length got over in time to pursue the trail five miles that evening. Next day, Monday, they progressed through the cane about thirty miles and on Tuesday resumed their march, five miles, to a creek, over which on examination no trail could be discovered. But knowledge of their customs induced the whites to suppose the Indians had waded up or down the creek, so as to leave no vestige of their footsteps. The company then divided, nine going up and nine down the creek. The latter had not gone very far, before they discovered smoke gently ascending. Every precaution was then observed in order to come as suddenly on the Indians as to prevent them destroying their captives.

Boone, who commanded the lower party, gave orders that not a gun should be fired until all could be made sure. The whites crept slowly on, until within reasonable shooting distance, one of the Indians rose from the ground. The anxiety of one of the men was such, that he fired on the Indian who showed himself, somewhat contrary to Boone's orders. The savage bounded, dropped what he held, and made off. The others sprang to their feet, when a volley from Boone and his companions left not an Indian to be seen. They did not drop dead, but made off; nor were they pursued, as the great object was accomplished. The fugitive Indians, one excepted, who alone of the party returned to their towns, must have died of their wounds or perished with hunger and fatigue.

"The pursuers rushed to the spot where they found the prisoners and the baggage of the Indians, and discovered that they had been cooking a buffalo calf for breakfast, which they had killed that morning.

"Now, an occurrence was near taking place which would have marred all the pleasure of the pursuers. Elizabeth Callaway was dark complexioned, and from fatigue and exposure very much so in her then situation. She was sitting by the root of a tree, with a red bandana handkerchief around her, and with the heads of her sister and Jemima Boone reclining in her lap. One of the men, in a moment of high excitement, as must have been the case with all, raised the butt of his gun to dispatch her, and it was about to fall on her defenseless head with a weight aided by all his muscular power, when his arm was fortunately arrested by one of the others who also supposed her for an Indian. Although no harm was done, a melancholy sensation was produced from which they did not soon recover. In fact, it is enough to make the blood run cold to think of the circumstance even at this time, when fifty-nine years have gone by, and the generation then in action have nearly all gone to rest.

"Another circumstance also took place on this occasion, which had strongly the appearance of the interposition of Providence in behalf of the prisoners. Immediately after they stopped to kindle a fire and cook, one of the Indians who had a gun (they were not all armed with guns) laid off his pack, took a little path and went away. He was about a few minutes, and returned without his gun, opened his knapsack and commenced searching for something he appeared to have forgotten (probably his powder), and while thus engaged, himself and party were discovered, and as already stated, fired on. This Indian no doubt had been sent out as a sentinel, and had he remained at his post would have discovered the whites, given the alarm, and allowed the others time sufficient to murder the prisoners and effect their own escape.

"I neglected to mention in its proper place, that two companies of whites were found at the fort, one of foot and one of horse - the former conducted by Col. Boone, and the other by Col. Callaway. The feelings of these two commanders in pursuit of their captured daughters can be but very faintly conceived, much less described. The horse company, by some tracks they discovered, took it for granted that Boone's party had succeeded, and returned to the fort without participating in the recapture.

"The girls, though much exhausted from affright, hunger and fatigue, were safely conveyed back to the fort. Their captivity, though brief, was painful to them and deeply afflicting to their parents, other relatives, lovers and friends, on account of their quality, their age, sex and tenderness. No indignity was suffered to be offered to them. Anything that savored in the least degree of such impropriety was immediately checked by one who seemed to be a chief. This individual is elegantly described in a romantic poem entitled 'The Mountain Muse' by Daniel Bryan of Rockingham County, Virginia. This work was published in 1815, and gives a good outline of the same we are now sketching.

"Mrs. Elizabeth Dixon, widow of Dr. Matthew L Dixon, died in Tennessee, in 1872, aged 82. She was a daughter of the Elizabeth Callaway, one of the captives, and her husband Samuel Henderson, one of the rescuing party."

***

15C 26-26(2), 27 LCD: **Col. Daniel Boone on Licking River, Ky. 1795-1796**

Christopher Mann, Independence, Mo., Oct. 15, 1888.

Mr. Lyman Draper

A few evenings since, I was the recipient of a letter bearing the above name and also the book. I thank you for your kindly remembrance of me. My health is good and also my mind.

I remember Daniel Boon while he lived in Kentucky on the licking [river]. I was a boy then about twelve years old. I remember his two boys well. They were around my size. He never raised any crops. He hunted & fished most of the time. I knew him in 1780. He would go from place to place to hunt. He had the logs & built a house. His boys did the most of it. He was never known to make a shot[?] without bringing down something.

The animules were not as wild as they now are. Had nobody to fear. It was not thickly settled. Daniel would sit in his cabin and kill Buffalo that came a round to lick Salt. They had licked a ditch 4[?] feet deep all around his house. I have walked in the ditch sometimes, over my head. He would boil down the water and make salt. The first [salt] I ever saw he gave dada.

This place inside of the ring the animules had made around the house was called Boone's Lick. I saw him before he lived in this house, and heard my Dada tell how many deer, buffalo, bear & etc. Boone had killed in a day. He was talked of as the old Back Woods hunter. No one knew where he lived. He _____ed no more after robbers made a raid on his house and the two boys killed them. One let the dogs out while the other shot. After we heard about this I desired to see the house. Dada was looking for land. I went with him and went by Daniel's but he told dada about it and said his boys done very well. He asked how far we lived. Dada told him about [?] miles. He said, old woman, we must move, they are crowding us.

I remember how his wife looked and the dogs, he had, six. He had a horse to carry his game on. He had a load of furs ready to take off and he feed his horse a half ___ and started nobody knew where.

He was dressed in leather. He was about the age and size of dada. I heard him tell dada he liked fish better than anything else.

I knew Griff Johnson[?] and Cornelius Washburn was my cousin. I knew Mike D_____ and lots of the men that you have the pictures of in the Book. They all followed us to Kentucky and we went togather to Virginia.

I could tell you lots about these men but nothing moore about Daniel Boone as he did not stay one place long to get acquainted and lived in a world of his own. I have seen him pass with his old horse loaded with game of every kind. He would go by when where we lived and would some times talk to Dada and tell what luck he had. He had traps of every kind to catch raccoons and etc.

Respectfully
Christopher Mann

This is by his daughter Alice, his words exactly. I did not copy it for I wanted you to know how well he could keep on one subject.

My Draper, My father is a great talker. He could talk to you all day and tell you many interesting things of his early days, how he worked and how he got his first pants & hat. He says if you ever come to Missouri, come and see him. You will be welcome. I read your book to him and nothing ever interested so much. I will write again.

Enclosed with the letter was an Independence, Missouri newspaper clipping dated Sept. 16, 1883 and titled "A Very Old Man." It states that Christopher Mann, born in Virginia, is the oldest man in Missouri. He "celebrated his 109th birthday yesterday, having twenty-six children, forty grandchildren, fourteen great-grandchildren, and five great-great grandchildren... He has made his home here since 1813."

15C 28 LCD: **Col. Daniel Boone – 1796.**
February 11 – Letter to Gen. Shelby – Scrapbook iii, p. 7, Collins' Ky., ii, 242

Fall of 1796, Col. Boone, his son Jesse and [____?]. Henderson went hunting up Sandy – but it was a dry autumn & they were unsuccessful; & as Nathan Boone does not seem to have been along, he does not mention it. See Col. ____ Rogers letters, 1862-63. Rogers met them while returning the last of September & early in October.

15C 29 LCD: **Col Daniel Boone – 1796**
June 2nd, 1796, Boone was on North Fork of Licking [River], as the statement of George Stockton & Michael Cassidy shows, appended to the following document.

Boone's Hunt on Greasy Creek of Sandy: See Col. Nathan Boone, William Champ's notes appended: & letters of Elijah Fields...

15C 30 Daniel Boone Deposition, Mason County, Ky., June 2, 1796

The Deposition of Daniell Boon of full age taken in Mason County on the path leading from ___uth's mill to the Salt works at Salt Lick Creek about 320 poles southwardly from whare it crosses the north Fork of Lickin at two white oaks by the Side of the path which hath old blases [blazes] and some old Picturs on said Blases.

This Deponent Sayeth that in the fall 1779 he was at the 2 Blased trees and there was an indian camp at the place at that time & that he, the said Deponent, Located 3000 acres of Land in the year 1780 for Nathaniell hart & in said hart's name to In____. The place he is now at whare the said Indian camp was, at that time, which camp was to be in the center of the Survey as near as may be & that the place whare he now is is whare the camp was, in the place aluded to in the Entry of 3000 acres made in the name of Nathaniell hart, and that him the Said Deponent is not Interested in said hart's claim for 3000 acres. This Deponent Surveyed the Said Entery for the heirs of said Nathl. Hart Deceast and made the Beginning course near whare this path to the salt works crosses the north fork of Lickin and this Deponent further Sayeth not.

Daniel Boone

Witnessed: Geo Stockton
Michael Cassidy

15C 30(1) Statement of George Stockton and Michael Cassidy, Mason County Ky., June 2, 1796.

Copy of original. Mason county, to wit

Agreeable to an order of the worshipfull court of Mason County, we the Subscribers met the second day of June 1796 in said county on a branch of the north fork of Lickin [River] on the path to the salt works from __uth's mill whare was two white oak trees with old

Blazes & some old picturs & Daniell boon made oath to the within deposition & in the presence of Stephen Furr & William Walker was marked the said two white oaks with new[?] Letters N H – D B – W W & P W & other papers was produced to us in which it assured there was Notises Given of the time and place of Taking the Deposition agreeable to an act of Assembly Concerning the Boundary of Lands. Given under our hands & Seals this Second Day of June 1796.

Geo. Stockton
Michael Cassidy

15C 31-31(1) William Champ interview, September 1863. LCD: Notes Taken of Wm. Champ, Kentucky. See Trip 1863, ii, p. 271-73.

Mr. Champ saw Col. Daniel Boone but once. Champ was sent by his father with a stock of cattle to winter high up on Licking. During the winter went with others on a hunt up Sandy. This was after Wayne's treaty [1795] while Indians still lurked somewhat on the frontiers, & was before the death of informant's father in 1799, & before Boone migrated to Missouri.

He met Col. Boone on head waters of Sandy. He had with him his wife, [and] two married daughters with their husbands. They had some half-faced camps. They ate their meals from a common rough tray, very much like a sap trough, placed on a bench instead of a table, each using as needed a butcher-knife to cut the meat, & using forks made of cane, with tines or prongs, & having only bread to eat with the meat.

It was a hunting camp. A great number of bears had been killed, & the skins were being cured or dried & the meat hung up drying all around the camp. Col. Boone said he designed taking the meat down Sandy by water, & up the Ohio & Kanawha to the Kanawha Salt works for market. He said he thought he had killed as he expressed it, "the master bear of the Western country." He was a monster for size – two feet across the hip bones, but was very aged & poor & if in good condition, must have weighed five or six hundred pounds.

As Champ was out wintering stock the next winter, & went hunting at the very head of Sandy, Licking, & Kentucky [Rivers], & there heard Indians yell. He & his party of hunters pursued, but the Indians scattered & disappeared in the cane. I should think it very likely it was the winter after Wayne's treaty he met Boone.

LCD: See Col. Nathan Boone's Notes. & Col. Thomas Rogers' letters about the buffalo boats for transporting meat & skins.

15C 32-35 Capt. Charles Yancey to Col. Boone, Feb. 29, 1796. From "Memorials of the Crawford Family," New York, 1883. Privately printed.

Louisa [Va.?], Feb. 29th, 1796

Colo. Daniel Boone:

Dear Sir: I am sorry to observe to you that I have heard that you were displeased with me on account of the debt due Mr. Ware. Far be it from me to take any advantage of you, were it in my power. I have ever been friendly to you and wished you better success in life than you have experienced, and I may in truth add that I have made some sacrifices to serve you, and that you wrote me that you would reward me in your country. I have often defended you in public against calumny and abuse when I have heard you accused. I also rode to Williamsburgh and bore my own expenses to serve you. I also paid for the clearing out of my lands in paper more than twice over, which I have received nothing for. The thousand acres warrant I first put in your hands cost me dear when the money was good, which you promised me should be laid on good land. But I have neither warrant nor land as yet.

A number of the locations you charged me for are not Surveyed or returned and may possibly be lost to us forever, and I am told Hughes' Survey of two thousand acres will the most of it be lost, owing, as I am informed, to its not being Surveyed according to location. Boone's Settlement and pre-emption, I am told, has claims on it, and, I fear, may be lost, at least in part, as I fear it was not located in time, and Bridges' pre-emption and Settlement, I am informed by William Lipscomb that he can find no deeds to him either in Fayette or Lincoln Counties, and that many settlers are on all those lands, and that it may finally be lost also, which different surveys, some of which I have sold, and cannot, I fear, make a proper right to, and it may cost much of my small fortune to make good.

Now, Sir, after this picture of my matters, can you entertain a hard thought of me? However, there is nothing like face to face. If God spares me, I will see you, or send my son to see you, before the summer is over, I hope, and will, if you please, have a settlement, I doubt not to your satisfaction. I hope that we shall be yet friendly, and ready to render each other that service that common justice requires. I add no more, but remain with good wishes to you, Mrs. Boone and family,

Your friend and Servant,
Chas. Yancey

LCD notes:

John Yancey was an early Virginia emigrant from Wales. His son, Charles, married a French lady named Dumas, and their eldest son, Capt. Charles

Yancey, the friend and associate of Daniel Boone, was born on Little River, Louisa County, Virginia, May 10th, 1741. He was married Feb. 2, 1762 to Miss Mary Crawford, and eight years thereafter they settled near Louisa Court House. He was a man of great thrift and energy of character, represented as of low stature, fleshy, with black eyes and a swarthy complexion – a man of irascible temperament, indefatigably industrious and stirring. He died of dropsy, Jan. 9, 1814, in his 73rd year. He was the father of ten children, several of whom died young. "Memorials of the Crawford Family," 29, 30, 84.

Capt. Yancy left to his descendants his fine homestead of some fifteen hundred acres, and much wealth in the wild lands of the country.

15C 36-36(1) LCD**: Capt. Charles Yancey**
Capt. Charles Yancey was born on the 1th May 1741 & died January 9th 1814 in his 73rd year.

15C 37 Elias Mollett. No date. The writer referred Draper to James W. Mollett, possibly the writer's son.

LCD**: Boone's Camp** Johnson County, Ky. Margin note: See notes of Col. Nathan Boone, pp. 205-7 for an account of this camp & hunt on Greasy Creek.

15C 38 James W. Mollett, Johnson County, Ky., June 30, 1884.

Mollett wrote that he was getting a "fair history" of Boon's Camp together for Draper. Boon's Camp today is an unincorporated town in Johnson County, Kentucky; the population was 73 when Mollett wrote to Draper.

15C 39-39(1) Rev. James W. Mollett, Sept. 9, 1884, Boon's Camp Johnson County, Ky

Boone's Camp Situated at the Three Forks of Greasy Creek, named by Col. Daniel Boone him Self where he located a camping ground at this place, near a large lick where he built his camp. Was then a wilderness of woods and high lofty mountains... Boone hunted here for years and camped here at the place called Boone's camp, and left marks on trees and rocks on his trace of travel... he used to bring his game to the camp. I live in four hundred yards of the camp ground – have found rocks marked Daniel Boone and trees marked the same way. They are some old people here who say this was on his road to Buffalo Creek where there was another large lick named David's Creek about a days hunt from Boons Camp. Greasy was named Greasy by Boone. It is said by the old citizens that he killed the largest and fattest Bear he ever killed in all his hunting. There is a post office here called Boons Camp in honor of Boone with Elias Mollett and M. C. Mollet... It is quite a village here now...with good school-houses and church houses, and the land produces well...

Yours truly
Rev. James W. Mollett

PS correct all bad spelling and excuse Bad writing for I am no scolar.

15C 40-41 Rev. James W. Mollett, Nov. 14, 1884, Boons Camp, Johnson County, Ky

Dear Sir:

The election is over and all peacible and all well, hope you the same. I will Now give you matter of

Boone's Camp as well as I can and in my way of spelling as you can understand its nature.

First Boone's Camp – at the camp ground is level for a few acres and is Surrounded by hills west of Boone's camp in sight of the tallest hill... South is a tall ridge divides Greasy, Buffalo _____, David's Creek. East is the head of Greasy and a tall hill dividing Greasy and Rockcastle... The old camp is on the Banks of the left hand fork we call it... one quarter of a mile from the forks...The Lick is the main tributary Stream of Buffalow. The Lick referred to is a Salt Water where Boone's Name is cut on a large Sycamore tree, on the right hand fork of Greasy, 1 mile from the Camp...

Yours in Christ
Rev. Jas. W. Mollett

15C 42-43-43(2) James W. Mollett, January 3, 1885, Boons Camp, Johnson County, Ky.

The writer said the land had been cleared and the marked trees, "they are gone." A hand-drawn map shows the area of Boone's Camp with the marked trees. The letter closed with a note:

PS if you can find a Christian harmony note Book in your country let me know what the price – my wife sends you her respects.

Sary A. Mollett

LCD margin notes are questions about Greasy Ridge: whether there was a fresh water spring near Boone's Camp, etc.

15C 44 James W. Mollett, Boons Camp, Ky., Feb. 7, 1885. This is a note giving a brief description of the country.

15C 45-45(1) Elijah Fields, Boone's Camp, Ky, Jan 22, 1885. Fields was Surveyor of Johnson County, Ky.

LCD: Boone's Camp on Greasy Creek, Johnson County, Kentucky.

Dear sir:

...I live about a mile from Boon's Camp where Daniel Boone Camped and Killed a Bear...at the 3 forks of Greasey Creek. Daniel Au___ camped with Col. Boone and they hunted to gather and killed their bear and carried to the Block House Bottom on Sandy River about 8 miles from where they camped... the Autier[?] family can give a true History of Col Boone... Major Autier[?] could give a great Deal of information...

Elijah Fields S. J. C.

15C 46-46(2) William[?] G. Wells, Jan. 26, 1885, Ward City, Johnson County, Ky.

Dear sir,

Yours of the 18th at hand... I came to this county in 1828. Boone's name was used as mutch then as Cleaveland is now. The Autiers[?] moved to this County about the time Boone came – Daniel Autier & Samuel and Mather settled at the mouth of Johns Creek* lived in the fort or block house... Daniel Autier was named after Daniel Boone...he visited the Aurier family often and hunted game on Daniels Creak & greasey creak... Daniel A_____ said he kept camp for Boone on Greasy Creak, killed a great many bear & dear, greased the bushes from whitch it took the name of Greasey. Years ago, I heard men who hunted a great deal say that they found Boone's name cut on trees... If you would write to Benjemon Spradlon you might get some information... 100 years old – lives at Paintsville...

Yours truly

Wm.[?] G. Wells

*LCD: See Shane iii, 243, showing this settlement made in fall of 1795. Graham's Station – Ohio Salt works that year opened...

15C 47 John Hawes[[?], March 28, 1853[?], Paintsville, Johnson County, Ky.
LCD: Young's Salt Works, Ky.

Dear Sir

...more than fifty years ago a man by the name of Young discovered a Salt Spring on a branch of the Lavey[?] fork of Sandy River called Middle Creek on the west side of said river about twenty miles above this place at which place....still a little salt [is] made... This portion of the county...was settled by James Young. The Country is broken and Hilly, the land very fertile and productive...

Yours Resp.,
John Hawes[?]

15C 48 Edwin Trimble[?], March 3, 1853[?], Prestonsburg, Floyd County, Ky.

Dear Sir

...your inquiry as to the exact locality of a place called Young's Salt Works... It is situated about ten miles due north of this place and the same distance west of the Big Sandy river. At this spring in early times...pioneers made salt. Since then a well has been sunk at the same spot where some salt is yet made. It is situated in a wild mountainous country. What connection Col. Daniel Boone had with these Salt Works...I have not been informed tho' I would think it highly probable...

Your most obt servt
Edwin Trimble[?]

15C 49-49(1) Prestonsburg, Ky. March, 1853.
Ink blots obscure letter.

15C 50 LCD: **Col. Daniel Boone – 1797.**
Shane's Collections, ii, Bath County, p. 51 and p. 84.

"Boone could write a good strong farmer's hand – was Deputy Surveyor to Col. Thomas Marshall in 1782 – 1785; and Deputy under me in 1797. Made several surveys. Came to my house and staid all night, several nights, and made out his plats, so that I know that he did it himself. Surveyed some 100,000 acres of land."

Col. William Suddarth [Sudduth?]
Boone's poverty – loss of Kentucky lands – Virginia's principal object, revenue, hence warrants for more good lands than she had – hence the overlapping surveys &c. Robertson's Scrap Book, 273, Butler's Ky. 138 near bottom.

Producing vexations & costly litigation, & Boone was a conspicuous victim.

15C 51 LCD: **Col. Daniel Boone – 1798.**
Boone living at mouth of Big Sandy. Shane i, Jessamine County p. 13. Nathan Boone's Notes.

In a large list of lands to be sold by the Sheriff of Mason County, Kentucky in September 1798 are 4000 acres of land on Fleming Creek.

And in Clark County, to be sold by the Sheriff, in August 1798, 1500 acres on Red River, & 5000 on head of Kentucky [River] – also for taxes - & both tracts in Clark, & the tract in Mason County against Daniel

Boone for taxes. And of Daniel M. Boone, 800 acres on Licking [River] in Mason County.

15C 52 LCD: **Daniel Boone, 1799**.

Land Losses in Kentucky

Boone's Old Age – Unable to Hunt
See Ohio & Mississippi Navigator, 1814, 248-249 Ditto p. 246, 248 – Major John & Capt. Michael Finley lose their homes by better titles.
Land Entries & re-surveys &c – Hening's Statutes, xi 441
Goes to Missouri: Shane i, Jessamine County p. 2, Shane ii – Fleming County p. 19, Bath county, p. 44; Collins ii – 300 &c; Nathan Boone's Notes.

The patriarch of his settlement
Breckenridge's Views of Louisiana, 117
History of St. Louis, I, 186-187

One of his laments of his old age was that he had no fortune to divide among his children. The hunter's life tended to poverty (Shane ii, Montgomery County p. 272 &c); but Boone's simple philosophy did not comprehend the cause, while he lamented the effect. Unfitted for other labors or duties: Collins' History ii, 453. Josiah Collins on Boone's character: Shane ii, Bath County, 85.

Very hospitable – but careless[?]: Writer in Illinois Magazine, Shane's Collections, ii, Montgomery County, 81

15C 53 LCD: **Daniel Boone, 1800 – 1804**

1800 – March – Adam & Jacob House killed by Osages on Renault's Fork of Merrimac. Billion's St. Louis, 298-299 Visited the Grand Osage & spent the winter there upon the headwaters of the Arkansas[?].

1802 The Mascoux (renegade Creeks) kill a man at New Ma___. One Indian shot. Billion, 334 &c, 373.

1802 Boone in Kentucky – Lulbegrud country: Shane I, Clark County, p. 43
Fall. Three killed by Osages on Grand Glaize. Billion, 374, 374

1803 February – Five Indians killed by whites. Billion, 375.

"The price of occupying those grants was frequently the hazard of their lives for years, although there was no open war." Shepherd's St. Louis, 34.

15C 54 B. H. Payne, Nashville, Tenn., March 2, 1879[?]

Dr sir
I am compelled to defer my writing in this way in consequence of my blindness, & my inability to get any one to write for me more frequently than I have. I sent you something since, a pamphlet by Reid[?] & some time previous to that my statement about Col. Boone. Did you rec'd them?

Daniel Boone, continued – I asked the old gentleman why it was that he left Kentucky where there was so much beautiful & fine land & go away off to Missouri. He said at home they crowded me too much. I could not stand it. I wanted to go where I could not be around so much neighbors; I am too much crouded now where I live in Missouri.

I asked him now near was his [nearest neighbor?] & he said about 40 miles. This is all I have to say about Daniel Boone that would interest you.

At some moment hereafter, when I may be able to command the services of a writer, I will communicate to you what I no about Gen. Simon Kenton.

Very respectfully your friend
B. H. Payne

15C 55-55(1-7) Terms of Settlement in Missouri, 1799. Lexington, Kentucky, Sept. 19, 1799. Columbia Gazette, Nov. 14, 1799.

Instructions to the Commandants of posts in Louisiana for their government in the admission of settlers from a foreign country, copied from instructions posted at New Madrid:

Instructions which shall be observed by the Commandants of the posts of the province for the admission of new settlers.

1.If the new settler comes from another post of the Province where he has obtained a possession of land, no other shall be granted; and if he intends to settle, he must purchase, or show a particular permission from me (viz. the Governor General) for the new concession; and in order to ascertain if he has obtained land before or not, the Commandant from the post from whence he came shall express it in the passport.
2.If the new settler be a foreigner, and not a farmer, or a married man, nor has any property in negroes or merchandize, nor money to purchase them, he shall

have no right to obtain a concession of land until after four years of good behavior...

3.Tradesmen shall be effectually protected, but no land shall be granted them until they have acquired property and lived three years in the service of their trade or profession.

4. Lands shall not be granted to any emigrant being a batchelor who has no trade until after four years; he making it then appear that he has been employed without interruption and with credit in the cultivation of land...

5. If, however, any of those mentioned in the foregoing article...presents a recommendation from some respectable farmer who shall have given him his daughter in marriage, in consequence of finding him industrious and steady... he shall have a right to obtain land...

6. The privilege of enjoying the liberty of conscience must not be understood but in regard to the present generation; for their children must absolutely be Catholics; and he who will not conform to these conditions shall not be admitted, and shall be obliged to retire immediately, although he be a man of great property.

7. At Illinois none but Catholics of the classes of farmers and tradesmen shall be admitted, and persons of ___who shall not have served in any public capacity in the foreign country from whence they came. The emigrants, not Catholics, who are already settled, shall be made acquainted with the contents of the preceding articles, in order that they may observe them; for such has been his Majesty's orders from the beginning.

8. The commandants with the greatest strictness are to watch that no Protestant preachers, or preachers of any other sect not Catholics, introduce themselves; for they shall be made severely responsible for the least neglect in this respect.

9. To every emigrant of the description to be admitted being a married man, there shall be granted two hundred acres... adding fifty acres more for every child he shall bring with him.

10. To every emigrant of property who shall come to this country with an intention of settling himself therein, being in the circumstances...mentioned, there shall be two hundred acres of land granted him, and besides twenty acres for every negro he shall bring with him; in such a manner, nevertheless, that the cession to any single proprietor shall never exceed eight hundred acres.

15C 56-56(7) Col. Boone at Fort Osage – April, 1816, from Niles' Register.

Portions of this article were sent to Draper by an unnamed writer at Fort Osage; it is found also in DM 16C 6. Included are a newspaper clipping giving a false account of the death of Daniel Boone, other clippings reporting the error, mention of the death of George Boone, and one item about the painting of Boone's portrait.

We have been honored by
a visit from Col. Boone...

Col. Boone - Extract of a letter addressed to the editors and published in the Columbian. "Fort Osage, Missouri Territory," April 29, 1816:

"We have been honored by a visit from Col. Boone, the first settler of Kentucky; he lately spent two weeks with us. This singular man could not live in Kentucky when it became settled. He has established a colony or settlement on the Missouri [River], about one hundred miles below us, which has been nearly destroyed by the Indians during the late war.

"The Colonel cannot live without being in the woods. He goes a-hunting twice a year to the remotest wilderness he can reach, and hires a man to go with him, whom he binds in written articles to take care of him, and bring him home, dead or alive. He left this [day?] for the river Platte, some distance above.

"Col. Boone is eighty five [eighty two] years of age, five feet seven inches high, stoutly made, and active for one of his years; is still of vigorous mind, and is pretty well informed. He has taken part in all the wars of America, from Braddock's war to the present hour. He has held respectable State appointments, both civil and military; has been a Colonel, a legislator, and a magistrate; he might have accumulated riches as readily as any man in Kentucky, but he prefers the woods, where you see him in the dress of the roughest, poorest hunter.

"I intend, by next season, if I can obtain permission, to take two or three whites and a party of Osage Indians, and visit the Salt Mountains, lakes and ponds, and see the natural curiosities of the country along the mountains. The Salt Mountain is but five or six hundred [miles?] west of this place."

Reported Death of Col. Boone – As he lived, so he died, with his gun in his hand. We are informed by a gentleman direct from Boone's Settlement on the Missouri, that early in last month, Col. Boone rode to a deer lick, seated himself within a blind raised to conceal him from the game. That while sitting thus concealed with his old trusty rifle in his hand, pointed towards the lick, the muzzle resting on a log, his face to the breech of his gun, his rifle cocked, his finger on the trigger, one eye shut, the other looking along the barrel through the Sights – in this position, without struggle or motion, and of course without pain, he breathed out his last so gently, that when he was found next day by his friends, although stiff and cold, he looked as if alive, with his gun in his hand, just in the act of firing. It is not altogether certain if a buck had come into the range of his gun...but it might have intuitively obeyed its old employer's mind and discharged itself. This hypothesis being novel, we leave the solution to the curious.

Chillicothe Supporter, Niles Register, Sept. 19, 1816.

Col. Boone – The account lately published... of the death of Colonel Boone, is, we have good authority to say, a fabrication. Col. Boone was alive in August. Kentucky Reporter. (Niles Register, Nov. 7, 1818.)

George Boone – Died in Shelby County, Kentucky, the last of the old stock of the famous Boone family – which has been as remarkable for its longevity as for its patriotism and adventurous spirit. Daniel Boone died at the age of 88; Samuel at 88; Jonathan at 86; Squire at 76; George at 83; Mrs. Wilcox (a sister) at 91; Mrs. Grant, a sister, at 84; Mrs. _____, a sister, at 84. Niles Register, Dec. 16, 1820.

Col. Boone –_The account of Col. Boone's death, published in Chillicothe paper, is entirely a fabrication, probably framed for the purpose of introducing the fanciful incident of the heroic woodsman breathing his last with his cheek pressed against the butt of his favorite rifle. We have lately seen a gentleman who was at Col. Boone's house in August last, when the old gentleman was perfectly healthy, and wore the appearance of not being more than sixty five years of age, although he is between eighty and ninety. His sight had failed him so much as to unfit him for his accustomed amusement and business of hunting. This is almost the only Symptom of old age... The chase with him was a passion which he indulged to extravagance. When the periodical hunting season arrives, he represents himself as laboring under the most restless anxiety...and he declares that nothing can compensate him for the pleasure he is deprived of in not being able to pursue the buffalo and deer as formerly to the center of the Missouri deserts.

The family of Col. Boone, consisting of his sons and daughters, with their wives and husbands, live near each other, and form a most interesting groupe. So far from the characteristics of savage life which they have been represented to possess, the sons are described to us as well bred gentlemen, distinguished by some of those grand features of mind which we so often found in our native sons of the forest. They own a fine estate in land granted to the individuals of the family by the crown of Spain. They are eminently useful to strangers who explore the lands on the Missouri and Osage, and the hospitality of every branch of this family is the theme of every traveler who extends his journey to the neighborhood of their settlement.

Pittsburgh Gazette

Col. Boone, says the St. Louis Register, has intimated his intention of moving higher up the Missouri, out of the precincts of the Settlements that are so thickly forming around him. Niles Register, Dec. 26, 1818.

Death of Col. Daniel Boone - The decease of this celebrated man was erroneously announced some years ago – but the latest St. Louis papers state that he died at Charette Village, on the Missouri on the 26th of September, in the ninetieth year of his age. When his death was made known to the General Assembly of the new State, it was resolved that the members should wear crape on the left arm for the space of twenty days, and to adjourn for that day, in respect for his memory.

He was the first settler of Kentucky, a great State, now containing from six to seven hundred thousand inhabitants. He penetrated its wilderness in 1775, and in 1799 removed to, and settled upon the Missouri. He soon after discovered the country now known by the name of "Boone's Lick," which is perhaps the most prosperous part of the new State. Until the last two years of his life, he enjoyed much health; when more than eighty years old, he was a keen huntsman, and made many extensive excursions in pursuit of game in places far distant from the usual tread of white men. Niles Register, Nov. 4, 1820.

Col. Boone's Portrait – it is with pleasure we learn that a portrait of this remarkable man was taken a short time before his death, by an eminent artist [Chester Harding – LCD] from which an engraving is about to be published. Niles Register, Nov. 18, 1820

15C 57-57(1) LCD: **Col. Boone Noticed**... Retires as Settlements Advance.

We lately observed that the "History of Col. Boone was that of thousands of his countrymen." As population advanced, he retired West, sometimes bounding several hundred miles at a time. The editor of the New York American, noticing a new work, which is about to appear on the Settlement of the Western Country, and mentioning Col. Boone, says; "Although a semi-savage in his pleasures and pursuits, he was not so in ferocity. His manners and disposition were placable and kind. His heart was frank, honest and sincere. He withdrew from society; not as a misanthrope, but as a philosopher. As civilization advanced, so he, from time to time, retreated."

An anecdote is told of his last retirement, which however incompatible with the dignity of history, may well be recorded, not only as descriptive of the man, but also of those to whom his remark was applied. "I first removed," said he, "to the woods of Kentucky. I fought and repelled the savages, and hoped for repose. Game was abundant, and our path was prosperous. But soon I was molested by interlopers from every quarter. Again I retreated to the region of the Mississippi; but again these speculators and settlers followed me. Once more I withdrew to the licks of Missouri – and here at length I hoped to find rest. But I was still pursued – for I had not been two years at the licks before a d_____d Yankee came and settled within a hundred miles of me!" Niles' Register, May 17, 1823.

15C 58 P. M. Burns, Deputy County Surveyor, Polk County, Mo. April 21, 1890, Boliver, Mo. Letterhead: Adams & Newton, Real Estate and Loan Brokers.
The writer gave detailed surveyor's calls for Big Spring. LCD memo regarding Big Spring is mostly illegible, mentions Campbell's Atlas of Missouri.

15C 59 LCD**: The Lower Big Spring** Campbell's Gazeteer of Missouri furnishes good water power, & is a point of considerable interest. p. 100

15C 60 LCD to P. M. Burns, April 23, 1890, Madison, Wisconsin. Letterhead: State Historical Society of Wisconsin.

Draper wrote that he could not locate Big Spring, having no sectional map of Missouri; he requested of P.M. Burns to give him the distance in miles from area towns.

15C 61-61(1) P. M. Burns, April 28, 1890, letterhead as before.

...The Big Spring is 9 miles south of the north line of Dallas County... I was at the Spring in the fall of 1872 ...it is about 50 feet in diameter ... [The area is] hilly & stoney, consisting of sharp ridges, all tending toward the river.. The Big Spring is about 20 miles in a direct line from the mouth of the Niagara.

Truly yours,
P.M. Burns

15C 62 P. M. Burns, May 18, 1890, Boliver, Mo.

The writer asked if there was more than one Big Spring on the Niagara, and stated that the locality must be near the mouth of Bryants Creek.

15C 63 LCD**: Col. Boone – 1804**
Gov. Delassus' estimate of him: Billions St. Louis, 367.
Office of Syndric – when appointed: Billions, 370

Delassus says (Billion, 370) that the year St. Louis was threatened with an attack by the Indians, he appointed Syndics. Jan 3, 1803, Tewanaye[?], a Mascon[?] Indian, was shot at New Madrid for assassinating Trotter, under influence of liquor; & Delassus feared retaliation - & perhaps this is what he referred to. Billion, 330.

Capt. William Hays killed: Dec. 1804. Pioneer _____ of Missouri, 30, 253; Shane ii, Bath County p. 32; Notes of ___ Bryan of California.

15C 64-64(1) F. Bell[?], April 17, 1885. St. Louis, Mo. LCD: Col. Daniel Boone, Justice of Peace & Character, 1805-1805. Stephen Hancock.

My Dear Sir,

I was much pleased to again receive a letter from you, as it is about an age since I last had that pleasure.

...Stephen Hancock in our county...at what date he came to St. Louis... His name is first found in our records on Oct. 28, 1815, on which day he purchased from William Massey 400 arpents of land on the waters of Bonhomme Creek in the back part of our count on the Missouri, where he subsequently resided for some twenty years. After several more conveyances to him in our records, I find the last one to be from a "John H. Rogers to Stephen Hancock of St. Louis County, March 24, 1830...

June 30th, 1804

This Day Came before me Justice of the Peace for the District of the Femmeosage, Francis Woods Peter Smith & John Manley and made oath that on the 29th of June of [illegible] at the house of David [illegible] a Certain James Meek and the Bearer hereof Bery Vinyant had some differance Which Came to blows and in the scuffle the said James Meek bit of a piece of Bery Vinzants Left Ear further the Deponent Sayeth not

Given under my hand and Seal the day and Date above Written

Daniel Boone (Seal)

Statement of Daniel Boone, 1804. DM 15C 65.

15C 65 Statement of Daniel Boone as Justice of the Peace on June 30, 1804.

This day came before the Justice of Peace for the District of the Femme Osage Francis Woods, Peter

Smith & John Morley and made oath that on the 29th of June of same Month at the house of David Bryan a Certain James Meek and the Bearer thereof, Bery[?] Vinzant had some difference Which Came to blows and in the Scuffle the said James Meek bit of a piece of Bery[?] Vinzant's left ear & further the Deponent Sayeth not.

Given under my hand and seat the day and Date above written.

Daniel Boone (Seal)

15C 66-66(1) Frederick L. Billon, April 20, 1885, St. Louis, Mo. LCD: Boone appointed Syndric, July 18, 1800.

My Dear Sir,

I received a few days since a certificate from your Historical Society of my election as a corresponding member of the same for which you have my acknowledgments...

Boone was appointed Syndic (civil magistrate) and commandant of the Femme Osage Settlement of Delasus on July 11, 1800, not only for his probity as a man, but doubtless as the only person of some little education in his locality, as you well know how few at that day in our wild newly settled country could write his name. Even Delasus himself, as a well educated, refined French gentleman, wrote Such a wretched scrawl that I have often spent hours, and with the assistance of a Strong convex glass, in deciphering some of his productions and I am somewhat of an expert on hieroglyphics...

The document, of which I _-------- is the only ________ of Boone's handwriting I ever saw and believe the piece to be found here. I thought it might prove a curiosity to you.

The private papers of Gov. Delasus, among which are many official ones, are in the possession of his only son, Augustus Delasus, a resident of __ Franc___ County[?] in our State, whom I have known since a little boy of seven years... Some years back, I had them for a long time in my possession and doubtless much time and labor in taking copies and translating all of them that had any bearing on the history and public affairs of our Territory, nearly all of which have appeared in print...

On this day, April 23rd, 1885, I complete my eighty fourth year and in observing it I am also honoring the natal day of William Shakespeare, James Buchanan & Stephen F.[?] Douglas, forming a quartette of "Irish" twins.

I have yet four years to go to reach the age of that old uncle Chau___ of mine whom you knew in ____ over 50 years ago, who died on Oct. 28, 1846 the day he attained eighty eight.

Respectfully &c
Fredc. L Billon

15C 67 LCD: **Col. Daniel Boone – 1807** – Boone's Lick Country.

The popular conviction is a mistake, that Daniel Boone made a settlement at an early day within the ____ limits of Howard County, Missouri, & manufactured salt at what was known as Boone's Lick, & hence the undefined region known as "The Boone's Creek country" took its name. The truth is, there is no evidence that old Daniel Boone ever owned or worked the salt springs; certainly none think he ever resided, even temporarily, in Howard County. It is probable, & yet the evidence of even this is not conclusive, that while commandment, in 1800 to 1804, of the Femme

Sage district, under Spanish Government, he may have gone on a hunting expedition into the territory of Howard County, & discovered the salt springs existing there.
Commonwealth of Missouri, _ _ B___ 1778 p. 178-179.

Daniel M. and Nathan Boone manufactured salt at Boone's Lick in 1807 – which gave name to the Blue Lick Country. p. 178

15C 68 LCD**: Col. Daniel Boone – 1808**
His hunt in the autumn & robbery:
Nathan Boone's notes; Allen's Biographical Dictionary, 104; Dr. __ Jones & others' letters &c.;
Scholl's account (of this hunt); Trip 1868, vol. 3, p. 218-220 – maybe it should be about 1802 or 1803-1804.

15C 69-69(1) P__ O'Connell[?], Montgomery County Kentucky Clerk, May 6, 1885, Mt. Sterling, Ky. LCD: William Watson Place – Boone Camp on Rat Creek, Ky.

Dear Sir

Yours of the 3rd Inst received... it appears from the records of this County that in the year 1808, John and William Watson, sons of William Watson, sold and conveyed to one John Fowler...a tract of land of 950 acres on Flat Creek in Montgomery County, Kentucky which land was surveyed and returned by Daniel Boone, Deputy Surveyor, by Virtue of an entry made in the name of William Watson and patented in the same of said Watson's sons – John, Mathus, and William, on November 8, 1788, from the Commonwealth of Virginia.

The land above mentioned is now, I suppose, the most Valuable in Montgomery and Bath Counties, and is owned[?] by Senator J. S. Williams, and the Hamiltons, who are the owners of the largest and finest herd of Short Horn cattle in the World.

Hoping that you in your valuable work on Kentucky history Shall do Justice to the name of the immortal Clay[?] and Eloquent Breckenridge.

I remain
Yours Very Respectfully
J. W. Priest[?] County Clerk
____ O'Connell

15C 70 Wade Hays's Statement [typescript], Los Angeles, Calif., Jan. 13, 1889.

LCD**: Col. Daniel Boone – Hunting Trip 1808 –** William Hays Jr., Los Angeles, January 18, 1889. Boone's early high opinion of California.

Wade Hays was Daniel Boone's great-grandson. The Yellowstone trip is mentioned here as taking place in the early 1800s. Next are notes from an interview that Draper conducted with Wade Hays.

Statement of Wade Hays, Esq.
A Descendant of Daniel Boone of Kentucky

My father's name was William Hays, born in Kentucky on Silver Creek in ____ [probably Madison County, Ky.] in 1784 and died in March, 1846 in Callaway County, Missouri. His [grand]mother was Daniel Boone's daughter [Susanna].

A few years after they came to Missouri, Daniel Boone and my father and others made a trip to the Yellowstone on the headwaters of the Missouri river. They were in that country about two winters after furs.

Daniel Boone had a very great idea of the Pacific coast; he described it very accurately, from some reason, I suppose, from talking with the Indians.

I had an acquaintance that came to this country years before gold was found and he told me that Boone was the cause of his coming to this coast. He started when he was quite a young man; his name was ____ Graham. He settled at Santa Cruz and lived and died there, owning considerable real estate. He and one hundred and ten men started from St. Louis and aimed for this coast. They were ten[?] years on the road and only ten of them came through and he had several narrow escapes. He was over eighty years old when he died. He told me that he never would have started had Boone not urged [him] to come, and told him that this was the finest climate in the world.

There was another circumstance of Boone's family that I never saw in print. He and one of his sons-in-law by the name of Stewart, and I believe the other man's name was Humphreys, went hunting in Kentucky, and the Indians found their camp, and wounded Stewart. He run and hid himself in an old hollow log and died there and was found several years after. His wife married again, but I do not know who. [Hannah Boone Stewart married Richard Pennington.]

My two brothers and myself came to this coast from Missouri. I left home the 3rd of April, 1849. My home was in Callaway County, and I went up to Holt County, Missouri. P. W. and Van Hays and myself made our out-fit there. Each one of us had a wagon and team and started from there on the 7th of May and landed in Sacramento valley on the 18th of October, 1849, at Lassen's ranch, then going direct to the Feather river mines. There we found Alphonso Boone, a grandson of George Boone, Jesse's son. And there were five sons with him. They had a small store. We bought him out and Alphonso Boone died there in February 1850. The sons all returned to Oregon. I do not know anything further of them. Now the old man was a brother to Governor Bogg's wife of Missouri.

There was four brothers of my father's family: Daniel, William, Boone, and Greenup. Col. Daniel Boone settled, when he first came to Missouri, 20 miles above St. Charles on the Missouri river, on the Femme Sage close to its mouth. Afterward moved up to the town of Marthasville. There was the place he died. Afterwards the relations in Kentucky came out to Missouri with a petition to move his remains to Kentucky, and there is where the mistake comes from in regard to where he died. His remains were taken to Kentucky after I would remember. I was born July 18, 1828.

Wade Hays

15C 71-72 LCD: **Boone's Hunt to Yellowstone, 1808.** Notes from Wade Hays, great-grandson of Col. Daniel Boone, and son of William Hays, Jr., Los Angeles, California, Feb. 25, 1890.

...As recollected by Mr. W. Hays as related by his father. Thinks his father was grown[?], about 24 years of age.

That Col. Daniel Boone, William Hays, Jr., Derry, the negro, several others were along. Started in the fall of the year [1808: LCD] & returned in the spring of the 2nd year following, spending one whole year & two winters hunting. Went to near the _____ of the Yellow Stone & two other streams – perhaps the Clark & Lewis rivers - & camped ___ Yellow Stone perhaps. Had good luck in hunting. Can't tell particulars. In some way got some mackinaw[?] boats – perhaps three - & started homewards with their furs &c. While the boats one evening were in the act of landing to stop &

camp for the night, Indians attacked them from both sides of the river, doing no harm – nor receiving any... went down apiece below ____ __ were attacked again. Thinks they were Snake Indians.

Then turned the boats into the river and went down, taking refuge behind a bluff at a bend of the stream, landed & camped for the night with sentinels. But they were followed no longer. Found buffalos plenty on this trip.

Recollects about Indians robbing the beaver traps of beaver & leaving the traps, hoping to repeat the procedure of appropriating the catch.

Hays left the party & returned home. Boone was taken sick, & had a dream or presentiment that he would die in a few days. Showed Derry where to bury him, under a stately tree, but he recovered.

Thinks perhaps this may have been another trip when Boone was sick, & Wm. Hays returned home.

William Hays, Jr. was born in 1784 – died in Missouri in March, 1846, aged 62 years. Was medium size, weighing about 150 pounds.

His children:

Preston W. Hays, born May 2nd, 1815. Address: Cedarville, M___ County, California – careless[?] about writing.

Sarah Benson, Portland[?], Callaway County [Mo.?], born June 18, 1819. This is her old Post Office... She is in feeble health; a daughter has written for her.

May Hays, born Jan. 3, 1821 – resides at Las Vegas, St. Magill County, New Mexico, is wealthy & cares only to make money...

Eliza Wood, born Aug. 29, 1823 – lives on southern borders of Missouri on Arkansas [River?] Post office not known.

Wade Hays, born July 1828.

Mary Dix[?], born Oct. 1, 1837, resides at Martinsburg, Audrain County [Mo.?].

[About] John Stuart: William Hays, Jr. said Stuart, after his disappearance, some or more years [later], his remains were found & ---- in a hollow log.

End

15C 73 Col. Daniel Boone visits Kentucky in 1808, And His Ghostly Visit to Henry Clay, from the Louisville Courier Journal, Aug. 31, 1884[?]

> **Aaron Burr wore his hair powdered and ending in a long queue, velvet coat and knee breeches with gold buckles, a satin waistcoat, and silk stockings...even then quite obsolete.**

In addition to the ghost story, there is an account of a grand ball held in Lexington, Kentucky to honor Aaron Burr as told by "Mrs. X." Fleeing prosecution and possible hanging after his duel with Alexander Hamilton, Burr made visits to Kentucky in May 1805 and October 1806. Between visits to Kentucky, Burr was the guest of wealthy Englishman Harman Blennerhassett in Ohio where he received some financial backing. In the fall of 1806, Burr appeared in court in Kentucky where conspiracy charges against him were successfully defended by Henry Clay, who later separated himself from defending Burr.

The Louisville Courier

The day after the address of the grand jury was given, tickets were taken about town announcing a ball at Captain Taylor's in honor of Mr. Burr on Monday. But there was a sad falling off, not from any fault of Mr. Burr, for he maintained his full dignity... A number of ladies were there... A second ball was held by ladies who refused to dance attendance upon Mr. Burr... in honor of the UNION. Among those attending was Gen. Green Clay.

Accounts of the balls are found in the National Intelligencer January 12, 1807.

Lexington Lore

"A Venerable Lady's Recollections of Very Early Days"

The oldest inhabitant of this good town is an ancient dame of high degree who was a beauty and a belle ...[so] writes a Lexington correspondent of the Chicago *Times*. She lacks but five years of completing her century, and yet is as bright and active as most women thirty years her junior.

Mrs. X. came to this locality from Virginia in the year 1800 and her experience covers the history of the Bluegrass region from that to the present time. I had the honor of a long talk with this fine old lady...and listened... to the reminiscences of Henry Clay as a young man... But most interesting of all was her gossip concerning the visit of Burr and Blennerhassett and the lovely wife of the latter, just before Burr's arrest in Lexington for treason. [Burr was arrested in Lexington, Ky. on Dec. 6, 1806.]

While these notables were here, they received marked attention from the local aristocracy, and, among other courtesies, a ball was given in their honor which was attended by my informant. "Col. Burr," she said, "was one of the most courtly and polished gentlemen I ever met, but the costume in which he appeared at the ball made him appear singular, for the dress affected by gentlemen at the time of the Revolution had even then become quite obsolete. He wore his hair powdered and ending in a long queue, velvet coat and knee breeches with gold buckles, a satin waistcoat, and silk stockings. A slender court-sword and a cocked hat completed the dress. He danced gracefully and talked beautifully."

Mrs. X remembered Mrs. Blennerhassett as a strikingly lovely person, who succeeded in charming the society of the place, and became such a favorite that Blennerhassett could scarcely have shown himself in Lexington in after years without being called to account for the heartless treatment he visited upon the poor young lady. Of that man...the old lady formed an unfavorable opinion. In fact, and in common with most of our great-grandmothers, her estimate of any foreign thing or body was not apt to be high.

"I did not take much notice of Mr. Blennerhassett," she observed. "He was like all the rest of those Frenchmen and foreigners with their exaggerated politeness, their bowings and scrapings and monkey tricks. Not only thought much of him – only for his pretty American wife, poor thing. [Margaret Blenerhassett was English.] We all felt so sorry for her afterward. You know Blennerhassett ran away from her and went to New Orleans. A few days afterward she followed him, only to find on her arrival that he had abandoned her for another woman. Shortly after the ball," continued Mrs. X., "Burr was arrested in town and taken to Richmond [Virginia] for trial. There was a great deal of excitement over the matter and we all felt a great deal of sympathy for the Colonel, because from what he told me and others, we understood that he was only proposing to revolutionize some islands in the Pacific, and entertained no designs whatever against his native country." Whatever were Burr's purposes, they little concern the present generation, who will probably only reflect that he didn't "get there," and thereby committed the one unpardonable sin in the religion of our times.

The following is a reporter's account of Burr's and Blennerhasset's plans for acquiring gunpowder. Family members said Boone was not in Kentucky in 1808, did not wear a coon-skin cap, and probably never met Henry Clay as stated in the ghost story.

Over in the mountains of Eastern Kentucky, and in a most romantic situation on the Red River, is an old mill-site now occupied by the lumber mills of an Eastern company, but for many years from the beginning of the century, the site of the first and only powder mill and forge west of the Allegheny mountains. It was at these old Red River ironworks that Burr expected to secure the powder and ball for his filibustering project, and during his visit to Lexington, he and Blennerhassett rode over on horseback to make the arrangements. I have had access to the books and papers of the old concern, and have ransacked them to find some evidence of the negotiation, but without avail. A very old man, whose father was in the employ of the works at the time, told me that the arrest of Burr created a great flurry at the forge, and it was believed that a voluminous correspondence was quietly and carefully disposed of. But these venerable day-books, journals, and ledgers tell other tales interesting enough.

[lines missing] ... on the order of Andrew Jackson, and there is little doubt that the same were properly fired at the British from behind the noble rampart of cotton bales at New Orleans.

In the day when the "old forge" was in its glory, it was a favorite stopping place of Daniel Boone. In a "blotter" for the year 1808 [illegible words] store connected with the works, there is charged to the great pioneer one York shilling for a quart of whisky and the most careful search fails to _____ any corresponding credit.

Daniel Boone, a national as well as a local hero, has been rather completely written about, but I have heard a story here concerning him, in a sort of post-mortem way, that I do not think has been before published. I had it from a distinguished member of the family associated with the incident, and, while it is strange, there are too many well authenticated statements of similar occurrences to lightly doubt the evidence.

...A cordial friendship formed a bond between the two very dissimilar men, broken only by the death of Boone... Henry Clay had become the leader of a great party; a Senator of commanding power and eloquence, a Presidential candidate, and an old man. His career was visibly drawing to a close, but yet he held death at bay pretty well for his years, and still maintained the quiet hospitalities of Ashland, where he sat in the library of that mansion one evening shortly before his last and fatal visit to Washington, surrounded by his children and grandchildren.

Back in the times when Burr wore powder and "shorts," when Andrew Jackson was a plumed knight, and people will personally remember how ill Lord Cornwallis looked on the day of his surrender, Henry Clay was a rising young lawyer – perhaps a member of the State Legislature. Coincidentally, Daniel Boone was the honored and famous pioneer, the aged father of the Commonwealth... He was already an old man, for a tree is shown near the Virginia line with an inscription by his own hand and still decipherable: "D. Boone cilled a Barr nere this tree, 1760."

A drenching thunder-shower pounded the roof of the house and rang chimes on the glass covering of the conservatory, which opened directly out of the library. The conservatory doors had been bolted and padlocked on the inside, and the house locked up for the night. While the storm was at its height, and immediately following a terrific peal of thunder, the family were startled at seeing a tall, lank figure stalk in from the conservatory. The unbidden guest was grizzled and weather-beaten, and grim of visage. On his head he wore the historic coon-skin, and his raiment was of buckskin from neck to moccasins. He carried one of the six foot rifles used a hundred years ago, and a powder-horn of huge size and antique appearance hung at his side. From cap, hair, rifle, and every part and garment of the strange visitant, water was streaming, and the first thought of those present was that he might be some wanderer from the mountains who had marched in, mountain fashion, without knocking, to escape the rain. But this did not seem a sufficient explanation, for the house was known to be carefully closed, and such costume had become extinct...

The figure walked across the room, and without a word, deposited his rifle in the corner and seated himself in a large arm-chair opposite and facing the table at which Mr. Clay had been writing. The statesman was pretty well used to the intrusions of political admirers and lion-hunters, but something about this particular intruder seemed to give him uneasiness. However, he said pleasantly "Friend, it is a wet night to be out," but the man in buckskin answered never a word, and continued to stare mournfully at his unwilling host for some seconds, after which he shouldered his rifle and departed as he had come.

Two gentlemen of the family followed instantly, but nothing was to be seen or heard of the wild huntsman. The doors were still bolted and padlocked; nothing had been disturbed, and what was even more remarkable, the dripping rifle in the corner had left not a trace of moisture on the floor where it stood, neither was the thickly-upholstered chair in which the figure rested the least bit dampened by contact with the streaming clothes of the visitor.

The circumstance made a painful impression on Mr. Clay, and after that night he was never known to refer to it; but his family knew that he had seen his old friend Daniel Boone, and that he regarded the appearance as a warning of impending death. Whether it was so intended or not, it is certain that the great political chieftain died soon afterward.

15C 74 Newspaper clipping (very dark, omitted here). LCD**: Col. Daniel Boone – visit to Henry Clay**

15C 75 LCD to Editor of the Times, Chicago, Ill. Sept. 2, 1884, and reply to a request from W. L. Storey.

Dr. Sir:

A Lexington, Kentucky correspondent of yours quite recently gave an account of Burr, Clay & Daniel Boone. Wishing to verify one statement of his, I should feel grateful if you will append his name & send it to me.

Very respectfully
Lyman C. Draper

G. B. West, 325 East High St., Lexington, Ky. Above is believed to be author of the letter.

Respectfully,
W. L. Storey

15C 76-76(2) G. B. West, New Orleans, La., Sept. 13, 1884
Letterhead: New Orleans & North Eastern Railroad Company... St. Charles Street, New Orleans. [LCD: care of] Jno. Glynn, Jr. General Agent.

This writer has Burr and Harman Blennerhassett, as well as Daniel Boone, purchasing gunpowder at Red River Iron Works which ran a gun powder mill in the early 1800s. Daniel Boone was then living in Missouri.

Dear Sir: Acknowledging your esteemed favour of 5th inst. which has been forwarded to me here:

I have seen the charge against Daniel Boone, "One quart whisky. 12 ½ cents" on the books of the Old Red River Iron works. I had occasion to go over the old books, papers, etc., when I explored and examined the property for the intending purchasers who now own it - The Kentucky Union Railway Company, Clay City, Powell County, Kentucky.

I am not certain as to the date and I related the incidents in the Chicago Times letter a year after I happened on the entry in question. I do not think that the military prefix was used, but you could find numerous instances in the archives of the time where it was not used. "Daniel Boone," or "Uncle Dan'l" I think were most commonly used than "Major" or "Colonel" and I am satisfied that he was called both and indifferently.

The Red River Iron Works occupied the western opening on the line of principal drainage, through the mountains of Eastern Kentucky making a natural line of travel from Winchester, Kentucky through Powell, Estill, Wolfe, Breathitt, Perry, & Letcher Counties to and through Pound Gap to Virginia. This route might be varied[?] by starting on a close parallel from Irvine in Estill county over a ridge to the county seat of Wolfe where the roads intersect. For many years in the early part of this century, I believe that Daniel Boone traversed this country very frequently. As the Red River Mills included a powder mill – the first, I think, west of the Alleghanys – and the only one in Kentucky at the time, I am about certain that Boone would naturally stop there for ammunition.

A short time ago an old man who was employed at the works in 1829 died at a very old age. His name was Samuel Vaughan – a truthful, reliable, and well-to-do man. He told me that his father knew Boone, and that the latter was often along that road early in the Century. Nearly all the records of the day – in fact all but the old blotter in which is the entry I mention – have disappeared. I suspect that the old powder mill and forge were expected and expecting to furnish material for the Burr-Blennerhassett Expedition, and when Burr was arrested at Lexington, it may have appeared advisable to destroy the books. However, that is mostly surmise[?]. If you would enclose the clipping of the Times article to Arthur W. Robertson, Clay City, Powell County, Ky. explaining to him the reason you have for desiring the information. He has charge of the record and would take pleasure in looking the matter up for you. Tell him that I suggest it.

As to the ghost story. I had it about ver. et. lit. from a near relation of the late Henry Clay, who sat in the family circle at the time of the occurrence. With this difference that my informant did not say that Mr. Clay at once recognized his supernatural visitant[?]. I was assured, however, that the "family" had no doubt on the subject. I was not told that Mr. Clay regarded the visit as a premonition of death. That, and the immediate recognition were added in the interests of art. I sincerely regret that I do not feel authorized to give you the name of my informant. When I return to Kentucky, I will see if I can obtain permission. With the exceptions noted, the first story is related as it came to me. I believe that the occurrence took place substantially as stated. And if the ghost wasn't Daniel Boone, his identification will be difficult.

With respect
Truly Yours
G. B. West

Thanks for your book which hasn't yet reached me.

15C 77 J. T. Keller, Dec. 20, 1884. Letterhead: Office of the Kentucky Union Railway Company... Clay City, Powell County, Ky.

... Mr. Robertson now lives in Canada. I have searched the old records you speak of and have been unable to find mention of Daniel Boone...

15C 78-78(1) Goldsmith Bernard West, Birmingham, Ala., Aug 12, 1885. Letterhead: Land Department, Vicksburg, Shreveport & Pacific Railroad, and Vicksburg & Meridian Railroad.

My dear sir:

Your esteemed favour of 8th wish [sic] has been forwarded to me from New Orleans and is just at hand. I regret that I cannot throw any additional light on the whisky for which I am afraid that "General Boone, backwoodsman of Kentucky" still owes 12 ½ cents to the Red River Iron Works. While in charge of that property I called the attention of one of his descendants to the matter, but the latter stated that the family knew nothing of it. At the same time, rather than to have that York shilling's worth of whiskey hanging over the reputation of his illustrious ancestor, the senator[?] made what amends he could in the way of conviviality. Following long established precedent, although an officer of the corporation to which the debt was owing, I did not turn my share of the conviviality over to the company. This was not perhaps, honest, but it was customary. I have no idea what could have become of the old blotter, which I saw last in the spring of 1883. It contained entries as far back as 1807 or 1808. I think it might be well for you to write to Hon. John R. Proctor, State Geologist, Frankfort, Ky., who is curious in the legendary lore of this state & might be able to put you on the track of some interesting date or tradition of Boone's time and of his adventure. x. x. x.

As to the ghost story, I repeat in confidence that I related it, as nearly as I could remember, as I heard it from Mrs. James D. Clay, relict of Hon. J. D. Clay, second son of Henry Clay and for long years the lady of Ashland. Mrs. Clay has had many sorrows! Shortly after I printed the story in the Chicago Times, her eldest son Henry was shot and killed. Generally the world has gone hard with her and I should hesitate to trouble her on the matter. But I think you could sift the story by addressing Col. Henry Clay McDowell, Lexington, Kentucky, the present proprietor of Ashland, enclosing a clipping from the Times, explaining my reluctance to call Mrs. Clay's attention to it, and asking him to find out from her how far the published story agrees with the facts. Mr. George Clay once called my attention to some unimportant inaccuracy in the narrative, but what it was I do not now remember. I received the volume you refer to and thought I had thanked you for it. I do so now at any rate and expressing my pleasure in again hear from you, remain

With respect,
Truly Yours,
Goldsmith Bernard West

15C 79 LCD. **Boone 1809[?]** A memo Dictated by the late Maj. Joseph McCormick, then of Manitowoe, several years ago, says, "He saw Col. Daniel Boone in

Louisville in March, 1809; & in June following, he again saw him at Charette, at his son-in-law's [Flanders Callaway's], & went out a few days hunting with him."

Hon. David Meriwether, Jefferson County, Kentucky, states that he saw Col. Boone about this time in Jefferson County.

James Bradley, descendant[?] of Samuel Boone (Daniel Boone's brother) born in Fayette County, Kentucky in 1810, says Col. Boone returned to Kentucky after going to Missouri.

1810 – petition to Congress for Missouri lands &c.
1813 – Confirmation of Spanish Grant

This grant, not confirmed in 1806 - & this explains the following in Vincent's Dictionary[?] of Biography: "His estates seized in 1805, restored in 1814."

Dr. Saugrain: See Trip 1860, viii. 147. (goes west in 1787).

15C 80 W. D. Hixson, March 12, 1991, Maysville, Ky. LCD**: Boone Revisiting Kentucky**. Boone 1810.

I have paid my debts...and no one will say Boone was a dishonest man.

Your letter concerning Daniel Boone's visit received and I regret that I cannot give a definite answer. Our Library is being improved and my papers are in such a position that I can not get at them. I have just examined the records of our courts (Circuit & County) and I can find no depositions of Boone taken here later than 1799. There are several taken after that date in Missouri... Traditions in the family in Missouri give it that Boone came to Kentucky to pay his debts.

In the U. S. Biographical Dictionary is a sketch of Col. Boone which says – page 838 – as follows:

"During his continuance in Office he made enough money by hunting and trapping to pay off every debt he owed in Kentucky, for which purpose he made a visit to his old house, and returned with fifty cents, saying, "Now I am willing to die. I am relieved of a burden that has long oppressed me. I have paid my debts and no one will say when I am gone, 'Boone was a dishonest man – I am perfectly willing to die.'"

Hartley in his life of Boone quoting from Audubon gives an account of Boone's visit to Kentucky to prove a corner to a large Survey.

Yours in haste
W. D. Hixson

15C 81 LCD: **Col. Daniel Boone – 1810**
His folks dissuaded him from hunting – he visits a camp of Indians – Shane's Historical Collections, xiii, 99. This visiting an Indian camp supposed to be _____, must have been shortly after the fight in which W. T. Cole & others shared in this year.

The Cole fight: Western Annals; Col. N. Boone's Notes
Shepherd's History _____, 46

15C 82-82(6) John Gibson, Sr *(1778 – 1869),* statement on Cole's Defeat of 1810. LCD: Erecting Forts in Missouri.

**I plunged my horse into the Creek.
I held to my gun and horse and he
came up snorting. The Indians
Shooting at me all the while.**

I, John Gibson, Senour, was Born in North Carolina, moved to South Carolina at 2 years old, raised there until I was Seventeen years old. am sory[?] for

Being raised in So Pisoned a place. I then came to Tennessee, Stayed there 6 years, then came to Missouri.

In the year the [Indians: LCD] commenced shocking [outrages: LCD] and murdering in Missouri. They murdered Patton, Smith, Gooch, and William Cole and others. Moredock & Stephen Cole escaped.

In 1811, Nathan Boone raised a Company of Rangers for 12 months. We went into Building forts in Different places over the Country to keep the Indians from murdering our helpless women and Children. We built Fort Howard, 17 miles from St. Charles; then we Built Cahoga, then we built Buffalo, then Fort mason, then we built fort Madison 24 miles above the mouth of Desmoines river; then we built _____ Deshain and built forts over the Country, We built Stouts fort; we built one at Troy, then crossed over the Missouri river to Bellfontain below St. Charles, then fortified at St. Charles; then came to Pinkney, then we built a fort at Charette Village; then came to Louter Island and built Fort Clenison; then up to Cole San Dessein, built a fort there; then we went up to Chariton Village and built a fort there; from there to Boon's Lick and built Coopers fort then to the Council Bluffs; then we returned back to St. Charles. Commenced building forts out in the country _____ the Missouri River. We built Pond fort, then we built Kennedy's fort on ____ Creek. We finished all those Garrisons in the year 1812 and had our women and children out of danger of the wild Savages.

Gibson's Escape

After building forts &c I went on an express tour in...1814 to Kennedy's Fort, cros'd out of Masas Creek, went up Masas Creek a mile and a half... my horse Began to snort and ____ I herd something like a Calf Blate [bleat]. I thought it was Scot and Carson that was to have went with me but they did not meet me. I turned my head and saw ____ some Indians. I put spurs to my horse. The Indians fired on me. My horse being feared went ____ at Speed. I come to a Creek. My horse being Feard so Badly leeped the creek clear. After crossing the Creek I looked before me and saw the Indians with there guns presented at me. I was surrounded by the Indians in a ____ of the Bluff.

I being acquainted with the Cituation of the ground, I rode to a low place in the Bluff. I found a perpendicular Cliff of some 3 feet. My horse being Scard So badly appeared willing to Scale the perpendicular Cliff. I gave him the spur and while he went up all but his hinder feet in struggling to get his hind feet up he threw one of his feet around a hickory shrub and scaled the cliff, they firing on me all the time. I was trying to rescue myself from them. I run my horse to the road leading from Louter Island to Camp branch. After I got into the aforesaid road, I saw the Indians in front of me. I turnd to the right towards lost creek. I saw none[?] of the Indians. I went up a ridge from lost Creek. I came to a trail that led out to Boon's lick road to the hickory grove there. I crossed the road and went to Kennedy's Fort. I rested... myself and my horse while delivered my Express [message] as commanding officer and received another. I was behind my time but took good care not to travel the same road back. I came by the way of McDermits mill. I got back to fort Clemson about daylight. I found the rangers prepared to start to hunt me. Carson and Scott had been to hunt me, and had returned and reported me killed. The Indians Came across to Sharot Vilage and waylayed Robert Ramsey's house about daylight, and murdered him and all his family except two little Children who hid themselves from the Savages in a cellar.

As the Indians made there retreat from there I was going down the Boon's lick road to St. Louis. I saw the Indians Crosing the road before me. I put spurs to my horse after they raised the yell and waived my hand back of me which was a token of more troops. They run hard and I crowded them as close as I dared to. One of them was giving out behind the rest. I got almost close enough to have shot him... I Scampered away out of Shooting distance of them. I went [to] Kennedy's fort, informed the rangers of a case and they put after them and followed to the Mississippi but did not overtake them.

In the Spring of thirteen [1813] the indians came across into an Island, about five hundred of them, made themselves bark Canoes, cross'd the river, pass'd up Bobs creek out to the Bluff, came down the bluff opicite fort Howard, there campt.

Seven of our rangers at Burnes farm kill'd and scalp'd them in plain view of the fort. The younger Daniel Boone was in Command at the fort; the officers held a council to see what should be done, then called on me for my opinion in the matter. I told them we had Better find where the indians cros'd and try and ascertain how many there was of the Indians. they asked me how we could find out how many there was. I told them we would go and see how many canoes they had. My spy mate would go with me. We would go ___ through the tall grass in the prairie. Struck the Mississippi below where the Indians had crossed. We crept up through the grass and willows to where the Indians had left ther Canoes. We spied about until we found there were no indians at the canoes. We examined them as to size. They had dry logs tied to each side of ther Canoes so they would not turn over or sink. I supposed ther was a sufficiency of room in those Canoes for five or seven hundred Indians to cross the river in. we went back and reported.

Then the question was whether we should give them battle or not. I told them that if 300 men would turn out we would give them battle, that we could whip them. Consequently, there was a call for 300 men. The number turned out immediately. We then elected Lieutenant Perkins as Commander. He counciled me on the matter. I told him that we would have to get at the Indians...in the tall grass. We got into the tall grass and marched into the Indians rear. We Closed upon them and gave them Battle. We faught them say from eleven o'clock until night. They harbored in sink holes. We then sent and got a keg of powder and aimed to move the battery but the indians were posted in so many places we could not annoy them much. They killed our leader and four others. We left them and went to fort Howard. We returned next morning to the Battleground. We found them all gone. They left ther dead on the Battleground. We found our leader and five others dead and Scalped. We took the trail of the yellow boys. We found 4 dead and wounded, Scalped all of them between the Battle ground and ther Canoes. One of those wounded Indians shot at me, shot through my hat above my head.

Sink Hole Battle – Ensign Ramsey's Fight – Callahan Wounded

We Returned to the Battle ground and found 86 more dead on the Battle ground. We took the Scalps of their heads. Shortly after this Battle the Indians returned and murdered Maxey's family, threw two of Maxeys Children into a boiling kettle of water. Then we started out, some twelve or fifteen of us. We found no Indians and was returning home and at a place called the Bushey narrows, the Indians fired on us, done no damage only to Shoot a man by the name of Foreman[?] through the heel. We faught them 3 miles on a retreat. We then met a detachment of four rangers. We then turned ...on the Indians and killed the last Indians in that crowd. Shortly after this some

Sauk Indians reported to us that there was 12 or 15 kickapoes Indians below the mouth [of] two rivers. Ensign Ramsey made a call for volunteers and some 20 or more men turned very quick. We started and marched to the place, made a Sauk indian guard Show us the place. When we got there we found the Indians in the Bush. We discovered the Indians and took some large logs for Brest works and made reddy and fired at a word and killed from 15 to 20 indians the first fire. The indians returned the fire and we retreated and so did the indins, leaving all ther dead on the Battle ground. We left our dead on the Battle ground. ___ we went out to next day and gathered up our brave boys. Brought them to the fort, buried the dead and took leave of the wounded.

In 1814 the Indians made a rade across or down the Missouri river to Best's plantation, wounded Calahan, come very near giting Best. They robbed Best's house of whatever they could have or carry away.

Sarshall Cooper. Joyce Campbell Collection

LCD: Callaway's Defeat – 1815

The next rade the Indians made was at Cooper's fort and Boon's Lick. Killed Col. Sashel [Sarshel] Cooper and many others. Stole a great amount of property and committed many Depredations. In 1815 the Indians made a raid into Best[?] Bottom and Stole from 70 to 100 head of horses. Calahan[?] being out on Louter Creek at his far

Seen the Indians going away with those horses, came in to fort Clemson and reported and made a call for Volunteers and got 40 or

Cooper's Fort.
Stephanie Brunda White drawing
https://www.coopercountyhistoricalsociety.org/forts

more. Directly James Callaway was appointed to Command the volunteers. Capt. Daniel Boon told Callaway to follow me. We left Louter Island and went up Massas Creek. Struck the Boons lick road where Jones now lives. There we took the Devide between the warters [sic] of Missouri and Mississippi, went up the devide 25 or thirty miles above Louter Lick. I Being foremost Discovered the horses in a grove of timber that ___ up to the prairie. I fell back and raised a flag as a Signal for the troops to advance. The officers called for a council and called myself and Keetly in to the council. We decided to march to the horses in single file and form a hollow square around the horses. I on the lead on the right with ensign Riggs[?]. Callaway marched to the Left with Keetly. We marched until we met around the horses. Saw no sign of any Indians. We Close up to horses in a hollow Square and found no

Indians. the Belled horses was tied up and some hobbled with hickory Bark. Blankets and equipment hung upon the Bush. We Discovered from the Sign that there had been from 200 to 300 indians about there. we Started back with the horses and goods and Chattles. Callaway wanted me to return on the Indian trail. Callaway's remark was "d___n the indians, they all gone to h__ll."

I start on the trail and after traveling some distance on the trail they had scattered out...I could see where one indian had Come into the trail. I could see where Different trails would Come into the road and then out again. Louter Creek was rising. We cross'd Louter Creek before it rose to Swiming water. After crossing Louter Creek I Discovered the Indian trail come in frequently. I halted and reported to Callaway. His reply was as before "d___n the Indians, they were gone to h__". Ensign Riggs, John Gibson, a cousin of mine and myself and Capt. Ramsey, ensign Riggs, old Capt. Ramsey John Gibson, Junior and some twenty others made ther way to the fort. We traveled on and I saw plenty of indian Sign and I pervaild to leave the trail. He would not agree to my proposition. We marched on across the prairie fork of Louter Creek about the time we all got across we had a Bluff on the south. The Indians was form'd on the west, the prairie fork on the north main Louter on the east and very high water[?] at that. We then had but only one gap to make our escape out of the Snar[e]. The indians fired on us from the ___, perhaps from 300 of them. They shot in among us where there was perhaps some 100 horses and from 20 to 30 men, killing nearly all the horses and all but men except my self and 3 others. I was wounded in the leg and my horse shot from under me. I mounted McDerment's horse, made for main Louter, passed by Callaway. He was wounded in two different places. He was making to the Creek. He called on me for help. I told him that I could not help him. He reach'd the Creek as I passed him, threw his gun into the Creek and Jump'd in himself. The Indians shot one ball, hit him in the back of the head and killed him. I put spurs to my horse and made for main Louter. Soon as I came to the Creek, I plunged my horse into the Creek. My horse, I thought, went down into the water 10 or fifteen feet. I held to my gun and horse and he came up snorting. I swam my horse to the eastern bank of the Creek, tangled in some willows. The Indians Shooting at me all the while. My horse being a horse of great power made his way out and I made my way to fort Climpson. I made my way through the hills and got into fort Climpson that night.

Next day made up a Company and went back to Louter to Bury our brave boys that the Indians had killed. Awful it was to behold the sight. We found the men Sculped, there heads cut off, stuck up on poles and ther entrails took out and stuck up on other poles, the varmints and fowls of the air had devoured them very much. We dug holes and laid them away the Best we could, laid logs over them. Then we Left.

1813. We had troops stationed at Prairie de Chien. The British came with the aid of the indians, came to the narrows & place between the Lakes and the Mississippi. The British Drew the keel boats out of the river on rollers, then cannon in them and roled them into the Mississippi, came down the Mississippi and attacted our soldiers at Prairie Du Chien. We faught them some days until our provisions and ammunition gave out. Our Commander, as brave a man as ever lived, was forced to surrender to the British. I was in a day and a half [to] travel with provisions and ammunition. Had [I] have got there in time, our troops would not have surrendered to the British. On getting ___ news I hastened back to St. Louis.

15C 83 John Gibson to Judge Henderson, June 6, 1868.

Judge Henderson –

If you are done with the manuscript I loaned you about the war of 1812-1815, I beg you will let Mr. Lyman C. Draper, at whose suggestion & for whose use I prepared it – have it.

John Gibson

15C 84-84(2) Report of the Committee, 1810, The Petition of Daniel Boone. Printed by order of the Senate of the United States. Italics are as in the original.

> **He possesses not one acre of that immeasurable territory which he so well defended.**

...at a period antecedent to the revolutionary war, Daniel Boon, the petitioner, possessing an ardent desire for the exploration of the (then) western wilderness of the United states, after traversing a length of mountainous and uninhabited country, discovered, and with a few bold and enterprising fellows, established, with a perilous hardihood, the first settlement of civilized population in the (now) state of Kentucky. That in maintaining the possession of that country until the peace of 1783, he experienced all the vicissitudes of a war with enemies the most daring, insidious and cruel, and which were aided by Canadians from the British provinces of upper Canada; and that during that long contest, he lost several children by the hands of the savages. That it appears to the committee, that although the petitioner was not *officially employed* by the government of the

United States, yet that he was *actually engaged* against their enemies, through the whole of the war of the revolution. ...he eminently contributed to the early march of the American western population...your petitioner is old, infirm, and though dependent on agriculture, by adverse and unpropitious circumstances, possesses not one acre of that immeasurable territory which he so well defended. The petitioner disclaiming all idea of a *demand* upon the justice of his country, yet requests as a grateful benevolence, that Congress would grant him some reasonable portion of land in the territory of Louisiana. The committee upon the whole circumstances of the merit and situation of the petitioner, beg leave to report the bill without amendment.

15C 85-85(1) The petition of Daniel Boone to the Honorable Senators and Representatives ... of the United States. Signed by Daniel Boone.

LCD: Copied from original manuscript for Charles H. Morse by Mrs. B. Boyd, Maysville, Ky. The second page of this document is in a different and less accurate hand-writing.

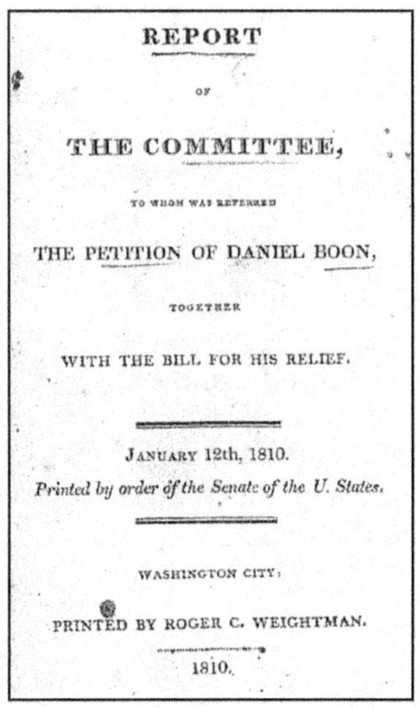

REPORT

OF

THE COMMITTEE,

TO WHOM WAS REFERRED

THE PETITION OF DANIEL BOON,

TOGETHER

WITH THE BILL FOR HIS RELIEF.

JANUARY 12th, 1810.

Printed by order of the Senate of the U. States.

WASHINGTON CITY:

PRINTED BY ROGER C. WEIGHTMAN.

1810.

Daniel Boone Petition, 1810
DM 15C 85

The petition of Daniel Boone, at present an inhabitant of the Missouri Territory, respectfully states

That your petitioner impelled by an ardent desire to explore the country lying West of the Alleghany Mountains, at a period when it was untrodden by civilized man, undertook at his own risque to search the then wilds of America... the result of his searches has been the settlement of the vast and fertile country watered by the Mississippi and Ohio. Your petitioner, not considering the formal sanction of his Government necessary, undertook & performed this task, replete with interesting consequences, without pomp or parade. But he conceives that his claim to the attention of his country is not diminished, by his having, at his own expense and risque, unseen & unknown, accomplished an object... for which Government has generously remunerated those engaged.

Your petitioner respectfully states that he once more approaches the Legislative body of his Country, with a hope they will grant him some small ___ of the millions of acres over which his discoveries have extended – and he makes this request from a full conviction of its justice... he has in common with society, a numerous family for whose welfare he feels an interest.

He refers your Honorable body to the fate of his efforts to obtain some remuneration from your predecessors in office...

Your petitioner, conscious of having contributed extensively to the benefit of his country, relies with confidence on that sense of right which governs your councils...

Your petitioner acknowledges that in the ardor of discovery, he has been inattentive to the means of acquiring property; and his numerous family have reason to lament that his own and their interest [had] not been more consulted... And he states...that the man who has opened the way to millions of his fellow men, has not even a space to deposit the remains of a body, almost exhausted with age, exposure and exertion. For as singular has been his fate, that although he has the highest evidences of approbation and confidence of the Spanish Government during their possession of Louisiana, and has made an actual settlement on the

Missouri river, yet such is the construction...he has acquired no right of soil.

Your petitioner concludes with a hope that the United States will display to the world, that they appreciate important and beneficial exertions of individuals, although they have been performed without ostentation.

Danl Boone

15C 86 and unnumbered page following
LCD**: Daniel Boone, 1810-1811-1812**

1811 March – Lately returned from a hunt with nearly sixty beaver skins: Bradbury's Travels, 16.

In Col. Nathan Boone's notes, there is nothing to indicate such a hunt, & such success.

1810 History of Howard & Cooper Counties, Missouri, p. 807 shows Boone in winter 1810 (1809-1810) on hunt, caught two beavers.
1810 Mr. Steele visits Boone – his going to an Indian encampment, Shane's Notes, vol. viii, p. 99
Mr. Peck in American Pioneer, I, 243, says Boone did not hunt any for ten years before his death. This is perhaps true so far as any extended hunt was concerned.

Maj. John Gibson. Wisc. Historical Society

1812 Kentucky Legislature Resolves – Trip 1860, viii, 148 &c.

15C 87 Maj. John Gibson interview, June 5-6, 1868 near Portland, Callaway County, Mo. LCD: Col. Daniel Boone

Notes of conversations with Maj. John Gibson...)

In these notes, as well as in the narrative immediately succeeding them written by Maj. Gibson himself, considerable allowance must be made from his exaggerations of numbers engaged in Indian fights, & numbers killed & wounded – perhaps not in all cases. He seemed truthful – yet I see allowances should be made. Compare notes of other pioneers in Notebooks of Trip in Missouri in 1868, & Col. Nathan Boone's Notes – Col. John Chew's in 2nd vol. Wisconsin Historical Collections - & Extracts in Manuscript Volume from the Missouri Gazette &c, 1812-1815. Also Gen. H. Dodge's Notes in this volume.

Maj. Gibson sustains a good reputation where known in Missouri: Hon. James S. Henderson of Fulton, Mo., spoke to me highly of him. LCD.

15C 88 Judge James S. Henderson, Fulton, Mo., Sept. 2, 1869. LCD: Death of Maj. Gibson

Judge James S. Henderson, of Fulton, Mo., under date Sept. 2d, 1869, writes: "Maj. John Gibson died suddenly May 24, 1869. Seven months before his death, he left with me his ambrotype to be forwarded to you, and [it was] overlooked. I now enclose it, with a short letter from the Major. Hope you will give his picture a place in your book. He was a man of substance, and of decided hospitality at his house, and did his country, during the war of 1812, good service."

15C89 John Gibson to James Henderson, Refor[?] Callaway County, Mo., July 30, 1868

Mr. James Henderson
Dear Sir

Enclosed you will find my Ambrotyp [sic]. I would have sent it sooner But could not get it taken. I want you to forward as soon as possible for I [have] not the address. Mr. Henderson if you think it necessary to have my name and age on the Ambrotype you can forward that also.

I was born April the 12th 1778. My native State is North Carolina. Forward this to Mr. Draper as soon as possible and you will oblige your friend

Yours &c
John Gibson

15C 90 LCD: **Daniel Boone, 1813**
Boone's land claim &c - trip 1860, viii, 150 &c. His settlement partially destroyed during the war: Western Spy, Cincinnati, July 5, 1816. Niles Register x, 261

15C 91-92 LCD: **Sink-Hole Battle, 1813.**

"St. Louis, May 27, 1815. Col. Russell has politely favored me with the ____ letters of Capt. Music, and Lieut. Gray of the Rangers, which give information that on Wednesday last (the 24th) a party of our men was attacked near Fort Howard by about 50 Indians. That the troops from the fort under Capt. Craig immediately repaired to the scene of action and engaged the Indians, that shortly after Capt. Music joined in the affair and a warm battle ensued. The numbers were about equal, but before the affair closed, a party of the Indians entrenched themselves in a Sink-hole, and perfectly secured themselves from the powerful exertions of our troops. At dusk the Rangers retired, and next morning found 5 Indians killed on the ground, and the appearance of many more having been killed. The action lasted a considerable time. We lost Capt. Craig, Lieut. Spears & 5 men killed – four wounded & one missing.

"Fort Howard is within a few miles of C__ _ ___.

"The commanding officer of this district has expressed his entire Satisfaction with the gallant conduct of both officers and men in the above affair. The Rangers, although they have received much censure, have generally acted well.

Capt. Whitesides (of Illinois) with a company of mounted military will cross the Mississippi today, destined for the neighborhood of Fort Howard."

St. Louis, Mo., June 3, 1815.

The Indians must have suffered considerably in their late attack on the Rangers near Fort Howard. Two more dead Indians have been discerned some distance from the battle ground, and a large quantity of blood marked their retreat to their canoes. Indeed, I think the Rangers behaved extremely well in this affair...Colonels Craig and Spears would have done better in combat with regular troops. They evinced such a contempt of danger and death that they despised the devious mode of Indian warfare. I am informed Lieut. Spears' family are by no means opulent. His widow should receive his pay without delay. x x x

Robert Ramsey still lives, & there are hopes of his recovery. Charleston, South Carolina City Gazette, July 6, 1815

15C 93 Obituary for Mrs. Mary Ester Marion, widow of Gen. Marion, 1815

Mrs. Mary Ester Marion, relict of the late Gen. [Francis] Marion, died at Pineville, St. Stephen's Parish, South Carolina, July 26, 1815, in her 77th year. She was buried near the grave of her illustrious husband, a lady of strong mind, benevolent & kind & conciliating.

City Gazette, Charleston, Aug. 9, 1815.

15C 94-94(17), 95 "Kentucky Scenery & Customs – 1813." From the Bardstown, Kentucky Repository. At the end: from Niles Register, Supplement, vol. 5, p. 177-180, Sept. 1813 to March 1814.

The Bardstown Repository was published from about 1812 to the 1820s. This article was copied from it by LCD. The author, name unknown, gave long descriptions of unsettled areas of central Kentucky. Much is omitted here, but the author's description of his visit to Bullitt's Lick (second paragraph) is included with the description of the buffalo and other animals' use of the Lick for their "nutriment" as the writer stated. He mentioned the steamboat as an "important invention." Draper wrote a second note mentioning Niles' Register perhaps indicating that the article was published again.

A few days since to relieve the ennui of close study, I determined on taking a tour through the adjoining county, which lies [near] Bardstown. A partial survey of an immense range of hills, which are called knobs, and of the face of the country which lies immediately above them, were among the motive that prompted me in this excursion. A thousand objects fell under my eyes to interest the votanist [sic] of natural curiosities, and excite the most grateful sensations in a heart that delights in contemplating majestic eminences and extensive plains...

The route I pursued led through the plain in which Bullit's Old Lick is situated. I have head a variety of interesting anecdotes relative to the enterprises of early adventurers in the country of which this place was the scene, when every species of wild animal known in this State, the rude and bloody savage, and civilized men, formed, as it were, but one Society!

...This Lick was the great point of concentration of the buffalo, the elk, the deer, and the interesting variety of animals that resort to Salt Springs as one great source of their nutriment and health.

... The joy of the buffalo at this spot was evidently manifested by the ceremony of rolling, and a thousand awkward gambols, that at once contributed to the playful frolics of an almost unnumerable herd... The ground about the Lick exhibits a luxurious and interesting appearance. The ground is very uneven...I supposed, from the licking of the buffalos &c, for some thousand years past.

...the tall oak which adorned the neighboring hills, and covered the deep plain, has been wrested from the forest, and made subservient to the purposes of public utility... pines under the destructive influence of human art, for now, here and there, is only to be seen a tall and solitary pine, that nods to every gale, mingles its sorrows with every passing breeze, and seems to mourn over this barren waste, stript of its gay attire...

...The green foliage of nature blends with the cerulean blue, and forms a spectacle at once brilliant and sublime...

If I recollect right, philosophic mention has been made of these matters by the celebrated Volney*, who travelled through the Western country some years since. He suggests that the whole tract of country which lies above this range of mountains, as high up as Pittsburgh, and bordering Lake Erie, was once the bed of an immense lake. He supposes that the summit of the hills...was sufficiently high and by some dreadful throe of nature, this dam or barrier was sent to its foundation, and a chasm produced through which the waters of the lake were discharged.

In this escape of the waters they...formed the bed of the river now called Ohio....The introduction and employment of steam boats will much facilitate the intercourse between New Orleans and the different States and Territories that border on the Ohio, Mississippi, and their tributary streams. This important invention will exert the happiest influence on their destiny, by contributing to their prosperity, and rapidly accelerating their advance to a state of solid glory.

*French philosopher who visited America in the late 1790's.

15C 96-96(1), 97-97(2) John Gibson's account of the Peoria Expedition of 1813 sent to James L. Henderson, near Portland, Callaway County, Missouri. Undated.

Black Hawk was in full blast fighting for his rights.

Troops, ammunition, Provisions, &c. We had an interview of the troops and agreed to meet at Peora on a certain day. The boats run up to draw the attention of the fort until the Land troops Could march up and form a hollow Square on the fort. The boats opened there artillery on the Indians. They fought a while until they found that they were in a bad ____. They then aimed to make the retreat. They came in Plattoons and aimed to break our lines ___ up the Illinois river. We were formed four men deep. we were a little too strong for the yellow boys, [they] fought Despuratly but we reinforced and got our line 10 men deep. We then stood our ground and mowed the red skins down as they advanced until no more would come. We then advanced and Closed up on the town[?] and found no indians except a parcel of helpless women and Children. Some of our boys killed some of the women and Children. I road as quick as I could to General Howard and told what was going on. He requested me to see the other officers and go and put a stop to killing the women and Children, which I done as quick as I Could. I Saved 466 women and Children. We then had possession of the Indian fort.

Then we commenced building a fort and built a strong fort. We hauled timber across the Illinois river Bottom, set our pickets double and filled between the pickets with rock. Pickets 14 feet high. Then we fortified the Block houses in a regular form. Then the Indian women and Children had to be taken care of. They [were] put on a boat and gave me charge of them. I started with them to St. Louis. A Change of Diet gave the Indians the diarrhea. I had to bury several of them in a watery grave between the fort and St. Louis.

After getting to St. Louis we had a Change of Diet. The Indians got well. Put them in a boat and gave me a ___ to take them [to] Prairie Du Chien and exchanged them for our Prisoner boys that the British had in their possession. I got 466 of our Prisoners in exchange for 466 Indian women and Children. Then I returned to St. Louis which put an end to the Peora campaign.

Black Hawk War

Black Hawk was in full blast fighting for his rights.

In 1832 the Indians became troublesome on the Desmoines River. Capt. John Jameson, Robert Read and myself raised a Company of 100 Volunteers, went to Columbia and was mustered into service under Col. Conyer. We marched with Capt. Hickman's Company to the Desmoines river, struck the Desmoines river at the point of a bluff near the Mississippi river. There we Commenced building a Large fort. Part of the troops building the fort and [part] reconnoitering around up the Desmoines river. We found no Sign of any Indians. we returned to Fort Pike, recruited and started out again, made a tour up as high as the head of Shariton river, returned back Down the Desmoines river to fort Pike. Saw no Indians or any sign of them except those on the north side of Desmoines river. The river is not wide at that point. We could see into the Indian houses. One man had more large hogs than any one man I ever saw. One man who Liv'd on the Bank of the river told us that he had a hundred and fifty head of large hogs. Branham and myself went over one day. We counted Sixty large hogs lying around a wallow.

Black Hawk
Charles Bird King painting c. 1837
Library of Congress

Black Hawk was in full blast fighting for his rights at the mouth of rock river. The volunteers whip'd him out, run him up a willow tree and took him Prisoner. Carried him to St. Louis and ship'd him all around the sea Coast of the United States to Show him the Strength of the United states in full when the war was over. They turned him loose and he went home.

Nathan Boone's Defeat, 1813

Nathan Boone, myself, White & Gilbert – we took 13 men and there horses to go [on] horse back so far as we thought we could be safe in so doing. We crossed the river at Capogia [Cap Du gray? – LCD]. Traveled on the head waters of Big Sandy. I being before, Discovered too many Mockansan tracks. I advised Boon to Send our 13 men and there horses Back. Boon decided that he would go down on the waters of big Sandy and strike Camp for the night. The Indians, I suppose, had been following us for two days. About midnight that night the Indians advanced, Closeing close up to White, one of the Sentinals. White fired on them. At the light of his gun the Indians fired perhaps upwards of 100 guns at him, shooting Boath of his thumbs of his hands and the Stock of his gun. They turned ther guns on our encampment but they overshot us. Of Course they did not do so much damage. We retreated as much as possible and all made our escape except one. He was so scard that he lay still; his name was John Robinson. They took him Prisoner, took him down to the Bank of the Creek. They Paddled his feet [to prevent him from running away], put ther kind of Dress on him and put one indian as a guard over him. Robinson Discovered the Indians go to Sleep. He Slipt off on his hands and nees into the Creek and swam off. He did not get fair [far] until the indian awoke and the Indians raised the alarm, some crashing[?] of Bush with the indians. He swam the river and Cleared himself of the Indians. he then traveled 7[?] days and nights living on Lizards, Bugs and any thing he could lay his hands on. Landed at Postash 11 miles below St. Charles without Clothes on his back or much Skin.

We then made our retreat the best we Could. Keetly and myself made our retreat for home. We turned out of camp and made a clear retreat. We traveled the first night all night. Next morning the

Indians fired on us all around us. I Concluded that I would git into a cavern in the rocks. We lay all day. Keetly and my Self Could have killed 18 Indians, but dare not fire our guns. Night Come and we traveled all night. Next morning ther was not much fireing. Next night we traveled all night. Next day we found that we Could travel in more Safety. We traveled on to Mississippi. There I tied Som Dry logs together and floated Down the river until daylight. Next morning, Shortly after day light, we Discovered several Canoes full of Indians in pursuit of us. I observed to Keatly that I would swim out with the raft as quick as I could. I done so and by the time I got to Shore or thereabouts, the Indians was Close after us. We made for the Bluff. We reached the Bluff before the Indians got in Shooting distance of us. We then Come on to a ridge and traveled about 4 miles. The Indians Could not trail us so well on that ridge. We were then tired, almost down and come into the head of a ravine, got behind a log. The Indians Came along not fair [far] from us without Discovering us. We lay still until night. Next morning we went to the river, tied some more logs together, got on them and floated down to Fort mason, home once more. The balance of Company Came in by small numbers until all was home once more except Roberson, who came in afterwards. Boone, Keatly, and myself went and reviewed the situation of the Indian town, Peora, then returned and reported the Strength and cituation of Peora. We then decided that we would go that fall and Storm Peora. The troups all were fitted out. Seven Keel Boats with ammunition, provision and apparatuses of 1500 troops on land. The seven boats spoken of above loaded with... [does not continue]

15C 97(2) LCD: **Black Hawk & Keokuck**

Black Hawk, half Brother Keokuck, had Seven hundred Indians drilling them at flint hill, 60 miles north of fort Pike. We supposed they were for the benefit of Black Hauck. They made no attack on us at all. We put the women and Children all in the fort and come home.

These I will Correct - an error: Campbell's Boat expedition was the beginning of the expedition for prairie Du Chien. You will please add this at the head of the Prairie Du Chien Campaign.

James L. Henderson: if you see any errors or date or otherwise, please Correct them to the Best of your knowledge or send me word and I will correct them.

Yours Respecfully
John Gibson

15C 98 LCD: **John Gibson's account of Campbell's Defeat near Des Moines River, 1813**

1813 we started to build a fort up the Mississippi river at Prairie Du Chien under Command of Maj. Campbell. Got near the mouth of Desmoines river. Something got rong with one of our Boats. The Boats were all stoped and ankered near the Shore. The Indians Came on us and fired [on] us and such a Surprise that we Could not do any thing in defense. They took our boat which had our ammunition on board. The Indians kill'd and wounded many more. We cut Cables and made our way to St. Louis. They shot Campbell through the abdomen; the rangers would have been glad he had been shot in the head for Casting anker so near Shore so as to give the Indians the advantage of us.

15C 99-99(3) Gen. Henry Dodge Interview. Notes of Gen. Henry Dodge, June 29th, 1855 at Madison

Gen. Dodge will please return this sheet, when read & corrected.

There had been considerable mischief done by the Indians at the Boone's Lick settlements where, among others, a man who was a potter by trade was killed. Being the only person of that trade in that region, his loss was seriously felt. The settlement was too weak to strike any effectual blow in turn.

Brig. Gen. Henry Dodge, then of St. Genevieve, who had been by President Madison appointed the successor of Gen. William Clark in command of the militia when the latter was made governor of Missouri Territory. Waived his rank of General and took the command as Lieutenant Colonel of Mounted Men. Was ordered by Gov. Clark to march with a body of men to the relief of the Boone's Lick Settlements in September, 1814.

Gen. Dodge's force consisted of 350 mounted men. There were also about forty friendly Shawanoes along, under four war captains: Pap-pi-qua, Wa-pe-pil-le-se, Na-kom-me, & Kish-Kal-le-wa.* The two former were aged chiefs fully seventy years old, & had both served in the early Indian wars against Kentucky. Pap-pi-qua, informing Gen. Dodge that he had aided in capturing Col. Daniel Boone, but that Boone was always too smart for the Indians, & easily effected his escape.

This force crossed the Missouri from the northern to the southern bank at the Arrow Rock, by swimming the stream or sending six men on horseback below the Horses, and following the Horses in Canoes... as a van-guard above & below the main body stemming the swift current. When about half way over, they struck the strong eddy, which soon wafted them over to the southern bank in safety. But two horses[?] were consumed[?] in crossing the river, with horses, baggage.

The friendly Shawanoes found & reported the locality of the hostile Miamis, who had thrown up a small fort. Dodge's men pushed forward several miles up the river, & in the night neared the enemy in what is now known as the Miami Bend, in Saline County, & soon surrounded them. Ascertaining this fact, the Miamis, knowing it would be folly to resist against such odds, proposed through the Shawanoes to surrender themselves as prisoners.

*See Sketch of Kish-Kal-le-wa in Hall & McKinney's History of Indian Tribes. LCD

Gen. Dodge called a council of his officers & asked their advice, commencing with the Coopers & other Boone's Lick officers. They all unanimously advised receiving them as prisoners. General Dodge then reminded his officers that in receiving the enemy as prisoners, their lives must be sacredly preserved, & he should hold them all personally responsible for their own conduct & that of their men, in this particular. The Indians now formally surrendered – 31 warriors, and about one hundred and twenty-two women and children – about 153 in all.

The next morning, while Capt. Cooper & many others were scouting around to make discoveries of hidden property, the Captain found the well-known rifle of the poor potter slain in the Boone's Lick region, when Cooper & his men came galloping to Gen. Dodge & the Captain, enraged, demanded of the General the surrender of the Indian who had murdered the potter, that he & his men might make a signal & terrible example of him. Gen. Dodge peremptorily declined. Cooper threatened, in behalf of his company who were dashing up on their horses, to kill the whole of the

Indians, when his men, as by common consent, cocked their rifles in shooting attitude. When the warriors seeing the threatening aspect, threw themselves upon their knees, & repeatedly crossing their breasts with great rapidity, & uttered their earnest prayers to the Great Spirit – or rather to the Sun, then just rising its morning splendor. Gen. Dodge heard the clicking of the locks of the rifles of the Boone's Lick [men] & fearing the consequences, but without even turning towards them, drew his sword & thrust its point within six inches of Capt. Cooper's breast, & reminding him of his sacred pledge to protect the Indians after their peaceable surrender, & that he would never consent to their being slaughtered in cold blood. If Cooper's men fired on them, Capt. Cooper himself should instantly suffer the consequences. At this critical moment, Maj. Daniel M. Boone came dashing up to Gen. Dodge's side, & said he would stand by him to the last – that he would never consent that the helpless captives should be inhumanly butchered, & taunted Cooper with the cowardliness and black treachery of the act he proposed to do. Dodge was firm, never taking his dark piercing eye for a moment from Cooper's. Boone presented a determined countenance as men always do when activated by noble purposes. Cooper at length yielded, Dodge ordering him to take his place in the line & march his men away. He doggedly obeyed, & as his men rode by, the Indians seeing the danger past, jumped to their feet with marked expressions of joy & gratitude to Dodge & Boone. The Shawanoes, too, were much gratified that the Miami were saved. Kish-Ka-le-wa visited Gen. Dodge at Fort Lawrence in 1835, ____ his old commander.

Gen. Dodge looks back upon his conduct in saving these prisoners [as one of] the happiest acts of his life.

Henry Dodge
Missouri Historical Society

15C 100 Henry Dodge, Dodgeville [?], July 3, 1855

My Dear Sir

Your letter and ___ of the 30th ulto I received on yesterday, the Enclosure I send you by the Mail. I have examined[?] it carefully, and find it generally correct. I have corrected it as to my Rank which was that of a Lieutenant Colonel of Mounted Volunteers and Militia – having waived my Rank as a Brigadier General to make me to command the ___ ___ which was a Colonel's Command... I selected six of my most active men, good swimmers on Horseback, sent them before the Horses. The Horses followed them flanked by Canon & in the rear by Canoes. Your memory must be good for you have mentioned particulars with great accuracy. I will endeavor during the Summer to write a Brief account of the Black Hawk war.

Truly your friend & obedient servant
Henry Dodge

15C 101 Memo from Gen. Henry Dodge, June 29, 1855

LCD: Copied from Notes placed among General George Rogers Clark Papers

Daniel M. Boone was a Captain on the Peoria Campaign in 1812 & a Major in 1814 under Gen. Dodge in the Expedition for the relief of the Boone's Lick country.

From Daniel M. & Nathan Boone, Gen. Dodge learned that their father, Col. Daniel Boone, got involved in land litigation in Kentucky, & lost, and became soured, & thinks he never re-visited Kentucky after settling in Missouri.

15C 102 Henry Dodge, Dodgeville [?], July 11, 1855

Sir

I find from examination that the Mounted expedition commanded by me in 1814 was under Brig. Gen. Benjamin Howard, United States Army. The General died during my absence with the mounted troops, and my report was made to Col. Russell, US Army, who succeeded Gen. Howard in command. I reported the facts to Gov. Clark, then Governor of the Territory of Missouri who had sent by the Military Commissioner for the Militia, Officers, of the Boon Lick Country. That was the name of that Country at that time. A lapse of more than thirty years makes it difficult to remember... facts connected with important Military Moments.

Very Respectfully
Your Friend and Obedient Servant
Henry Dodge

15C 103 Address by Gen. Dodge, Burlington, Iowa Gazette, June 7, 1883. LCD: Address by Gen. Dodge [at a Golden Wedding celebration].

> **Governor Dodge rode between the kneeling Indians and the leveled rifles and cried "you shoot them, it will be through the dead body of your General."**

He described his connection with the Black Hawk war... He said the whites always treated the Indians fairly... told of the capture of five hundred Miami Indians by a command of Kentuckians, under his father, Governor Henry Dodge. A number of articles of dress taken from the massacred wives and children of the soldiers were found with the Indians, and this so enraged them that they took advantage of the temporary absence of the General and decided to kill every one of the Indians, including women and children.

Learning of this, Governor Dodge jumped upon his horse, and reaching the scene, rode between the kneeling Indians and the leveled rifles and cried "you shoot them, it will be through the dead body of your General." The countrymen of Boone, brave, hardy frontiersmen, loved their commander and obeyed him. Many years after, in riding through a reservation, Gov. Dodge found his horse surrounded by Indians who kissed his feet and gave other expressions of their simple gratitude for saving their lives.

The general stated that five of his father's uncles and his only brother were killed by the Indians, the latter a brave officer in the Black Hawk war and spoke several Indian languages. He was captured by the Apaches and burned at the stake in New Mexico where he was stationed as an Indian agent.

15C 104-105 LCD: Daniel Boone, 1814, 1815, 1816 1815

Hunt up Gasconade: Note-Book "H", p. 138.

St. Louis, March 8, 1815 Capt. Callaway was attacked and killed by the Indians – the Savages lay in ambush. Five men are missing, and two wounded. I have given the alarm along the frontier.

Boone's Lick, March 10 – Last night an Express arrived here from the upper Settlements of St. Charles County informing that the settlements are attacked by formidable bodies of Indians. On the 1st inst., they stole a number of horses, and killed a negro. A number of the inhabitants pursued the Indians, and retook the horses. At the same time they were attacked by three times their number. They charged without hesitation and after a smart action of about fifteen minutes, retreated with the loss of one man killed. The loss of the Indians was considerable – they were seen bearing off their dead.

Since the above was put in type, we learn that those who have been killed and wounded belonging to Captain Callaway's Company, and at Boone's Lick have large families depending on them for support. Capt.

Callaway was known to all, and his loss will be regretted by all who estimate worth and sterling courage.

Charleston City Gazette, April 18, 1815.

1816 – [Boone] On hunting trip to Fort Osage. Louisville Courier, July 11, 1816.

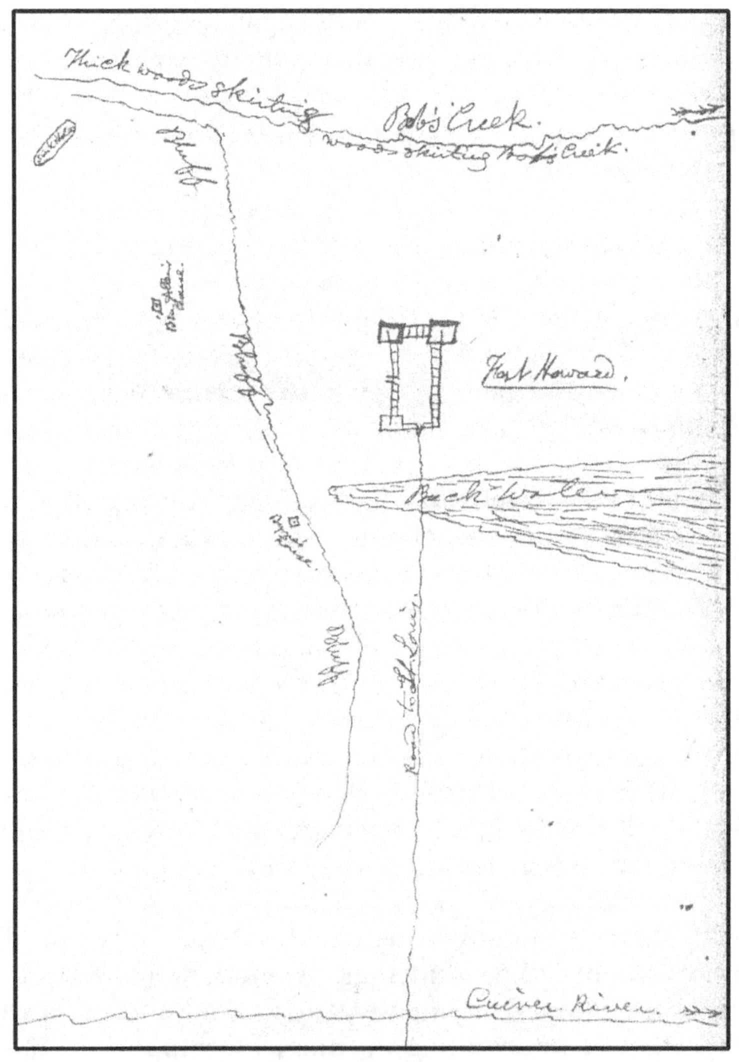

Sink-Hole Battleground showing Fort Howard.
Drawn by LCD. DM 15C 106.

15C 106 Plat of Sink Hole battle in Missouri, May 24, 1815 [describes] Fort Howard, Thick woods skirting Bob's Creek, Road to St. Louis, Bluff, Byne's[?] House.

15C 107-107(19) John Gibson interview, June 5-6, 1868. Notes of Conversation taken of Maj. John Gibson of Callaway County, Mo., near Portland, June 5th & 6th, 1868 by L. C. D.

> **The Indians took off Robertson's clothes and put a breech-cloth and blanket on him & paddled his feet till they were sore so he should not run away.**

John Gibson was born in North Carolina in April 1778, early removed to Pendleton County, South Carolina, and settled in Missouri in 1810, having resided in Bedford County, Tennessee from 1804 till 1810.

In 1813, in the Spring, when the Indians attacked Cote sans Dessein, on the Missouri [this was in Spring of 1815 – LCD], Col. Daniel Boone and two Frenchmen with him in a canoe, trapping beaver at the mouth of Ox Saux creek, about seven miles above Portland on the Missouri & about ten miles below Cote Sans Desscin. In the Indian attack on Cote Sans Dessein, Mrs. Roy distinguished herself in the defence – was very brave – shot seven Indians through the port holes.

Col. Boone trapped at the mouths of Charotte, Chariton, Osage, Gasconade, Cedar, Moriteau, and all three of the Avoux [?]. Spent much of his time trapping & would get canoe loads of furs – there at different times.

Indian Philips often went with Boone – more frequently, perhaps, than any one else, except the

Frenchmen. Can't tell his origin – suppose he was at some time with the Indians.

In the Spring of 1811, Gibson remembers meeting Col. Boone, who then went to St. Louis with Indian Phillips with a load of beaver fur.

Major Gibson moved to his present residence in December 1817. Phillips died at his (Gibson's) place at Loutre Lick previously. If Daniel Boone & Phillips went up the Missouri in Spring of 1817 – or in 1816, then[?] Philips died early in the fall of 1817. Came to Gibson's sick, & died in a few days. He was pretty much a savage in feelings and appearance; a medium sized man – five feet eight or nine inches – a great walker.

James Richardson started with Lewis & Clark on their expedition to the Pacific, was taken sick & returned – never was well afterwards & went out some with Col. Daniel Boone hunting & trapping. He had been nine years in the mountains as a hunter & trapper – a good, reliable man. He died of consumption at Gibson's not long after Phillips' death, in 1817, probably. He left a family. Of Jenkins Williams, knows nothing. Of Indian Rogers & Joab Barton, can give no particulars.

Dr. Muir was a foreigner. Gibson was at his house at Fort Madison in 1832. Muir said he had travelled in many countries, & never found anywhere so much true hospitality as among the Kickapoo Indians, & so he married an Indian wife. She acted the lady – had two daughters, very pretty, & sons, well educated, musicians. He seemed wealthy & finely fixed. He entertained Gibson & a party of 24 in 1832.

In Spring 1816, Nathan Boone raised 100 Rangers – informant was one – James Callaway (son of Nathan Boone's sister) was another. [They] were out three months ranging from St. Charles & on that frontier. No Indians were discovered during that period.

Isaac Van Bibber – Nathan Boone's Defeat, 1813

In summer of 1812, when Boone's men were discharged, Capt. Isaac Van Bibber's company of light Horse was ordered out to serve till a new company of Rangers should be embodied. Nathan Boone soon enlisted a new company of Rangers who served a year – Gibson again of the party. Ranging service was widely extended – up Missouri River to head of Grand, Salt, Perche, all northern tributaries of the Missouri.

In 1813, preparations were making for an Expedition against Peoria, & Nathan Boone was desired to take a small party & go & reconnoiter there. All mounted - seventeen of them – reached the waters of Big Sandy, a western tributary of the Illinois River. Here it was, according to the plan, that thirteen were to return with all the horses. Boone, Gibson (informant), one Gibbett and one White were to proceed on, on foot, Spying. It was thought the escort had gone as far as it was prudent – too far as the Sequel proved. Some signs had been seen that day. The horses escort were to go as far as it was safe & then return.

There they camped raining, put up blankets. Indians came on the whites in the early part of the night. 150 Winnebagoes or Kickapoos fired on the camp. Whites fled & left everything. Horses fled. Just before they fired on the camp while creeping up, White, as one of the sentinels, saw them & fired. They fired by the blaze of his gun, & shot both of his thumbs off & lock & trigger of his gun, but he brought in the barrel. No other one was wounded.

John Robertson, who did not run from the camp, was taken prisoner. After getting all the plunder, the Indians took off Robertson's clothes, and put a breech-cloth and blanket on him & paddled his feet till they were sore so he should not run away. This was on the bank of Sandy. The Indians had been two days dogging the whites, & were now very weary & sleepy, & now lay down & went to sleep, & so did the sentinel having Robertson in charge. Robertson sought the favorable opportunity to take French leave – crept carefully down, snake-like into the creek, and swam off some distance & got out the other side (casting off his breech cloth & blanket as he entered the creek), escaped. He was eleven days getting in – wandered to the Illinois & finally reached Portage De Sioux. He lived on bugs, frogs, & a snake or two – suffered much from gnats.

The French at the Portage were kind to him, & he soon recovered. He re-entered the service, & subsequently settled in St. Charles and was living a few years since

The Indians, in attacking Boone's party, shot into the tops of the tents. The next Indians got some eight or ten of the men of Boone's party & the whites got the rest on their retreat. [They] retreated in squads & singly, all got in safely to Fort Howard from which they had started, crossing the Mississippi on rafts. Gibson & Thomas Kiteley on a raft, floating down the Mississippi. The next morning discovered, taking the lead, his horse dodged. An Indian with a broken thigh fired & just grazed the top of Gibson's head. He dismounted, & with tomahawk in hand, the Indian seeing his antagonist approaching, first threw his knife & then his tomahawk, both missing their aim & then clubbed his gun – game to the last. But Gibson rushed up & tomahawked him in his covert in the grass.

The Indians had gone to their canoes, some three miles to the Mississippi, from where they had fought – found several of their dead bodies & the trail bloody.

Tansy Fight

July 4, 1813. Ensign Ramsey of St. Genevieve County, & others scouting came to Freemore's Lick, twelve miles above the mouth of salt river. They found several pretended friendly Sauks, making salt. One of these Sauks told about a party of hostile Indians & Ramsey's party concluded to go & get some scalps, an easy way to secure large rewards. Found a few Winnebagoes in a hurricane place where bushes had grown up into a thicket directly on the bank of the Mississippi about 60 miles above Fort Howard. Nine went, taking the Sauk with them.

The large part had stopped at Buffalo Fort about 30 miles above Fort Howard, in the fore part of the day. The Sauk pilot went with the remaining nine & showed where the hostile Indians were, but would not himself go & fight, saying the Indians would kill him if he went. The whites crept up – shot several Indians off logs on which they were unconcernedly sitting. Others were playing games. Indians when shot at, seeming to rise up all around. Whites only fired once & received a fire in return. Seeing the unequal contest before them, the survivors fled.

Levi Tansey was shot across the wrist. He swam several streams & heating himself, his wound became much inflamed. Informant, Gibson, put a slippery elm bark poultice on the wrist & cold mud, but they got but very little rest or food. It was a foot Expedition. Tansy's arm mortified, and he died after his return.

One Foreman was shot in the heel, and Gibson treed & kept the Indians back momentarily so Foreman could get off. Duff & Ramsey were killed on the spot. Ramsey was a fine little man. Jourdan Whiteside was wounded & died. Thinks more than Duff & Ramsey were killed on the ground.

No doubt but the pretended friendly Sauk deceived the whites & led them purposely into the trap, representing the hostile Indians as a small party when it was really a large one. The Sauk, most officious, never returned to the Fort for liquor and tobacco as before – was well he did not, for Gibson and others had resolved on killing him at sight. Thinks Ramsey belonged to Capt. Craig's Company.

The Jourdan Defeat

In Spring of 1813, Capt. Robert Jourdan had a log rolling about a mile from Buffalo Fort and a large [number] of people with Gibson, a spy, & some of the Rangers, went out ___ed in the log rolling till towards night. While returning, having got about a quarter of a mile ___ found themselves in an Indian ambush. The Indians posted at the heads of some ravines near the path, and behind logs and fallen trees, fired on the unsuspecting whites, killing nearly all. Among them Capt. Robert Jourdan and two sons, John Jourdan and one son, a Mr. Templeton and a son of the settler, John and Lindsay Lewis [LCD: brothers of Mrs. Daniel M. Boone, son of Col. Daniel Boone], Samuel Watson, among the Rangers, & several others. Not all killed at the first fire, but some of them when the Indians rushed up and finished their bloody work. All the whites were on foot except informant Gibson, whose horse was wounded in the side, but both horse & rider escaped. Gibson, when the party was fired on, was riding ahead of the others. A large party of Indians.

As soon as Gibson could dash to the Fort, men were rallied there & hastened to head the Indians, but the latter reached their canoes & escaped. Thinks about twenty in all were killed – all except Gibson.

Callahan Wounded

In 1814, Jacob Groomes & Mr. Callahan – Groomes residing 8 miles up Loutre Creek from Loutre Island, had a fort there in which he lived in winter. The two started with some horses to Best's Bottom to have them placed out of the reach of the Indians. This was in the summer - & brought them horses from Groomes' Station. They had scarcely got started from the Station when they were fired on. Callahan slightly wounded, & the horse he was riding killed & fell on him. Groomes had a young man with him. They managed to keep the Indians back till Callahan got loose. Groomes gave Callahan his horse & all escaped.

Gibson's Adventure

In the Spring of Summer of 1814, Gibson was taking some dispatches from Fort Clemson (on Loutre Island) to Fort P____ in upper end of St. Charles County on Baneck [Perrugue? LCD] Creek, a tributary of Daidenne Creek. As he went along mounted, his horse looked back as though he heard something, & so did Gibson, like a calf bleating. Gibson looked around & saw an Indian taking aim at him, when Gibson spurred his horse & dashed through the creek, guns firing all around him. He dashed up the bluff, one place four feet up a ledge on the top of which the horse got his fore feet, but could not at first get up his hind feet. But locked one of his fore feet behind a hickory sapling, & then made a vigorous effort & succeeding in jerking up his hind feet, soon lost sight of the Indians. Gibson delivered his messages, & returned the same night [by] a different route.

Fort Clemson was named after Col. Clemson who belonged elsewhere & had some reputation. Gardner's Dictionary of the Army says: Eli B. Clemson, of Pennsylvania, was appointed Ensign and Second

Lieutenant of the 1st infantry, 3rd March, 1799; First Lieutenant April 1800; Captain March 1807; Major 1st Infantry Jan 20, 1813; Lieutenant Colonel 16th Infantry, March 9, 1814; disbanded June 1815. Assistant Commander of Aug. 27, 1816; resigned 1st Dec. 1819. Died in Illinois in 1845. LCD

Fort Clemson was built (continues Mr. Gibson)) in the Fall of 1813, after returning from the Peoria Campaign.

Rangers

No ranging in the winter. Spies Rangers supplied themselves with horses, food, clothing, wore buckskin mostly, & would in the fall lay in a stock of wild meat & dry it.

Col. Henry Dodge's Expedition

Major Daniel M. Boone was along – the only expedition on which he served. James Callaway was not along, nor Captain Ramsey, nor Col. Ben. Cooper. Informant, Gibson, was on the campaign. All went up the Missouri in boats & had hard work to get up.
"We scared the Indians mightily," says Gibson.

Miami Fort, built by the Indians, was a little piece back from the southern bank of the Missouri, a little above Arrow Rock. There the Indians were. Landed a piece below in day time, & slipped up through the brush – quite a number of the men had improvised ladders out of poles and bark. Reaching the rude picket fort, scaled it. Inside found several shanties & found several old squaws & children and dogs. Scouring around, found others hid – a few perhaps were warriors, but mostly women & children, & not to exceed forty or fifty altogether – a dirty, filthy, miserable looking set. None was killed – no gun fired.

Col. Dodge ordered Sarshall Cooper & company, who had joined Dodge at some point below the Boone's

Lick Settlement remaining at their homes. A part of their force had to remain at home for their own protection...

Gibson thinks there was no good reason to suspect Cooper & men of any intention of killing the Indian prisoners. It now looked as if a real fight would ensue between Dodge's St. Genevieve troops and the Boone's Lick men. Gibson thinks if any thoughtless, unguarded men of Cooper's Company threatened to kill the Indians, Capt. Cooper himself was too high-minded to have countenanced such a design. Thinks Dodge drew his pistol on Cooper.

The Miami Fort was burned & the Indian prisoners taken down to St. Louis and subsequently exchanged at Prairie Du Chien.

Campbell's Expedition 1814

This was not Gov. Clark's Expedition. While boats were anchored out at the Rapids of the Mississippi & Indians were in the weeds & bushes on shore nearby, the latter shot at the whites on the boats. The whites not having much chance to fire back, cut their rope cable lines. Peter Harpole, a chunky Pennsylvania Dutchman, who lived near Perruque[?] Fort, a great hunter, had been a Ranger all through the war – a young man – he bravely shot at & fought the Indians, & was in the act of peeping through a port-hole to see where best to get a good shot, was himself shot through the head, the brains oozing out. He lived till the boats reached St. Louis. William Breeden had his tongue nearly all shot off. He was living quite recently in Osage County, Missouri. Got his land warrant for his services. The Indians captured the ammunition & provision boat, having killed a part of the men, when the survivors fled to a near boat.

Campbell was shot through the belly – hid among some barrels, & disgraced himself. A Major, but was dropped from the Service. Don't know anything further about him.

[John Campbell, Virginia, Ensign First Infantry June 13, 1808; second Lieutenant December 1809; First Lieutenant January 1813; Captain, May 1814; commanded in an engagement with the Sauk & Fox Indians, and was wounded, July 1814, near mouth of Rock River; disbanded June 1815. Gardner's Dictionary of the Army. LCD]

Some two days previous to this attack on Campbell's boats, the Indians had been dogging the boats on their way up & sometimes shot & killed a man. Campbell proposed a treaty with them, & they held a council on the western bank (Indians on both banks) & gave them largely of presents.

Gibson was slightly wounded on this expedition. Boats returned from the Rapids.

Lieut. Perkins, from St. Genevieve region, a brave, fearless little man.

The Rangers did a heap of work & hard service building many forts.

Isaac Van Bibber – Thomas Keightley Indian Phillips – Gibson – Ramsey

Isaac Van Bibber was surveying under Maj. Nathan Boone after the war & died a few years subsequently to the peace of 1815. Had no family. He was a nephew of Maj. Isaac Van Bibber, who was a brother of Mrs. Nathan Boone. Jesse Van Bibber was "a mighty good hand with a gun." Spied six months.

Thomas Keightley spied the longest of any one with Gibson. He died before the war closed. Was on Campbell's Expedition, very brave & useful. Lived on south side of the Missouri, joined Nathan Boone's company. Nathan Boone was "very popular, & greatly beloved." So was First Lieutenant Lamme of Nathan Boone's Company in all the early part of the war. He was not on the Peoria Expedition, however, perhaps sick at the time.

Indian Phillips – He was a dirty fellow of no account, & only fit for the woods as servant or camp-keeper. Col. Daniel Boone could get him as his time was valueless & his services, such as they were, could be easily obtained.

A negro woman looking on at a dance given to the rangers, seeing one young soldier jumping high, exclaimed, "O Lord, see how high he jumps – he'll be fit for Captain next year!"

Major Gibson is five feet, ten inches, spare, active, light complexioned. Still vigorous and quite active in body & mind at ninety. Has been Justice of the Peace some twenty years, Major in the Militia, & commanded a company in the Black Hawk War.

[William Ramsey born in 1741, served in Revolution, an Indian fighter in Kentucky, removed to Missouri in 1802. Ensign Rangers, Feb. 1814 – declined. Died in Boone County, Mo., May 24, 1845. Gardner's Dictionary Army. LCD.]

Howard's Expedition – Indian Captives

Three or four canoes of Indians pursuing them. They put to shore & escaped & reached Fort Madison in four days and nights. Others were longer, hiding at first by day in a bluff, saw Indians passing them. Took several hundred Indians, women & children prisoners at Peoria – over 400 who were hid in their huts & out of the way of Howard's cannon firing on them from the boats. Nathan Boone was a Major on this Expedition.

At first, the men commenced cutting down the prisoners & Boone and his influence had a stop put to it. These Indians prisoners were taken to St. Louis & finally sent to Prairie De Chien & exchanged for white prisoners taken there when Lieut. Perkins surrendered. Perkins lived in Missouri, in St. Louis County – very brave, had a family – surrendered Prairie De Chien, as the British brought cannon & yet fought as long as ammunition & provisions lasted. Perkins was next year, 1814, killed at Sink Hole battle (1815? LCD).

Two Indian Prisoners taken.

In summer of 1813, Gibson & Jesse Van Bibber were watching for deer at Buffalo Lick where Buffalo Fort was located in now Ralls County on Buffalo Creek. The Fort [was] not far from the Mississippi bank, & below the mouth of Salt River. [They] were out spying. Gibson saw an Indian creep through the bushes within eight or ten feet. When Gibson presented his gun and ordered him instantly to drop his, & Van Bibber quickly did the same with another who showed himself almost at the same instant. They had their prisoners tied in a moment. This was about one o'clock in the afternoon & then made them trot forty miles to Fort Howard that evening. Gibson & Van Bibber - $80 apiece reward for their prisoners, & much praise.

Gibson & Jesse Van Bibber had waylaid & shot two Indians on the waters of Salt River not long before & got $40 each for the scalps, given to encourage the destruction of Indians by the spies & frontiersmen not taken in battle.

Ramsey's Family Killed

Robert Ramsey, wife & family lived two miles above Old Charette Village on the Missouri River – had lived there several years. Were from Kentucky, son of Capt. William Ramsey who served in Missouri during the War of 1812-1815. Were attacked by Winnebagos & Kickapoos, & all killed. Several of them, only two small children who hid under the floor undiscovered, escaped. The Indians took the scalps of the killed & the plunder, across the Prairie towards the head of __aivre – when Gibson, carrying Express from Fort Clemson (on Loutre Island) to St. Louis, seeing them, yelled and put after them & waived his hand behind, when the Indians put off at their best speed on foot & together – about a dozen or fifteen. Thus Gibson chased them three or four times, when one began to lag behind, & by this time seeing no others coming, the Indians got re-assembled rallied, and put after Gibson, who in turn had to retreat & easily on his fine horse out stripped them. He said it was a source of real delight to him as long as he could keep them on the run.

Callaways, Bryans and others pursued them clear to the Mississippi, but they had reached their canoes, & had gone.

In about 1814, Isaac Best's family, residing on the north bank of the Missouri above the mouth of Loutre, and not far opposite the mouth of the Gasconade, hearing of Indians, got his family out of his house & took them to Fort Clemson.

Best & William Callahan were at Best's house & dogs espied Indians creeping up through the corn towards the house. The dogs & these two white men kept the Indians at bay till Mrs. Best & Mrs. Callahan & children ran down & got into the canoe & escaped. In the fight, Callahan was shot through the thigh, a flesh wound, & they both escaped to Fort Clemson. Indians robbed the house.

Indian Phillips and another did go close to Best's house & saw the Indians emptying & shaking feather beds & escaped.

The Coopers of Missouri

In 1810, Benjamin, Sarshall, Braxton Cooper & others came from Kentucky & stopped a year at Loutre Island & raised a crop. Sarshal Cooper was the principal man of this party – from Madison County, Kentucky.

The Coopers were early settlers and defenders at Fort Boonesborough, Kentucky, and noted pioneers in Missouri.

Cole Fight, 1810

Thinks Cole, Patton, & Gooch were killed & Moredock, who lived in that region. Came from Kentucky with the Coopers & had two brothers. Thinks Isaac Van Bibber was along, & Paddy Woods, & both escaped. The latter was living in Howard County two years ago, some twenty miles east of Fayette, Missouri. One Bynum was also along, who for many years was clerk of the court at Fayette or Columbia & only a few years dead.

Indians had stolen horses from Best's Bottom & there started the pursuing party, others joining them at Loutre Lick. Were defeated at the edge of Loutre Prairie, seven or eight miles from Loutre Lick. Were attacked in the night & defeated. Thinks if Van Bibber had been more prudent, the said defeat would not have occurred.

Capt. William Ramsey was from Kentucky – an old Indian fighter there. He lived & died in St. Charles County many years ago – was a fine man – left a family.

Callaway's Defeat

About 150 Indians, Callahan saw them when they stole horses at Best's Bottom, above Loutre Island - ___ 75 horses. John Gibson (informant) called Duck River John, having lived half a dozen years on that stream in Tennessee, to distinguish him from his cousin of the same name, also engaged in the same service. Said if forty persons would volunteer, he felt certain he could lead the way & recover the horses – some 40 or 50 horses altogether. Capt. William Ramsey, Capt. James Callaway, & others started & went some fifteen miles the first day. Did not follow the horse trail, but tried to head them. The next day, towards noon, Gibson & Keitley discovered a gang of horses ahead. (When Gibson proposed to go, Daniel M. Boone said to his nephew, James Callaway, who had been chosen leader, "Now do you follow Duck River John") - & waited till the men came up. When they divided, Callaway [was] leading one half and Gibson the other. Made a wide wing, & surrounded the horses. In closing up, they found the horses hoppled & tied. Indian blankets hung up in the forks of the trees of the thicket where the horses were – the whole gang.

It was evident that the Indians expecting pursuit on the trail had left the horses and gone back to waylay the trail & defeat their pursuers. The horses were found about 30 miles from Fort Clemson. Gibson advised against returning by the trail. Capt. Ramsey strongly advised against it also. Jonathan Riggs said "Now, we ought to be admonished by Capt. Ramsey, an old experienced Indian fighter."

After retreating on the trail a dozen miles and evidences of Indians every now & then seen, Ramsey, Daniel & William Hays, Jr., Riggs & others broke off...& took a woods cut home. Callaway unhappily persisted in keeping the trail & near night, when about 14 miles from Fort Clemson, with the swollen Loutre on the east of the trail – an abrupt bluff on the South, the Prairie Fork on the north, which the whites were permitted to ford. The Indians on the west & in the rear. There was a narrow plateau or track between the bluff & river for single-file passage, but this was guarded. The first onslaught was a heavy fire, perhaps from a hundred, killing several men, cutting down limbs from the trees & killing and wounding a large number of horses, who were pitching & groaning. The whites were too few to resist, & fired scarcely a gun, but each made a dash to escape. As the gap was occupied by the Indians & the bluff could not be ascended, they could only plunge into the swollen stream. Capt. Callaway was shot through the left arm, and broken – the ball passing through a watch (which cost $60, belonging to informant, Gibson) & the passing on through his side. Gibson was shot through the left leg & had his horse shot from under him. He got Francis McDermand's horse, McDermand having been killed. Callaway called to Gibson to aid him to escape, but there was no chance & Callaway pitched his gun, muzzle foremost into the Prairie Fork, & it stuck in the mud in the bottom. Then he jumped in himself (his horse having been killed). Being on foot, the Prairie Fork was nearer than the main Loutre. The Indians fired at him in the stream & shot him in the back of the head & he sank. Gibson plunged in on horseback & both horse & rider went under several feet. The horse soon rose to the surface snorting. The willows lining the bank protected him & he got over without further harm. Reached Fort Clemson that night having to re-swim Loutre Crek.

The horses were mostly killed. Callaway, McDermond, McMillen, John Gleason, Andrew Vumault & others were killed. Out of twenty perhaps, only four escaped: James Gleason, who was slightly wounded on the toe, Newton Howell, John Causley – both latter unhurt, with informant, escaped.

Next day Gibson went [with] others – found Callaway's gun, butt up. Heads, hearts, livers, entrails cut from the bodies of the slain & hung upon poles. Birds, wolves &c had badly disfigured the bodies. Buried all but Callaway's, on the spot. Callaway's was not found till some ten days after & then some two or three hundred yards below in main Loutre. His jeans coat fastened to a willow, & body floating.

At the time of the fight, main Loutre was 15 or 20 feet deep & the Prairie Fork was barely fordable, & rising.

Sink Hole Battle

Maj. Gibson says Craig was not the commander as J. Shaw says in his Narrative in Wisconsin Historical Collections, vol. 2, but that Lieut. Perkins was commander – a very noble man. Major Daniel M. Boone was at Fort Howard, near half a mile off, but not in the fight, was not popular – crusty - & was in no fight, nor on any expedition except Gen. Henry Dodge's.

Sink-Hole Battle, 1815

Seven men went to Burns' cabin after a grindstone. Indians ambushed & killed them. The Indians then showed themselves on the bluff as evidently a banter to come out & fight them. Scattered along quite a distance, so as to make a formidable appearance. The whites crept up towards & around them through the grass & got in their rear. Had a sharp tree fight, which lasted most of the day, and a number of Indians were killed. Then the Indians retreated & went to the Sink Hole & killed six or seven (whites) & wounded two.

Don't remember who suggested the moving battery but a pair of truck wheels was taken & a plank breast-work fastened uprightly upon the truck several feet high. A keg of powder was carried behind with a fuse attached to be lighted & keg thrown into the sink hole for explosion among the Indians. There were some trees in the large sink hole and some lesser sink holes around where Indians shot from & picked off some of our men behind the battery – Lieut. Perkins among them & so had to abandon it. It was now dusk & were pushing up the battery with pikes & within about a dozen feet of the Hole.

Thinks Craig was killed behind a white oak. Informant, Gibson, was twice grazed during the day. Next day Gibson & a large party followed the Indians' trail, when they had advanced half a mile, with Gibson mounted as a spy.

15C 108 Daniel Boone's grant, from the St. Louis Globe Democrat, 1924, and presented to the Wisconsin Historical Society by Alva N. Turner through Miss Louise Kellogg and others connected with the library.

A correspondent writes: "I have read several communications in your column relating to the log cabin of Daniel Boone and the grant of land made by the Spanish Governor... [this is] the exact location of the grant. It is in St. Charles County, forty-eight miles from St. Louis on the M. K. T. Railroad, and is known as the Richard Matson farm, Mr. Matson having been a descendant of Daniel Boone. His widow has in her possession the old Spanish land grant. The station of Matson is on this farm and the old cabin is about a quarter of a mile northwest from the station on a knoll overlooking the river."

APPENDIX

Original order of Richard H. Collins' Depositions as sent to Lyman Draper. All were recorded in Kentucky except Daniel Boone's and Flanders Callaway's depositions which were recorded in Missouri, and Patrick Henry's, recorded in Virginia. Page numbers are from Collins' *History of Kentucky*, volume 2. The town of Washington is near Maysville.

p. 526 Peter Shull [Scholl], 1818
p. 94 Henry Hall, 1804
p. 94, Simon Kenton, 1824
p. 446-7 Simon Kenton, 1824
p.566 Simon Kenton
p. 664 Simon Kenton 1821
p. 563 Simon Kenton, 1814
p. 550 Hayden Wells, 1797, near Washington
p. 550 William Triplett, 1797, near Washington
p. 549 Capt. Thomas Young, 1804, 1810
p. 551 John McCausland, 1798
p. 234 Daniel Boone, 1794 at Point Pleasant,
p. 555 Daniel Boone, 1795 in Fleming County
p. 559 Daniel Boone, 1797
p. 563 Daniel Boone, 1817 in Missouri
p. 466 Daniel Boone, 1796
p. 656 Jesse Coffee [Cofer/Copher], 1805
p. 656, 664 Stephen Hancock, 1808, Madison County, Kentucky Courthouse
p. 656 William Cradlebaugh, 1808, Madison County, KY Courthouse
p. 94 Simon Kenton, Capt. Thomas Young, and William Triplett, 1796, before the Land Commissioners
p. 179 William McGee, 1804
p. 179 David Mitchell 1804

p. 180 Josiah Collins, 1804 on Mill Creek
p. 425 Benjamin Berry, 1804 on Mill Creek
p. 425 James Guthrie, 1804
p. 466 563 Col. Robert Patterson, 1818 at his home
p. 466 Maj. George Stockton, 1805, Flemingsburg
p. 467 Jacob Sodowski, 1818, at his home, Jessamine County.
p. 467 John Riggs, 1797
p. 549 Capt. Thomas Young, 1810
p. 555 Capt. John Waller, 1797
p. 453 Levi Davis, 1801
p. 563 Daniel Boone, 1799
p. 563 Septimus Davis, 1799?
p. 563 John Curry, 1799?
p. 563 Peter Harget, 1814
p. 655 Flanders Callaway, 1817, Missouri
p. 664 Jesse Hodges, 1817
p. 666 Jesse Hodges, March 4, 1818
p. 496 Patrick Henry, 1777, Virginia

ACKNOWLEDGMENTS

I wish to thank especially Lee Grady, Reference Archivist at Wisconsin Historical Society for help deciphering Draper's original notebooks. For her editing and organizing portions of the book, I thank Margaret Crabb. For making this into a book, my gratitude to Tracy Holton.

Thanks to Nancy O'Malley for her insight. I am grateful to Lloyd Callaway for reading this work, to Joyce Campbell for contributions to the illustrations, and to Harry Enoch for counsel.

Archives/Reference Librarians, Brad Allard and Jennifer Mattern at Clark County Kentucky Public Library were most helpful. Most of the transcribing for this book was made from copies/scans at that library.

For assistance with formatting, I thank Tristan Wilson in Technical Services at Madison County Kentucky Public Library. For other assistance, I thank Jennifer Cole at Filson Library, and Kathy Nell at E-Systems for saving the book more than once. Lauren Salwasser at Missouri Historical Society assisted with finding images. Thanks to Debbie Riley at Heritage Books.

Given the difficulty in transcribing of the handwriting and discerning the intentions of many persons, errors are inevitable, and those are solely my own.

INDEX

www.ingramcontent.com/pod-product-compliance
Lightning Source LLC
LaVergne TN
LVHW020531100826
845148LV00010B/1424